JOE VITALE
BACKSTAGE PASS

As told to Susie Vitale

HR

HIT RECORDS

Proofed & Edited
Kathy Swihart Kane

Format and Layout Design
Joe Vitale Jr. Parallel Dimension Graphic Design

Cover Photography and Design
Susie Vitale and Joe Vitale Jr.

Published by Hit Records, LLC
Copyright Hit Records 2008

Printed by Bookmasters
Ashland, Ohio USA

First Edition

ISBN number 978-0-9816719-0-1

Table of Contents

Foreward
By David Crosby, Stephen Stills & Graham Nash

Acknowledgements

Joe: I'd like to thank my wife Susie for writing this book. Without her love, support, drive and dedication, this book would have never been written. It is impossible to express my deepest thanks for the incredible work that she's done. I love you, honey!! I also need to thank my son Joe Jr. Again, none of this would have even been possible without his love, support and sheer dedication to do all that he could to make this happen. I love you, Joe. I'd also like to thank David Crosby, Stephen Stills and Graham Nash for writing the foreward. It's been a wonderful 32 year journey with CSN. I thank Bill Szymczyk for all the years of friendship and loyalty to me as a person and as a musician. In reading this book, I'm reminded of just how much you've done for me. I love ya "Coach". I need to thank Joe Walsh for all the music and some of the funniest chapters in the book. To all the fabulous musicians I've had the honor of working with....Thank you Ted Nugent, Peter Frampton, The Eagles, Crosby, Stills and Nash, Dan Fogelberg, John Entwistle, John Lennon, Zakk Wylde, Michael Stanley, Ringo Starr, The Beach Boys, Neil Young, Bill Wyman, Rick Derringer, Boz Scaggs, Jay Ferguson, Al Kooper, the massive amount of incredible players both live and in the studio, including my first band, The Chylds. I thank my dear friends, Doug Breidenbach, Thom Lowry, David Santos, Tom Bukovac, Mouse and Alan Rogan. And of course I'd like to thank God for the life and talents He's blessed me with. The orneriness was probably not in the original draft.

Susie: I want to thank Jesus Christ, my Lord and Savior, my A-440 and the North Star of my life. My greatest prayer is that somehow my life would glorify Him. My husband, Joe, thank you for all the years of this crazy life we've shared together, the countless cherished memories of these past 39 years, for our unbelievably kind, brilliant and talented son, and thank you for all the laughter, adventures, our wonderful families and the great friends we've made on our journey through this life together. I love you! Thank you, Joe, so much, for sharing your memories and stories with all of us.

Our one-of-a-kind son, Joe Jr., thank you for all the hours and hours of work you put into this project which made this book possible, and all the fun and laughter we've shared along the way. We absolutely could NOT have ever done this book or the albums without you. It will be a great moment when we hold the first printed book, and see the dream as reality. Kathy, thank you for all the hours and hours of expert and extremely careful reading and re-reading…and re-reading, editing, proofing, corrections and questions…this book would not nearly be as good as I hope and pray that it is, without your help. Thank you, Mom, Kathy & Gary Kane, Jim &

Carol Swihart and all my precious family and friends for their support and encouragement. Especially, thank you Mom and Dad, the best parents God ever gave a family, for teaching me stability and tenacity, and for the love-filled childhood you gave me. I love you all so much.

Very special thanks to Tim Leonhart at Bookmasters.

Thank you to the fantastic photographers who have allowed us to use their images.

Henry Diltz   www.morrisonhotelgallery.com
Jann Hendry
Beth Jordan-Kroll
Steve Jorgensen
Tami Jorgensen
Rick Kohlmeyer   www.Backstagegallery.com
Julie McNulty
Joe Merante
Paul T. Neves   ptn59@yahoo.com
Buzz Person
Jeff Pevar   www.pevar.com
Claudette Sooter
Michael Stanley   www.michaelstanley.com
Joe Vitale   www.joevitaleondrums.com
Susie Vitale
Joe Vitale Jr.   www.joevitalejr.com/photography
Tom Wright   www.morrisonhotelgallery.com

Over the years I've received many photographs from friends, fans and photographers, which sometimes aren't marked with the photographer's name on the back. I have tried my best to identify them and, if I used them in this book, to correctly give photo credit. If I have inadvertently omitted a photographer's name or given credit incorrectly, I sincerely apologize. Please email me and I will post the correction on my website: www.joevitaleondrums.com.

Foreward

By David Crosby, Stephen Stills and Graham Nash

For the last 40 years Crosby, Stills and Nash has made fine music together... for at least 32 of those years our friend Joe Vitale has been our drummer..... This man has seen it all... the good, the bad and the ugly... now Crosby hasn't always been good and Stills has sometimes been bad but I don't think that I'm... well never mind.

When one writes a 'Tell all' book people seem to want the gory dark details of life on the 'road' but when I read Joe and Susie's book, "Back Stage Pass" I realized that they had concentrated on the positive, funny, extraordinary side of life making music.

Joe's memory is astounding, often remembering details that even I had long ago forgotten, bringing things into greater perspective and reminding me, once again, what an unbelievable life we have lead so far and drilling into my very being just how grateful we all should be. This is a remarkable story, well worth the price of admission.

Ladies and gentlemen here's your Back Stage Pass.... Enjoy... I know I did.

Graham Nash
On the road, with Joe, in Alabama, 2008

****

Joe knows everybody in Rock and Roll and has worked with most of them... he has more funny stories than you can count ...a fun and fascinating read...

David Crosby

****

I have had the honor of working on music and traveling the globe with one of my best friends, Joe Vitale, for 30 years. Besides being an awe-inspiring drummer, he is a gifted songwriter, keyboard player, flautist, sound engineer and electrician. My wife is always excited about Joe coming out to work with me, because there are always at least three things around the house that we've paid several people to fix, yet remain un-fixed, but she knows only Joe Vitale can and will actually fix this stuff AND crank out a mean marinara.

He's built my home studio three times. We had to move. Twice. And then we decided to go ahead and build a 24 track analog room, which is as good as anything I had to work with in the 70's, and which sounds better than the stuff they have today. He would just mutter, "I gotta solder," and viola; we have a full-blown studio; with clean wiring throughout. Not only that, he and Dougie Breidenbach, otherwise known as Bunion Brothers Construction Inc, turned a useless porch into a drum booth. They just went to Three Guys and bought some wood and a couple windows and built the darn thing. You'd think it was part of the house.

Joe's secret, which he reveals in this book, is that hidden beneath all this competence and talent beats the heart of......a comedian. Joe Vitale possesses the wicked sense of humor of a born troublemaker. That's why I can't even think of anybody else playing drums for me. As it is with most any Italian worthy of being Italian, we have moods and tempers to deal with, and are prone to argue - mostly about where the groove is. The fact that I always win is a testament to his professionalism.

Herein lie the tales of life on the road with some of the most interesting and talented, not to mention great, icons of rock n' roll - ever. Being a super rich, bored rock star, armed with a chain saw and a great idea isn't enough. You need technical help. If you want to glue ALL the furniture in a suite to the ceiling, you need someone with a grasp of physics, who knows how much of what grade of epoxy you need and where to find it. And the discipline to tell you: "Forget the Piano. It won't hold." That's Joe Vitale.

This is the PG-rated version of tales from the Dark Side. All the stuff we wished we'd thought of, and very well might have, but were too drunk to pull off. Without the help of this zany Italian, armed with a superior knowledge of math, physics and construction; and a grand appreciation of a well executed prank, none of this would have been be possible. Luckily, I have neither the means nor a compulsion to trash a perfectly decent hotel room. I cherish my relationships with first-class hotels and the people that run them. Crappy ones, on the other hand........well, suffice to say, I tolerate them, but sometimes I wish I had the nerve. But I don't. I much prefer the wicked sense of humor that accompanies the story-telling abilities of Joe Vitale. It's all about timing. Here's to you, Joe Bob; You De Man.

Stephen Stills

CHAPTER ONE

Introduction

People are always asking me what it's like to be in the music business and to have played with some of the greatest musicians in rock & roll. That question covers a lot of territory, since I've been playing drums professionally since I was eleven. Over the span of my career, I've played with groups ranging from my Dad and brother in the Tony Vitale Trio, to playing with Joe Walsh & Barnstorm, The Eagles, Dan Fogelberg, Peter Frampton, Crosby, Stills and Nash, Ted Nugent, and Neil Young, just to name a few.

During my forty-eight year career, I've traveled literally millions of miles and played drums with the best musicians in the business, for hundreds of thousands of people. I've played in countries all over the planet, and have fans on every continent. But there's been a price to pay for the career I've had. I've performed when I've had broken bones, after being bitten by a black widow spider, when I had pneumonia, and I even had to fly out and play a show the day of my brother's funeral. I didn't have a honeymoon and although I've taken my family on the road, I've never taken them on vacation. I've missed countless birthdays, anniversaries, holidays, my parent's 50th wedding anniversary party and my sister's wedding.

And stories? Oh yeah, I've got stories. I haven't included one from every tour or record that I've done, just some of my very favorite stories from over the years. The experiences I've had during my career have been more interesting and exciting than I ever could have hoped for or dreamed of when I was just starting out. And just when I think I've seen it all, I'm amazed at something, like petting a koala bear or seeing the Southern Cross for the first time on my last trip to Australia with Crosby, Stills & Nash. After all the decades of playing the song, there in the pitch black sky was the constellation Stephen Stills had written about all those years ago.

I can look back in time with the pictures I've taken and see glimpses of myself having the time of my life with people young and living like there was no tomorrow. Life is fragile, and for some of them there was no tomorrow, and they've since passed away. But some are still going strong and are part of my life today. Good friends. Fabulous musicians. What great times! So, here are some of my stories. Some are funny, some are interesting, and some are just what happened. People who were there may remember things differently, but looking back, here's how I remember it.

CHAPTER TWO

Early years

I'm Italian...now there's an understatement. My grandparents on both sides came from Italy through Ellis Island and eventually settled in Ohio. They came on the quota system, learned English and had to have someone sponsor them. They worked very hard. My one grandfather mined coal and the other worked on the railroad. Nana Spataro was known for her cooking and Nana Vitale was known for her crocheting.

Italians are big on respect. In this book, you'll notice that I always capitalize "Mom" and "Dad" even though it's not correct English. I do that out of respect. I think parents deserve that. Both sides had big families full of respect...my Mom had five brothers and sisters and my Dad had four. When my Dad was ten, he started entertaining people with his accordion. It was during the Depression and he played at the soup kitchen after school for twenty-five cents for three hours. With those twenty-five cents, he was able to buy enough food for an entire meal for his family.

It was always very loud with lots of stories, laughter and great food whenever my family got together...which was all the time! There was usually music, too. My Dad was a barber and played the accordion with local groups. I always say my Mom played the radio. She actually played the sax and met my Dad when she went to Gattuso's Music Center to buy a strap. My Dad worked and gave lessons there at the time, and he wanted to see this cute little Italian girl again, but she was from a very strict family. He sold her a broken strap so she'd have to come back to return it. She did, and they started dating.

My Dad's music career was going well. He played in local groups and one night, when he was about twenty, he got the call of his life and was asked to fill in with The Tommy Dorsey Band locally at Moonlight Ballroom. About a week later, he got a call to come on the road with the band, which was a dream come true. Unfortunately, he had already signed a contract with The United States Army.

My Dad spent four years in the army and fought in the South Pacific, including Guadalcanal. He was a radio operator, often from a muddy foxhole. I have a diary he kept while he was there. He experienced horrific and terrifying things first hand. He shared some stories with us over the years, but although he was very proud of the service he'd given our country, he mostly told funny stories and kept the darker details to himself. He was badly damaged by his war experiences and spent a lot of time with other veterans who shared the scars. He made lifelong friends in the service. And when he got back, wearing his uniform, he married my Mom.

My Dad's side of the family is from Sicily, and my Mom's is from Calabria. The Calabrese side had a Christmas tradition of everyone getting together on Christmas Eve. The dinner table was covered with a red & white Italian tablecloth and thirteen kinds of food…one for each of the twelve apostles and Jesus, just like the Last Supper. Italian women make food and feed you to express their love. So, bursting with love, it took my Nanas, Mom, her sisters, and my aunts, two days to cook the food, using several stoves at different homes.

A lot of the fish were fried, and the aroma hung in the air for days. We had smelts, oysters, calamari, linguine with clam sauce, bacala (cod), and zepolle (deep fried dough with anchovies in it)… and pasta, pasta, pasta. We also had escarole salad, broccoli, cauliflower, and green and red Jello. The Italian bread was always warm and served sliced in a basket covered with a mopina (cloth napkin). Homemade Italian wine flowed, followed by annisetta. Mountains of homemade cookies of all kinds, including pizzelles, were piled high. It took days to bake all the different kinds. We ate them with spumoni and my Nana Spataro's ricotta cake.

Of course, we had a nativity set, which was from Woolworths, and we put it up under the Christmas tree. Combining cultures, my brother and I set it up beside the train tracks that surrounded our tree, in case anyone from the stable wanted to go for a ride. Sometimes the neighbor, dressed as Santa, made a stop at the house. Friends of the family dropped by and, of course, had to sit down at the crowded table and have something to eat and drink. My Mom never sat and ate a full meal, but perched at the corner of the table so she could jump up and hover around, serving everyone. My Dad played Christmas songs on his accordion and everyone sang along. On Christmas day, we opened our gifts and then went to mass.

I asked Santa for a drum.

I have home video of the last Christmas Eve my Dad was alive. After dinner, he sat at the end of the room in front of the fireplace, his accordion was placed on his lap and he played. He was dying of pancreatic cancer and would only live another ten days. Everyone was crying and would step out of the room so he wouldn't see the tears. I've never watched the video or looked at the photographs from that last Christmas Eve, and I doubt that I ever will.

I had an older brother Frank and a younger sister Joanne, who was born later when we moved to Florida. I was the standard middle kid who didn't get enough attention...I guess today you'd call me hyperactive. I was in trouble all the time, mostly from kid pranks. My brother was always a willing accomplice. We did things in the moment, not considering future consequences.

When I was a baby, I used to empty my Mom's cupboard, get her pots and pans out and hit them with her wooden sauce spoons. I was really peppy and left a few scratches and dents, but she still let me play with them. I still have a couple of those old pans. To my Mom, her pots and pans were like my drums are to me, and she really didn't like my daily destruction of them. So, my very first Christmas my parents got me a drum…I even have a picture of me with it. It made big loud bangs, way better than the pans. It was love at first sight, and it changed my life forever.

I love drums. Maybe it's the noise they make or being able to hit something. C'mon, I'm Italian. Ever notice how many drummers are Italian? We're very emotional and we have to blow off steam. Then again, maybe it's the attention I craved that I've always gotten when I play them. When I first met Susie, I actually told her I was married to my drums. Yeah, I really did. Whatever it is, I love 'em. Till death do us part. It's as much my identity as being Italian. It's who I am and what I'm all about. I even wrote songs called, "I Play The Drums" and "Speaking In Drums."

I was fascinated by drums. I have a picture of me drooling over a drum set at a wedding reception…I'm in the background and it was actually a picture of the bride and groom, Frank and Alice Corbi, cutting the cake. I must be about three by then. Check out the wonder on my face. I can hardly keep my hands off those drums. Interestingly enough, the set actually belonged to Carl Mitseff, nicknamed "Keek", who became my drum teacher years later in the 60's.

Music was always a part of our family gatherings. I can remember being about four and my Dad having groups of his friends and relatives over every week to watch the Friday Night Fights, sponsored by Gillette, of course. The men gathered in our small living room and watched on our black and white round-screened TV. They shouted, smoked cigars and cigarettes, drank beer, and ate cheese, salami, pepperoni and Italian bread. The women went in the kitchen, drank coffee, ate Italian cookies and talked. I played with my cousins. The room was filled with smoke, loud shouts and cheering. Gathering with family and friends...the typical kind of fun people had in the 50's.

As I said, my Dad was a musician, and so were a lot of our friends and relatives. When the fights were over, they'd get their instruments and play music in the living room. They never got tired of playing music together. They all had sheet music with their names written on the front. I still have a couple boxes of it.

My Dad had a lot of experiences playing gigs, and I loved hearing my Dad's old musician stories. My all-time favorite is the trombone story. Joe Walsh liked it so much that he always used to tell it at shows and sometimes on the radio. My Dad played with a trombone player named Dick Beiter. Yeah, that was really his name. His group played a lot of dances and parties at a lot of different places, including a mental institution, Massillon State Hospital, and another hospital called Molly Stark. Dick apparently wasn't listening very carefully when my Dad called to tell him where the gig was, so he showed up that night at Massillon State Hospital.

They'd played there a lot before, so he went right in, carrying his trombone in its case. He went to the gym, got the trombone out and started warming up, as he always did. Some attendant heard it and came in and said, "Hey, who are you, sir, and what are you doing here? …and by the way, where'd you get that trombone?" Dick said, "I'm in the band that's playing here tonight for the dance." Of course, there was no dance, so they thought he was one of the inmates.

They wanted him to go back to his room and tried to take the trombone. Dick got really upset and kept insisting that he was in the band that was playing for a dance there…and he wasn't about to give them his trombone. More attendants came. The more they didn't believe him, the more frustrated and upset Dick got. Finally, they wrenched the trombone away from him and Dick lost it. They wrestled him to the floor, put him in a straight jacket and gave him a shot to knock him out. Meantime, my Dad was at the gig at Molly Stark, wondering where Dick was. My Dad called Dick's wife, the highway patrol and hospital emergency rooms. No one knew where he was. Dick spent the night there and it wasn't straightened out till the next day. From that story, I learned that you gotta pay attention to that itinerary.

I saw my Dad playing music for people, and they seemed to really like it. He got attention and approval and had a lot of fun. I started to follow in his footsteps. It's really silly, but I remember being at Gibbs Elementary School in Canton, Ohio, and playing a plastic clarinet for my kindergarten class, so I

must have been five by then. I don't remember what I played, or how bad it was, but I already enjoyed playing music for people. It was in my blood from my family experiences.

I Play The Drums

People always ask me how I learned to play the drums. I started when I was really young. My brother had a lot of allergies, so we moved to Fort Lauderdale, Florida, in 1955. By that time, my Christmas drum was long gone, having been beaten to death, so the following year I started taking drum lessons on a practice pad, with Joe Salvi. I was seven. I'm so glad he was my first drum teacher. Joe was a friend of my Dad and had moved to Miami because there was a lot of music work in the 50's. He was a great drummer and teacher, and was also a violin virtuoso, which is an odd combination of instruments.

I had lessons once a week and never practiced. I ran over my lesson in the car on the half-hour drive to Joe's and I always did well. We used Charley Wilcoxon drum books. When I moved back to Ohio, I eventually took lessons in Cleveland from Charley himself. I still have those books with Joe's handwritten notes, and one of the notes has stuck with me all these years. It read, "Ten minutes of concentrated practice is worth more than two hours of goofing." Goofing? Me? Why would he write that? Thus, concentrated practice in the car seemed to me to have Joe's stamp of approval.

The lessons were rudiments and exercises and took a half an hour. He gave me my lessons, which cost about a buck, for free, and my Dad, being a barber, cut his hair, which cost about two bucks, for free. Every couple of weeks he got his hair cut, so it worked out really well.

I started playing snare drum in the Fort Lauderdale City Youth Orchestra that year. I thought that it was really geeky, but my Dad said that to be picked for this was a big honor. We had too many rehearsals for just one performance, and I had to wear this stupid bow tie. And check out the guitar player in her frilly little dress! As I remember it, we weren't too good. I didn't join the following year. I knew

what good musicians were supposed to sound like.

My family was full of musicians. My Dad played accordion, my Mom played sax in high school, my Uncle Paul Spataro played upright bass, keyboards and sang, my Uncle Mario Solito played accordion, my Uncle Vince Vitale played bass, and my brother Frank played accordion, bass and keyboards.

My Uncle Paul, my godfather, moved to Florida and drove down from Canton, Ohio, with a set of drums he bought for me for my eighth birthday. Uncle Paul always took a special interest in me and encouraged me like I was his son, and I knew I could count on him for anything. The drums were silver and blue Ludwigs. Joe Salvi even added a few more pieces to it. It was the most exciting day of my life

up to that point, to have a real drum set of my own. Joe Salvi started teaching me how to play set. I played that same drum set into the mid sixties.

And that brings me to my first gig, at an assembly with my brother at St. Clements Elementary School in Florida. I was in the fifth grade. My brother played accordion and I played snare. Our show was three songs. We played "When The Saints Go Marching In", "Ah Maria", and "The Beer Barrel Polka"…great set list….and what a finish…we

rocked the house! The nuns snapped their fingers and tapped their toes under their black habits. The kids thought we were great! We were the most popular kids in school for a good two weeks. I knew I'd never get enough of this!

My interest in music after that gig rapidly accelerated. I was on a mission. As you all know, rock & roll was born in the 50's, and I started listening to artists like Elvis Presley, Little Richard, Chuck Berry and Fats Domino. When I used to go roller skating, they played rock & roll over the big speakers, and it sounded unbelievably great. But when I got home, I had to listen to music on our cream colored plastic Philco radio which had a very small speaker and didn't sound very good. I wished that the music on the radio sounded as good as the music on our TV. Then I had an idea.

I was about ten by then, and I loved electronics. One day when I was home alone, with my limited knowledge of electronics, I took the speaker out of the TV and attached two wires to it with my recent birthday gift, a soldering gun. At the time, my Mom, who knew me well, felt that giving me a soldering gun was a very bad idea. Oblivious to the dangers of electrocution, I hooked the speaker up to our radio. It was fabulous!

However, I now had a problem…the TV no longer had a speaker. So, I took the tiny speaker from the radio and put it in the TV, wired it up, and it worked. I didn't think anyone would notice the difference, and when my Dad questioned as to why the TV sounded funny, I looked innocent and made no comment. A few days later, when the morning sun shone into our Florida room, it backlit the TV, and the silhouette of the small speaker showed in the big space where the other speaker had been. It didn't take anyone long to figure out I did it. Yeah, I was in trouble again. And what did I learn from this? I learned that I needed equipment!

I needed something to burn off some of my energy and drums seemed like the ticket. Like I said, I was hyperactive or something and sometimes did things either for attention or just to have some excitement. Yeah, even then. This is a foreshadowing of things to come on the road. When I was in the first grade at Northside Elementary School, I set off the fire alarm. Now, I'm just telling you this, I'm not recommending it. The kids were daring me to do it. Back then you didn't have to break the glass on the alarm, you just pulled the lever, so I did. When a fire alarm goes off at a grade  school, it's serious, and a lot of fire trucks show up. Five big red fire trucks came to the school. It was really exciting! Of course, they found out who did it, and I had to face the principal and my parents.

I moved on to St. Clements Elementary School, where I made a big splash. One day my Mom sent me canned sardines in my Superman lunch box. I was just a kid, and I hated sardines...what was she thinking? I took them into the bathroom and crammed them down the drain, sending them to a watery grave... a nice Italian touch. I never considered that the drain would back up, sending water all over the place. Water all over the place...just like the water fights in hotels with Joe Walsh in my future. With very little detective work they found out I did that, too. I mean, who else would have access to sardines? I was becoming a regular at the principal's office there, too.

My parents got my brother and me bikes for Christmas that year, which gave me a wider range to find trouble. The neighborhood kids had a regular contest, called, "Meet you at Sixth Street." We'd all take different routes and try to get there first. I was riding as fast as I could and blew through a stop sign. Unfortunately, there was a Wilton Manors police officer coming in my direction. He made a U turn, turned his siren on, and actually pulled up behind me, pulling me over. Youth crime wasn't like it is today. I got a  ticket and I had to appear in juvenile court with my parents. I pleaded guilty and was sentenced to a one hour class of bicycle safety. My parents took my bike away for a month, but I was soon riding into danger again.

During our game of "Meet you at Sixth Street", one of the boys discovered an abandoned shack near a canal, where we started hanging out…you know, like secret meetings and stuff. We got the bright idea to fake a note from our parents and buy a pack of Salem cigarettes. We forged a note and sent little Tommy Burns on the caper. Unbelievably, he was able to buy the cigarettes. We met at the shack to smoke them. It was getting really smoky in there, so someone opened the window and saw that an alligator had crawled up on shore for a nap, right between the door and our bikes. We were trapped!

It was hot and in the middle of the afternoon, and the alligator must have been really tired. We yelled and threw things at it, but it wouldn't budge. Time ticked away. Our parents started worrying that none of us were home, since it was getting near dinner time. My Mom called the police and my Dad, who came home early from work. We were stuck in that shack for about four hours. We were so scared, that we seriously discussed never going home again. Around dusk, the alligator got up and slid down into the canal. We went home, reeking of cigarette smoke, and lost the use of our bikes for another month.

Once we got our bikes back again, we rode everywhere. There was a lot to do outside in Florida, and my brother and I were oblivious to the natural dangers. One day we rode to an area we had never been to before, where we came across an abandoned cement trough...it looked just like a boat. Coincidentally, my brother, Frank, and I were into boating. Like all kids in Florida, we learned to swim at a very young age. Unfortunately, that gave us the confidence to drag the trough over to the nearby canal and launch the makeshift boat. We used two scrap boards for paddles, and just like Huckleberry Finn, we started out on our adventure.

It was wonderful! It was a hot summer day and we started paddling toward the deepest part of the canal, when we noticed that there was a crack in the bottom of our boat and we were taking on water...a lot of water. By now we were at the center of the canal and it quickly became apparent that we were going down. Looking around for any kind of help, my brother spotted two hungry alligators on the opposite shore, looking for an adventure of their own.

We knew we'd never make it in our boat, so we abandoned ship and frantically swam toward shore with the alligators close behind. As soon as we hit land, we ran to our bikes, and, dripping with canal water, peddled home as fast as we could go. We arrived home, still terrified and soaking wet. My Mom asked how we got wet and we just said, "We fell in the canal." We learned nothing, but I had boating in my future. I never dreamed at the time that one day I'd record an album with Joe Walsh on a yacht in Florida.

OK, so boating didn't work out so well at the time. We thought that maybe we should stay away from the canal for a while and stick to the field, which had ground cover as high as our heads, that was near our house. We found a small clearing and set up camp with sterno and a can of pork and beans and started heating up the food. The fire wasn't working very well, but we noticed that there were a lot of very dry pine needles on the ground.

We gathered them up and built a really great fire, which quickly started spreading to the surrounding area. We tried to put it out with our little canteens of water, but there wasn't enough water to stop it. My brother and I took off, and the neighbors who saw the smoke called the fire department. Three trucks came. This disaster worked out really well for us. By the time they were able to put out the fire, so much of the field had burned that we now had a natural clearing to play baseball. We cleared an even larger area, and made a baseball field.

We recruited a bunch of the neighborhood kids and formed two teams. For a while, playing baseball was our life. I still have my glove. We couldn't wait to get home from school, do our homework and hit the field. The Florida sun was baking hot and we didn't have any shade on our field, so we thought we'd build a dugout area for our teams. We rounded up wood and dug holes about three feet deep in the sand. Then we put a heavy wooden roof over the hole and all got into the dugout. It was great to be in the shade! But, the sandy unsupported sides started caving in, and the hole began to rapidly fill with water. The heavy roof was trapping us in the hole, so we had to dig out like groundhogs. We decided to go without the dugout of death, and played at the field the rest of the time we lived in Florida. When I moved back to Ohio, one of the neighborhood boys was named Thurman Munson. Yeah, THE Thurman Munson…as in New York Yankees. He loved baseball as much as I loved my drums.

Back to Ohio

We lived in Florida from 1955 to 1960, and then we moved back to Canton, Ohio, so my Dad could get more work. I had a paper route for a couple of years, which is not a fun job in Ohio's snow. After the Florida sunshine, we didn't find the winter snow and cold magical at all. Even sled riding, snowball fights, ice skating and building snow forts didn't make up for the cold. I hated it. My family rented until we could find a house to buy, so I went half my 6th grade year at St. Paul's, then went to St. John's for the rest of that year and my 7th and 8th grade years. Regardless of the climate, my need for entertainment continued.

The nuns at our school used to serve us milk in glass bottles and I heard that the empty bottles made a really funny noise when you flushed them down the toilet. I'm a musician. I love noise. I flushed one down. It worked! It made the noise! I enjoyed it so much that, one by one, I flushed a whole bunch of them down the toilet, which eventually backed up.

When a toilet backs up, a kid's natural inclination is to keep flushing it, to try and get it to unclog and work again. I thought a few more flushes might get things going again. Water flowed everywhere. Then the sewer backed up into the cafeteria and did about $700 in damages. More water damages…my destiny. My amusement turned to fear when the parish priest showed up the following day and went classroom by classroom, trying to get the culprit to confess to the crime. I tried to look as innocent as possible and my big Italian eyes worked again. I looked totally angelic and they bought it.

I really didn't care much about spelling and English, and couldn't see how important they would be for lyrics, so I generally did just enough work to get by. But even when I was trying to do well, my Italian heritage sometimes affected my academics. One night we were sitting around the table at dinner and my Dad asked me how my day at school had been. I had to tell him that I'd been knocked out of the spelling bee in the very first round. "What word did you miss?" he asked, so I explained that I'd misspelled the word "sandwich." He asked me how I spelled it, and I said, "I spelled it just like it sounds… s-a-n-g-w-i-c-h….sangwich." That's how my Dad always pronounced it, so I thought that's how everyone else said it, too. My Dad immediately was angry and came to my defense. "Rose, isn't that how you spell 'sangwich?'" he demanded, reaching his hand out as if appealing to reason. My Mom looked first at my Dad, and then at me, like we were complete morons. Then she just shook her head, looked down at the sauce and said, "How about another meatball?"

Not that I was holding a grudge, something all Italians are intensely trained for early on, but I wanted to get back at the nuns at school… didn't everyone? The nuns wore long black habits back then, so when they were writing on the blackboard with their backs to us, we used to flick little sticky spit balls at them. It was easy game…a large, slow moving target. The little white spit balls would stick to their backs…sometimes there would be almost a hundred of them and it looked like a moving snow storm. OK, I still laugh at that one. Like I said, my need for entertainment caused me to always be in trouble at school. Today I think of it as expressing my creativity.

I clearly needed an outlet for this need, so my parents had me take more drum lessons…you know, something physical to wear me out. I continued my lessons on drums with Keek, who had the same deal with my Dad as Joe Salvi…drum lessons for haircuts. Keek came over to my house and gave me drum lessons every week for the next several years. He was a fantastic teacher. He had a big band that sometimes played at Meyers Lake's Moonlight Ballroom.

Meyers Lake had an amusement park, beach, fishing, boat dock, restaurant and ballroom on its shore. All the big name big bands played at Moonlight Ballroom in the 40's and 50's. There was even a large outdoor ballroom called Moonlight Gardens, where the summer nights were lit with neon and the air was filled with the aroma of beer, cigars and petunias. The bands played outside and people sat on red and white metal folding chairs at little white tables, or danced "under the stars" and, sometimes, fell in love. The warm summer-night breezes were filled with the sounds of music, the roller coaster, the carousel, laughter and crickets. What atmosphere! But, I cared only about the music.

A really great memory I have is when I was about twelve and Keek's band was rehearsing at The Parkway Nightclub for their gig at Moonlight Ballroom. It was a big deal to play at the ballroom, and Keek wanted to sound as good as the national bands that sometimes played there. He had some 78 rpm records and charts of songs his big band was playing that he brought to some of my lessons, and then he worked with me so I'd know how to play them.

One Sunday afternoon, I was watching them at rehearsal when Keek called me up to the bandstand and gave me his sticks. He was so good to me. I got to play with a seventeen-piece orchestra. It was absolutely thrilling. I was reading music and playing with all these professional guys. I was only twelve, seventh grade, and scared to death, but I knew some of the guys, who were friends with my Dad, and they were really nice to me. Did it make an impression on me? It was throwing gasoline on a fire! I can still remember how excited I was and how wonderful it was to play with professionals.

Two years later, I went to Lehman High School where I joined the band and learned even more about playing with other musicians. I heard about this drum teacher who was really good at teaching rudiments, so for a while, I took lessons with Bob White. He helped me get a solid foundation and excel in marching drum technique. I was in the Lehman High School Band all four years, which included marching band, pep band, and orchestra. On Friday nights during football season, I used to walk three miles from my house to Fawcett Stadium, play at the football game, and then walk home again, alone in the dark. We had horrible outfits that were really hot, with  giant hats that looked like something the Pope would wear. I was lucky I wasn't beat up on the way home.

The summer of 1964, when I was going to be a sophomore, we marched in the very first Pro Football Hall of Fame Parade. It was

August and about 90 degrees, and we wore our wool uniforms. The end of the parade route used to wind through Stadium Park and up the hill to The Professional Football Hall of Fame building. A lot of band members never made it up that last hill. Even playing drums for the entire parade, I always made it. Eventually, they mercifully changed the parade route.

I'm glad that I was in the band and that I took orchestra. I have a picture of me playing tympani and I also learned a lot about other instruments like bells and vibes, which I ended up using later on in my career. High school band helped me grow and mature musically, and was a great foundation for learning to play with other musicians.

I joined the Musician's Union in 1963 when I was fourteen. Now, normally in the 60's, you weren't allowed to join unless you were sixteen, and, even if you did join, you weren't allowed to play nightclubs. But, I passed the test…yeah, you had to take a test back then to join. You had to go to the union office and they asked you music theory questions. Then they put music in front of you and said, "Play this," and if you couldn't read music and play it, they wouldn't give you a union card.

As long as my Dad was alive, whenever I was really excited and telling him about a new gig with someone and what a big star they were, like Peter Frampton, Joe Walsh, CSN or The Eagles, my Dad would narrow his eyes, squint through his glasses and say sternly, "Can he read?" It was his criteria for success or failure. Eventually, I overcame my frustration with this reaction and just thought how "old school" it was.

My Dad had been a member of the Musicians Union for years, and I was playing with his band, so even though I was under age to play in nightclubs, my Dad was there, so it was OK. So, there I was at fourteen, playing in a band called The Tony Vitale Trio with my brother and Dad. We played at weddings, parties, and in this jazz club, The Fox and Hound Club, in The Belden Hotel in Canton. I didn't care much about school, and even though I had a high IQ, it didn't interest me and I didn't study very much. I did really well in math and took college level courses in high school, but I didn't do very well in English and history. Thank God for my Aunt Kate, who always typed, and I'm sure corrected, my papers for me. I cared only about music.

I had my drums set up in my family's living room, and that's where I practiced. I got a lot more practice in during the summer when I was out of school and home alone during the day. I did do a few things besides music. I played football in the 8th grade with the St. John's Crusaders. Our colors were green and white. At my size, you can imagine how good I was. I played offensive guard…and my playing was pretty offensive. You know the type, stocky and low to the ground. And what loyalty! I was on the sidelines warming the bench every game.

I was too small to play football and too short to play basketball, so baseball was my game. I played short stop, and I mean SHORT stop, in Little League and did pretty well, so I enjoyed playing. Thurman Munson lived in my neighborhood and was always coming by my house wanting to play baseball…even in the winter. There'd be a knock at the door and it would be Thurman Munson carrying a duffle bag full of gloves, baseballs, bats and catcher's equipment. He'd say, "Hey Joe, let's throw the ball around a little bit." I'd say, "Thurman, it's January." And he'd answer, "Ah, just put a coat on and let's play some baseball."

He'd commentate while we played catch, "Mantle steps up to the plate…Wow! He hits a long drive into center field." Then as he'd throw a towering high ball, he'd continue, "Vitale goes back and HE… MAKES…THE… CATCH!" He also liked it when I'd throw as hard as

I could with him in the catcher position, pretending to be Yogi Berra. All the players' names he used were Yankees, except mine. When we were finished playing my Mom would feed us…he loved my Mom and her cooking.

The cool thing was that we didn't know the future…that he would someday catch for The New York Yankees as team captain. I can't believe I used to play catch with Thurman Munson, and went to high school with him and his future wife, Diane. Years later, I really loved seeing him catch for the New York Yankees and was so proud that he did so well, and that we had been friends. He was a great guy and I really respected him. As I said earlier, he was as crazy about baseball as I was about drums.

Besides baseball, I was also in the Soap Box Derby for four years, when I was eleven through fourteen. Back then the rules were really strict and you had to build the car all by yourself. They really checked up on you, but also were there if you needed the answers to any questions. No girls were allowed.

I built four cars, and in order to pay for the supplies, Ewing Chevrolet got sponsors to help the kids with their expenses. Each kid would get a sponsor and then you'd put the name of your sponsor's company on your car. It didn't cost much, probably about $50 for the wood, paint, wheels and axles. It was just advertising and a nice thing for the businesses to do to support the local kids. I think the deadline was May 1st, since the Derby was in July. The first year I was running a little late, so by the time I got a sponsor there weren't many companies left to choose from. My first car read "Atomic Sewer Cleaning."

My Uncle Frank Spataro, who had a junk yard and auto repair place, was my sponsor the next year, so my car that year read "A-1 Auto," which was quite an improvement. The third year was the Soap Box Derby's 25th silver anniversary, and for that and my fourth year, my sponsor was "DePasquale's Silk Screening." It was great, because they were the ones who did the lettering on my cars and it made them look really professional.

I built my cars mostly with hand tools. I didn't have many power tools…I had an electric drill and that was about it. I think now the Derby allows adults to help, but back then, you were supposed to do it all yourself, so the cars were a little rough around the edges, a little funkier. I didn't win, but I built them all myself and I learned a lot doing it. I've still got my entry trophies, pictures, helmets and tee shirts from my soap box derby years. Building those cars helped me learn the basics of construction, which eventually made it possible for me to build several home studios for myself, the studio Joe Walsh and I built in Nederland, home studios for both Stephen Stills and Graham Nash, and gobos for Neil Young's studio.

Even though I was raised in the city, another thing I enjoyed doing was our own style of camping. Sometimes in the summer, my brother Frank, the Palumbo boys and I used to sleep on the front porch at night. We lived in the city on Woodland Avenue, right near 12th Street, which was relatively safe back then. We would walk to the Your Pizza Shop and buy a pizza and Cokes, and then bring them back to eat outside on the porch while we talked and waited for my Dad to go to sleep. Then the night began. We went out and walked through the neighborhood looking for adventure, rode our bikes, and dodged the police. It was fun because we knew we weren't allowed to be out that late.

Spending the night on the porch was just like camping, but we wanted to have a real outdoor adventure. I'm not sure what he was thinking, but my Dad, not exactly an outdoorsman himself, drove us…me, my brother and the three Palumbo boys, Jimmy, Rodney and Dennis, to a deserted country woods south of town on Route 43, and dropped us off. It was late afternoon on Friday after he got home from work. He said to meet him there on Sunday afternoon at 1:00 PM. Yeah, two days later. Today, this would be considered some sort of crime. Back then, it was an adventure!

He left us with sleeping bags, pup tents, Spam, bread, chips, cookies, peanut butter, pork & beans and hot dogs and buns. We had our small canteens full of water. Remember, this is before cell phones. We didn't know the people who owned the property and we didn't have their permission to camp there. We hadn't checked the weather forecast. It was really odd for someone who was such a strict parent to drop us off in the country with no supervision. I was in the eighth grade, but, except for sleeping on the front porch, I was totally inexperienced as a camper.

We picked up our Army back packs and hiked into the woods for about an hour. We had never been there before, so we had no idea where we were going. We found a place to camp near a lake and built a campfire. This fire went better than the one in Florida. We made hot dogs the first night, then put up our tents. We talked until dark, and I mean DARK. Although we had flashlights, an Army knife and a hatchet, we were pretty scared when we heard "things" rustling in the bushes that night. It was colder than we expected. Remember, we were city kids. We finally fell asleep.

The next day we got up and had Spam for breakfast. Then we left our campsite and walked around by the lake. We came back and had peanut butter sandwiches. We noticed we were already starting to run out of water. It was starting to get hot, so we got into our bathing suits and went swimming for a couple hours. We returned to the campsite and made more Spam and pork & beans, and talked until dark. That night we heard some people walking around near our campsite and we were really scared. Jimmy thought they might be Indians. No one bothered us, though, and we finally went to sleep.

We got up Sunday and had the last of our food, which was cookies, and we were more than ready to go home. We walked down to the meeting place at least two hours earlier than we were supposed to. We were done with camping. My Dad picked us up on time and took us home. We never went camping again. Nothing in my childhood outdoors experiences prepared me to go hunting with Ted Nugent or to spend time with Joe Walsh and Dan Fogelberg in the mountains of Colorado. I was totally a fish out of water.

In the summer of 1963, my brother and I caddyed at Congress Lake Country Club located about twenty minutes north of Canton. My cousins, Tony and Frank, had told us about caddying for a summer job. My Uncle Vince Vitale used to let them drive his '57 Chevy to the golf course. Unfortunately, they were only fourteen and fifteen, and had no driver's licenses, but, hey, things were different then. It was probably safer than hitchhiking, which is what my brother and I did. My parents let us hitchhike up Market Avenue with our lunchboxes and sometimes we had to walk the last mile to the course. We made about $2.50 an hour, so by the end of the day we usually earned about $11 with the tip. Then we had to hitchhike home.

We tried not to go on Wednesdays, because that was the day doctors came to golf. They had the biggest bags with the most clubs and accessories, and gave the smallest tips. Thursday was women's day, and we loved that. They had light bags and paid us the best. Sometimes they drove carts, and had us walk along with them carrying their bags. Then they'd ask us which club to use. We could hardly contain ourselves when they asked us, "Caddy, can you wash our balls?"

One time we rode up to Congress Lake in the '57 Chevy with my cousins, and brought our accordion and drums. We set up and played music at the caddyshack. The golfers complained because it made too much noise. How could a polka band on the thirteenth hole be distracting?

Caddying was hard work and we did it about three times a week for a couple of summers. When we weren't working, we used to walk or ride our bikes everywhere because my parents only had one car, which my Dad took to work. Sometimes we took the bus. The #2 McKinley bus went out to Meyers Lake Amusement Park. Everyone who lived in Canton during those years loved Meyers Lake Park and has stories to tell about being there. There was a roller coaster, a Stein & Goldstein carousel that now sits in Bushnell Park in downtown Hartford, Connecticut, a Laugh In The Dark with a Laughing Lady, a neon light covered tower with silver rockets that flew over the lake, a ferris wheel, kiddieland, a miniature golf course, and all the rides common to the time.

The admission was free and we only paid for the rides we rode and the food we ate. There were candy apples, cotton candy, pop corn, hot dogs, french fries, hamburgers, ice cream and snow cones. If you were old enough, you could smoke a cigar and have an ice-cold beer by the lake in The Beer Garden. The beach cost $5 for an entire summer swimming pass. The crystal-clear, spring-fed lake water was icy cold and had large chunks of gravel on the bottom that killed our bare feet. In the hot summer sun, the beach smelled like mowed grass, lake water, wet rubber bathing suits and Sea & Ski tanning lotion. That grassy beach was in my future, but not just for swimming.

The southwest edge of the park near the parking lot held the Lakeshore Restaurant and the Comet. The Comet was a wooden roller coaster, which made this tremendous racket combined with the screams of the riders every time it went down the first hill. If you walked under the Comet's structure, you could find coins, papers, and even false teeth! And right beside the Comet stood Moonlight Ballroom. Meyers Lake was full of entertainment, excitement, romance and dreams. We went whenever we could. I loved that place. Everyone did. We thought it would be there forever. I spent a lot of time there on weekends and that park was what I was thinking of when I wrote, "Roller Coaster Weekend." By the time my first album was coming out, the park was closed forever and the roller coaster was being torn down. Sometimes people ask me if that was the roller coaster on the front cover of my first album. Sad to say, it wasn't.

So, here I was, a Midwest Italian kid who loved music with dreams of becoming a professional, and somehow believing that dream could come true. On Sunday February 9, 1964, my life changed forever. I, along with millions of other American teenagers, watched

The Beatles on The Ed Sullivan Show. It blew my mind, focused my dreams and confirmed my "mission" to become a professional musician. It was attainable. I was fourteen and started fanatically practicing playing drums to rock & roll music, with headphones on so my Dad wouldn't hear. It was the perfect time in history to be a teenage musician in America. Although I had dreamed of a career as a professional musician and had never wanted to do anything else, I was now consumed with that dream. I still wanted a career in music, but now I wanted a career in rock & roll music. Looking back, I see that my whole life, I was moving down a path straight toward my dreams.

"Searching for the Path"   *Photo by: Joe Vitale Jr.*

CHAPTER THREE

<u>The Knights</u>

My freshman year at Lehman High School there was a band called The Knights. Tom Krammes and Lowell Stein played guitar, and Tom's brother, John, played drums. They needed a bass player and asked if I knew one. After seeing Ed Sullivan, I REALLY wanted to be in a rock band, so I said that I played bass. I had never played bass guitar in my life. I borrowed a bass from my cousins, who owned Gattuso's Music Center. The Knights played several gigs... I especially remember playing two at Lehman High School, one at Cholley's, one at an All City Dance at the YWCA, and one for my cousin Lynette's eighth grade graduation party at Belle Stone Elementary School. Lynette led the charge and got all the girls to scream when we played. For a moment, we had a glimpse of rock stardom and we were The Beatles. My mission became even more clear.

I had to sneak off to rehearse and do gigs with this band, because my Dad hated rock & roll. A few days later, there was a story about the All City Dance in the local newspaper, The Canton Repository. My Dad saw my name in the paper and hit the roof, so I had to quit the Knights. I was a drummer and I really didn't want to be a bass player, so it's just as well that my career with them was so brief. But, my mission was far from over.

The Echoes

It was a hot August weekend during the summer of 1964. I was now fifteen years old and going into my sophomore year in high school. Sometimes life takes unexpected turns in ways you could never anticipate. I had no idea that playing with The Tony Vitale Trio at the Magnolia, Ohio, homecoming would launch my career in rock & roll.

Magnolia is a very small, picturesque country town south of Canton, which, at the time, had one traffic light. Standing right along Main Street near that light is a large red restored historic building, The Magnolia Flour Mill. A river and canal flow side by side along the outskirts of town, so Magnolia is surrounded by a tall earthen dike with massive iron gates, which can close across the road to prevent flooding. Literally right outside of town was an airport with a blacktop runway where drag races were held on Sundays in the summer. They're still held there today.

It was a typical small-town homecoming with lots of foods, rides, exhibits and entertainment. The event had one stage, the bandstand, and all kinds of musical entertainment. It stood on the edge of town near the dike and baseball field, and people could sit in the grass or on their folding lawn chairs and listen. There were bluegrass and country western bands, a dance band, our band, which played polkas, and a band called The Echoes, which played rock & roll.

The Echoes had Tim Hogan on rhythm guitar, John Berecek on lead guitar, and Al Twiss on bass, and they all sang. Their drummer, John Gardner, had already left for college to become a dentist. When I started to take my drums down after The Tony Vitale Trio played, the guys from The Echoes asked me if I'd mind leaving them up and playing with them. Mind?

We played typical top 40 songs, including "Wipeout," a favorite of mine since it featured drums. I was on top of the world playing with a rock & roll band. It ranks right up there as one of the best days of my life. They thanked me for playing, and we exchanged telephone numbers. I went back to high school that fall thinking about this wonderful experience I'd had. I daydreamed about it in study hall. But when they didn't call for a long time, I started to think that they never would.

The Echoes finally called me in January of 1965, and asked me to play a gig with them in Louisville at Cholley's Rollatorium, a fairly rowdy roller skating place that had teen dances. I was so thrilled. We started rehearsal at Cholley's at night after school. I couldn't drive yet, so they'd pick me up. We rehearsed for a few days and then we played the gig. I'd told  my parents that I had a gig at Cholley's, but for some reason they didn't ask who I was playing with. We played Beach Boys, Beatles,

Chuck Berry and other top 40 tunes. To this day, it was the most fun I ever had in my life, because it was all new, fresh and innocent. I'll remember that night forever. After the show, they asked me to join their band. I said, "Absolutely!"

I went home and lay in bed most of that night wondering how I would quit my Dad and brother's band, The Tony Vitale Trio, to play music that they both hated, with The Echoes. It was too powerful, though, and I had to do it, even though I knew it would be "High Noon" at the Vitale house when I told them. It was. I told them a week later and it was a horrible scene. My Dad shouted, "You'll never go anywhere in rock & roll and when you're sixty you'll be playing in dives!"

For me, the 60's were wonderful, golden years. Life made sense. The nucleus of high school life back then was muscle cars, the radio, rock & roll music, dances, cinema drive-ins, the local high school game, and the local

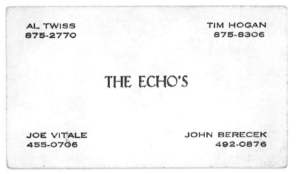

AL TWISS
875-2770

TIM HOGAN
875-8306

THE ECHO'S

JOE VITALE
455-0706

JOHN BERECEK
492-0876

hamburger hang-out which kids cruised through. At Lehman High School, it was "The A" which was short for The Avalon. The Lincoln High School kids went to Eckard's, which at one time actually had waiters on roller skates. We went to movies, bowled and played miniature golf. We didn't have computers or video games and we only had three channels on TV. No remote, either, so we had to get up to change the channel. Most homes eventually had a private phone line, and one black rotary dial telephone.

Teenagers weren't using drugs or drinking that much, so there were teen dances everywhere, every weekend. Songs were about love, cars and dancing. Everybody danced. The wilder kids smoked cigarettes. If someone was what we call "hot" today, we said that they were "tuff." Occasionally, a fight broke out over someone's boyfriend or girlfriend. There were almost no gangs, except in movies like "West Side Story."

Sound systems weren't so great and DJs used scratchy 45's, so most dances had live music. That worked out well for me. There were teen dance places everywhere, especially at swim clubs in the summer. I really liked the name of one place we played called "Suntan Acres." Yeah, back then, suntans were good. We set up right by the pool or on the beach at local lakes, and played. The kids danced around the pool or in the sand on the beach. At the Lake Cable dances on Wednesday nights, the girls would dance in the sand and burn their bare feet on the still smoldering cigarette butts smokers had tossed on the ground. When we played at Meyers Lake beach, we set up on the shoreline with the lake behind us and the kids danced on the grassy beach. Once we played there with The Standells, who had the hit song "Dirty Water."

In the winter we went ice skating, bowled, went to the local high school game, and the dances were moved indoors to high school gyms and dance clubs. They were always packed. All kids wanted to do was dance. Well, almost. If you were in high school in the 60's, you know exactly what I'm talking about. It was a wonderful time.

Season's Greetings

'The Echo's

I couldn't have been playing with three nicer guys, which made The Echoes such a great experience. I was so proud to play in such a popular band that played so well. We considered ourselves a band and a team, and I felt that I totally belonged in this group. These guys became my lifelong friends.

Tim Hogan was a soft gentle soul who sang like an angel. He not only sang with The Echoes and The Chylds, but he also sang at his church. Every band needs a singer who can hit those high notes. He was that kind of singer. He played rhythm guitar and keyboards with us. He was a dear friend.

John Berecek was our lead guitar player and a solid musician and singer. He and Tim had a Lennon-McCartney type blend, so when we covered songs by the Beatles or Beach Boys we could sound really great because of the vocals. John will always be a good friend and I talk to him every few months. We still enjoy talking about our days together in the Echoes, and later, The Chylds. John still plays his guitar and loves music.

Al Twiss, our bass player, was the rebel and a great guy to have in the band. He had lots of energy and always had new ideas for us to try. He constantly worked on our set list bringing new songs to the table all the time.

I played drums and also sang lead and back up vocals. I was recruited to get a lot of the chord changes for songs we were learning, which wasn't easy at the time, but it forced me to learn keyboards. Of course, I was the jokester in the band. Although all of us came from different walks of life, the chemistry and personalities immediately gelled from day one.

Lake Cable 2007

We started playing all over the area and got a huge amount of fans and recognition, so "The Echoes" made a 45 single at Akron Recording called "Around And Around." We paid for the recording ourselves and bought a thousand copies of the 45 for about twenty-nine cents each, to sell at our gigs. We got our money back, even with selling them for about fifty-nine cents.

The Chylds

We were really in demand since there were only a few bands in town, and we were approached by an artist manager named Nick Boldi. We decided to sign with him, because by that time we were at a point where we needed management. He hooked us up with Carl Maduri, who was Nick's partner in a music publishing company. They got us a deal with Warner Brothers Records, who wanted to change our name, since they thought it sounded a little dated at the time, like a 50's band.

Nick wanted us to be called "The Wild Childs," but we weren't that kind of a band, so that didn't last long. At one point, we wore ties and coats. Then we cut it down to "The Childs" and with the British Invasion, and the different spellings of everything, we called it "The Chylds" with a "y."

When I was in the Echoes, we dressed alike and had one outfit. We had black pants with light green jackets, white shirts and ties, or sometimes turtlenecks. We looked too collegiate and "clean cut," so when we became the Chylds, we wanted to change our image. We got brown corduroy suits and wore them with Beatle boots to look more British. I had a Beatle haircut. My Dad was also my barber, so we had yet another frequent clash. It was a constant struggle to keep my hair as long as possible.

Nick, who wore sharkskin suits, was kind of stuck in a 50's Vegas generation thing, and had this Wild Chylds vision of us. Anyway, he had a lady named Clara...we called her "Clarabelle"...I'll never forget her...she lived in a trailer and literally had one tooth on the bottom row. One tooth. So, Nick had her make two harlequin type outfits for us. We looked like court jesters or jokers from a deck of playing cards, with the top half black and the other half hounds tooth, and the bottom having the opposite sides half black and half hounds tooth. The other suits were the same design and were half orange and half white. I don't even want to go there. There are pictures of how terrible those outfits were, and I still have mine buried deep in the back of my closet. Their awfulness is beyond description. The suit probably still fits...not like I'd try it on.

WARNER BROS.
RECORDS

"CHYLDS"

Nick R. Boldi
Personal Manager

L to R Front: Al Twiss, John Berecek, Tim Hogan. On Piano: Joe Vitale

The horrible suits were even duplicated on a set of handmade dolls some of our fans made us. The girls dressed the dolls in the black and white suits….they must have taken a lot of work. I still have those dolls. We had several fan clubs of really nice girls who followed us, wrote to us, and had parties whenever it was one of our birthdays. My sister, Joanne, was, without question, my biggest fan and always was supportive of my career. I can't tell you how much that's meant to me over the years.

Having all these fans could have really gone to our heads, but we also had gigs that helped us remain humble. John recently reminded me of the worst gig we ever played with The Chylds. Occasionally we traveled a short distance out of Ohio for gigs, and one of those gigs was a dance in New Castle, Pennsylvania. The song "Liar Liar" was becoming a big hit, so some of the kids started yelling it out

The Chyld's Dolls

as a request. We really didn't know it well enough to play it at a gig, so we couldn't play it for them.

The guys had heard the song a few times, though, and played a few bars, kind of asking the kids if that was the song they were talking about. They cheered wildly, thinking we were going to do the song. Unfortunately, we only knew the first few bars and then had to stop playing. Then the crowd went wild again, but this time they were furious. They started pelting us with eggs. OK, who brings eggs to a dance? Where'd they get them? We didn't know. We just knew that all of the sudden, there were eggs flying everywhere.

Al decided to turn it into a baseball game and started trying to deflect the eggs using his guitar neck like a baseball bat, but that only revved the kids up to throw more. It was a horrible gig and very humbling. What a mess! The equipment, our clothes, the stage...all covered with smashed eggs, and all over a song we didn't know. It took several weeks to get all the egg out of the nooks and crannies of our equipment. Meantime, we were moving on to bigger things.

We made several singles with Warner Brothers Records and made the national charts. My future wife, Susie, and I had crossed paths when the Echoes played at the Lake Cable dances, but we hadn't met. Susie lived in Canton and went to Lincoln High School, one of Lehman's rival schools. To Susie, the band was just something to dance to. But even though she didn't know me then and wasn't a Chylds fan, she bought our record "I Want More (Lovin')", with me singing lead.

By now we had started opening shows at Memorial Auditorium sponsored by WHLO, "640 AM on your radio dial." We opened for The Beach Boys, Mitch Rider and The Detroit Wheels, and Terry Knight and The Pack, which evolved into The Grand Funk Railroad. We also opened for The  McCoys with Rick Derringer at a dance at Glenwood High School. We felt bad that the guys from both The Chylds and The McCoys were still in high school, but The McCoys had a song "Hang On Sloopy," that was #1 in the country. They were already a big time band and came in with big amps and limos. Later, by the way, in 1985 "Hang On Sloopy" became the official rock & roll song of the State of Ohio, which is the only state in the country to have an official rock & roll song.

Although I have to admit we were jealous of The McCoys, they were actually very inspirational to us, because they were our age and had made it to the top of the charts. It made my dreams seem attainable. I was really competitive and always wanted to be better, so I started standing up to play drums because the McCoy's drummer did. It was really hard to do, by the way. I also threw my sticks in the air and twirled them, because Dino Dinelli from The Young Rascals did and it was so cool to watch him. I loved the Young Rascals' music!

We also opened up the show for The Beach Boys, one of my all time favorite bands, about three times at the Canton Memorial Auditorium. I never dreamed that someday I'd be friends with them. That was back in the days when fans didn't have to take out a loan to go to a concert. Reserved seats for those shows were $5.00 and general admission was $3.50. You can't even park for that now. Even the Beatles, sponsored by WIXY 1260 AM, only charged from $3.00 to $5.50 for their concert at The Cleveland Stadium in 1966.

John, Tim and I got three of those tickets. It was August 14th and I was seventeen. John said he got the tickets at Recordland, across from The Onesta Hotel. The concert was at 7:30 PM and was billed as rain or shine. Of course I wasn't allowed to go, but John and Tim picked me up and we drove to Cleveland Stadium in John's Pontiac station wagon. That was back when the stadium held 70,000 people. We got there and found our seats. As I remember it, it was a beautiful August summer night. The Beatles had this little PA system set up on the stage with them. Probably since no one was going hear them play anyway, the promoter just put mics in front of their PA, so it broadcast over the regular stadium PA system. I remember the Cyrkle opened up for them, but everyone just wanted to hear the Beatles.

Finally the Beatles came out in their suits with their Beatle boots and haircuts. From my seat, they were about the size of an ant. Witnessing this, though, was larger than life, like nothing I'd ever seen before or like anything I've seen since. The girls screamed so loud throughout the entire show that we literally didn't hear a note, but what we saw was what we wanted…we wanted to play for 70,000 screaming fans. I can hardly comprehend that now, going to a concert where the fans are screaming so loud that you can't hear the music the entire show. I don't think we'll ever see anything like that again. It really was an inspiration for us, though, and fueled our rock & roll band dreams. My mission was now turbocharged.

Things just kept getting better, and over the next few years we recorded several singles. As I said earlier, we even got on the national charts. In 1965, we recorded "You Make Me Feel Good," in 1967, "I Want More (Lovin')" and "Psychedelic Soul," and in 1968, "No More Tears."

I can't begin to tell you how exciting it was to hear our tune on the radio for the first time. Anytime we ever heard a song we'd recorded played on the radio for the first time it was exciting, but the very first time we ever heard our very first song on the radio was another dimension in time and space. The Chylds had played a WHLO Appreciation Days gig and we had given the DJ, Uncle Joe Cunningham, a couple of copies of our 45. He said they'd listen to it and try to get it on the play list. A few days later, I was riding home in the car with my Mom and, as always, we were listening to WHLO. I had listened to WHLO non-stop since we had given them our single, hoping to hear it.

They announced that they were going to premiere the Chylds new single in the next hour. I was stunned…in shock…I couldn't believe what I just heard. I turned to my Mom and said, "Did you hear what they just said?" and she said, "Turn the radio down. It's too loud." We had pulled into the driveway and I stayed in the car because I didn't want to risk not hearing it during the time it took to get into the house. I sat in the car for the next half hour and I was listening to all these great 60's songs, getting a little nervous and questioning if our 45 would be good enough. All of the sudden, the DJ, Uncle Joe Cunningham, said, "Here's a brand new one from Canton's own, The Chylds "I Want More Lovin.'" I had a rush no drug could ever deliver. It was crazy. Our song was being played on the same radio station that had just played The Beatles, The Rolling Stones and The Beach Boys.

It's impossible to put the feeling into words. Being on the radio was what all bands were striving for. Let me put it this way…in the mid-sixties, if you were in a rock & roll band, you were cool. If you had a record on the radio, you were REALLY cool. After that day, my phone rang off the hook. What was most important was that the radio station's phone was swamped with requests for it. I felt that we were on our way!

Having a single out on the radio opened the door for us to play bigger gigs and open for national acts. Because of our singles on Warner Brothers Records, Nick Boldi and Carl Maduri were able to get us on several local TV shows. One was originally called "The Big 5 Show", and had become "Upbeat", on ABC, channel 5, with Don Webster.

Nick Boldi wanted us to look our best, so he had us wear our hounds tooth and black suits. Oh, to go back in time!

Back then, no one other than Ed Sullivan was live and everything was lip synced. It was very difficult to lip sync for that show, because the only thing they had as a monitor was a small eight inch speaker hanging above us, and it wasn't very loud. We got there, set up and waited for our time slot. After three minutes of filming, it was over. I was the lead singer and  we did the song, "Psychedelic Soul," which charted nationally and was somewhat of a hit locally. The show was taped in front of a live audience one week in advance, so we got to watch ourselves on the show the following week. I thought we did a good job, and it was even more exciting than the first time I heard our single on the radio.

All the major acts of the time appeared on this show at one time or another. It was a huge break for us. After that TV appearance, it felt like we were local celebrities and the attendance at our shows increased even more. Here I was, still in high school, and I was on this big local show on TV. There is no known footage of our performance on "Upbeat." I was sad to hear that those films had been destroyed. But, then again, thinking about our wardrobe, maybe it's for the best.

Speaking of wardrobe, recently a drummer friend of mine, Bill Peterson, and I were talking about the time the British group, Eric Burdon and The Animals, were playing at Memorial Auditorium. We went to People's Drug Store and bought long hair wigs for about

$5.95. We put the horrible wigs on, wore flowered shirts, and drove around in the car trying to impress and, hopefully, pick up girls with our unbelievably bad fake British accents. Some of the girls came over to the car and talked to us when we asked them for directions to the Auditorium, pretending we were going to play at the concert. No one bought it. I only wish I had a picture of us.

Bill Petersen & Joey Berecek

My brother had moved on to another band, and sometimes he was playing a gig and I was left at home with a night off and time on my hands. That was never a good thing. Joe Andaloro was the drummer in my brother's band, The Frank Vitale Quartet. They played weekends at The American Legion Hall on Cleveland Avenue. There weren't very many parking places over there and we lived nearby, so the guys used to drop their equipment off at the hall, drive over to my parent's house and leave their cars, and then walk over to the gig. Sometimes, if the weather was bad, they'd all go in one car. Joe had a really great car, a brand new burgundy 1967 Chevelle Super Sport 396 with beautiful black leather seats. I was seventeen and I really wanted to drive that car.

I wanted to imagine what it would be like if that car was mine, so I went out just to sit behind the wheel. I leaned back into the leather seat. Ah-h-h-h-h. Then I had an idea. I'd discovered by accident that, at the time, all Chevy keys would go into all Chevy locks. If I jiggled the key, on rare occasions, it would turn and start the car. This rare gift was bestowed on me that first night. I took my Dad's '64 Impala car key, put it into the ignition, jiggled it, and started Joe's car. I couldn't believe it…it worked! In my head, I heard angelic choirs singing.

I turned the car off. Then I thought that maybe I could just drive it around the block. Once. I didn't ask Joe if it was OK to take his car, because it wouldn't have been. I drove the car around the block and brought it right back. It was everything I imagined it would be and more. So, I went driving around all evening. I went to "The A" drive in and everywhere else I could think of. I knew when my brother's band would be finished playing, so I brought the car back in time. It was fabulous driving around in such a cool car. If you had a cool car in the 60's, you had girlfriends. Sometimes I'd pick up three or four girls at a time and drive them around. This went on for weeks whenever I didn't have a gig.

Finally, one night, I narrowly escaped getting caught. We were under a tornado watch and the weather was getting really nasty. I brought the car back and as I pulled into the driveway, I noticed that the power had gone off in the whole area. That included The American Legion Hall where my brother's band was playing, except they weren't playing anymore. Because of the tornado watch and the power outage, they'd shut the dance down. The guys were headed over to the house on foot to get their cars and load up their equipment. No more than five minutes had gone by since I returned, when Joe arrived. As he went by his car, he noticed that it was hot. I had made myself scarce...and besides, why would he ask me about his car? It was a close call and scared me so much that I stopped having my Muscle Car Weekends.

Years later, in the mid '90's, I went to an Alumni All City High School Basketball game, where Susie was cheering as an alumni cheerleader for Lincoln High School. I ran into Joe, who had eventually become the principal at one of the Canton City Schools. We were catching up on the past, so I thought Joe would enjoy my story about driving his car around all those years ago while he played at The American Legion Hall. He didn't enjoy it. In fact, I could tell that it really made him mad. C'mon, it was forty years ago. I forgot to mention that I also never put gas in his car after an evening of cruising. I said goodbye to him and started back to my seat. Then I stopped, turned around and asked, "Hey Joe, what kind of car did you drive here tonight?"

Sometimes people ask me what gig I consider to be the worst of my career. There's no question in my mind that it was the circus gig. Since I was a member of the Musicians Union, once in a while I'd get a call to do a gig and if I wasn't working, I'd take it. So, I got this call and they said, "Hey, you read music, right?" and I said, "Yeah," so they said, "We have a show for you at The Canton Memorial Auditorium with The Ringling Brothers Circus." The circus carried a band with them on the circus train that went from city to city and the drummer was sick, so they needed someone to fill in. I thought this might be fun, so he told me that there was a rehearsal at 3:00 PM and the show was at 7:00 PM. I had to wear a suit and tie and the whole bit. When I got there and looked at the marquee, it read, "Ringling Brothers Circus," and I thought, "What am I doing here?"

I brought my whole drum kit down to the gig. The first thing the band director did was look at my kit and say, "You won't need that, that and that...all you need is a bass drum, a snare drum, a high hat and one crash cymbal. And make it a loud one." I knew I was in trouble when I saw the other drummer's kit over to the side. It had this gigantic twenty-eight inch bass drum, a big fat snare, one cymbal, and a high hat. It was ancient stuff, and the guys playing in the band seemed really old to me, although they were probably only in their thirties.

I can't remember the titles of the music, but it was circus music and playing it was fun. It was almost like polka music, and I was good at polkas. So, I was playing the music, and reading the charts and I kept watching the band director because he was directing us. All of the sudden he stopped directing the band, looked over at me and said, "Why are you watching me?" I said, "Well, you're the band director," and he said, "No, no, no, no, no! Watch the CLOWNS. Your job is to watch the clowns, and every time they jump or do something silly I want you to hit the crash cymbal."

The clowns don't ever jump or do things in time, so it was just random crashes. If you've ever been to the circus, you know how it works. The clowns threw something up in the air and if they caught it, I hit the crash. If they fell, I hit the crash. I wasn't familiar with the show, and it drove me crazy. It was the worst and hardest gig I ever played in my life. I had to play in time with the circus band, but I had to hit the crash cymbal whenever a clown randomly did anything, which was always out of time. I missed a few cues because while I was watching the clowns, I'd start watching the circus. I thought, "No wonder this guy was sick. He was probably sick of this gig." I played for about three hours, plus rehearsal, and they gave me $12, which was union scale back then. I had to pay work dues on it, so I made about $10.

I was still going to Lehman High School and was in the band, which went to the Ohio State Competitions each year. I competed in both solo and ensemble, and I got first places all four years. Our percussion section in pep band, which played at our Lehman High School basketball games, was known throughout the city. The band director featured us and really let us cut loose. The kids from the other schools used to clap for us at the games. My future wife, Susie, who I still didn't know yet, said the kids from her school loved to hear us when we played for All City Night basketball games at the Field House.

I was chosen from all the first place competition people in the state of Ohio to have a free drum lesson with Joe Morello, because I had collectively so many first places. Joe was a famous drummer who played with Dave Brubeck and has a well known drum solo in "Take

Five," a song that's in 5/4 time. It was really exciting to have a lesson with this legendary drummer who was famous for his techniques in approaching different time signatures. In twenty minutes, he showed me some of the secrets it had taken him a lifetime to perfect. I still use some of the things I learned that day. The contest was sponsored by Charley Wilcoxon, who lived and taught in Cleveland, and was the author of my first drum lesson books.

Since I found out that Charley Wilcoxon lived in Cleveland and gave lessons at The Arcade, I signed up and started taking lessons in the spring of 1966. Saturdays everyone else got to sleep in or do whatever they wanted, while I spent $5 for a two and a half hour Greyhound Bus ride to Cleveland. I took my half hour lesson, which cost another $5, and then waited on the corner and caught the bus again for another two and a half hour ride home. By that time, the day was pretty much over. It was well worth it, though, and he raised the bar for my drumming and brought it to a whole new level.

I graduated from Lehman in June of 1967 and enrolled in Walsh College for the fall semester. It was not what I wanted to do. Not only had I bought a great car, a burgundy '65 Mustang, and a new set of drums, but I had also saved a lot of money playing with The Chylds. The last thing I wanted to do was spend it going to college, but my parents insisted. I spent the summer playing gigs all around with The Chylds. One of those gigs ended in drum tragedy.

In the beginning of that year, the winter of 1967, I'd gotten a brand new set of psychedelic red Ludwig drums. I first saw them in the store window one day when I drove past Gattuso's Music Center. The color was perfect for the era. To me, it was like seeing a Corvette Stingray for the first time. They were beautiful! I immediately stopped and went in. I sat at them and imagined myself playing them at a gig. There was a sign that said, "Do not touch", but I touched. I had to make them mine. A few weeks later, they allowed me to put $200 down and make payments.

I had a five piece set, with a snare, bass drum, two mounted toms and one floor tom. Later, I added a second bass drum. Here's the story behind that. It was this set of Ludwig psychedelic red drums that I had the summer of 1967, when I played at Chippewa Lake Park for WHLO's Appreciation Days. Normally, I loved playing dances at the park. There were several area bands playing that day.

We were unloading our band's equipment and sat all our gear behind the van, while we brought it to the stage. Another band's large truck was parked behind us. They were done playing and were leaving, so they backed up to get out of the parking space…right over a couple of my beautiful new drums, smashing them to bits. My drums! My new beautiful uninsured psychedelic red Ludwig drums! It was hit and run, I tell you. They just took off. I was furious and horrified. I had to borrow a couple drums from another band to play the show. That week, I had to order two new drums from Gattuso's Music Center, so while I was at it, I ordered a second bass drum for my set, and started learning to play a double bass drum kit. No matter what happened, I used it to further my mission. Little did I know that six years later I would play this same drum set on "Rocky Mountain Way."

I'll always remember and be grateful to people who took an interest in my career and helped me. Charlie Gattuso Sr., who owned the largest music store in town, Gattuso's Music Center, had a great relationship with and really cared about the area musicians, high school bands and music programs. Being an accomplished musician himself, he always tried to help young musicians. I had noticed that Keek and Chuck Stan had really great sounding ride cymbals, and I decided that I had to have one, too. I had started playing this unbelievably fantastic sounding twenty-two inch ride cymbal at the store. I loved that cymbal and I had to have it. Unfortunately, my Dad said he couldn't afford to buy it for me, and my parents were making me put most of the money that I made playing gigs away for college.

One day when I went to visit my ride cymbal, it was gone. I couldn't believe it. I said, "Oh no! Did someone buy my cymbal?" and Charlie said, "Yeah, but I have another one in the back." He really liked to kid me. I went back with him and he said, "I bought it," and then he gave it to me. I can't tell you what that meant to me. I still have that cymbal, by the way, and every time I see it, I think of Charlie. Later on his sons, who were my cousins, Charlie, Denny and Rick, ran the music store and gave me great deals that made it possible for me to get the endless amount of equipment I've always needed. I'll always be grateful to them, too.

My new Ludwig drums were really getting a workout. We played gigs all over northeastern Ohio, and a lot of the time we were out late at night driving home. Gary Hawk and Roy Stephens drove the band van with our equipment, while we rode in cars. On August 26, 1967, we were driving home on Route 62 in Salem, Ohio. Our bass player, Al Twiss, was driving and fell asleep at the wheel. We hit a telephone pole head on, going about 50 MPH. I never wore my seatbelt and was asleep in the passenger seat. I hit my face on the dashboard, which knocked me unconscious. I must have hit the windshield, too, because I remember a doctor picking glass out of my face later at the hospital.

I remember very little about that night. Whoever found us, called an ambulance and we were taken to the Emergency Room at Salem General Hospital. They called my parents in the middle of the night, the call every parent dreads. My parents immediately drove to the hospital and got me. I have a brief recollection of being in the back seat of the car with my Mom, who was trying to stop the bleeding, on the way to Timken Mercy Hospital in Canton, and then nothing again. I woke up in the hospital surrounded by my family and in tremendous pain.

I was injured to the point that I couldn't play or sing for a couple months. Bill Peterson took my place until I could play again and John Berecek's brother, Joey, sat in and sang to cover my vocals. The Chylds fans were wonderful and I saved some of the cards and letters they sent. The support was fantastic. I couldn't wait to start playing again, but the band was about to go through some serious changes. I started Walsh College and went back to playing in the band in the late fall of 1967, but everything was starting to fall apart.

Over the next three months, all three of the guys got married and were pressured to move on and get a "real" job, and not fool around with this rock & roll stuff. Since there were only four of us in the band, that left me. Actually, we were making good money and they could have made a living playing music, so I guess it was the security thing.

I can understand that none of them wanted to take the chance, since we didn't know how long it would last. On the other hand, I knew that this was what I was going to do for the rest of my life. I was committed to take the gamble and risk the consequences if it didn't work out for me.

First we lost Tim Hogan and we replaced him with Dave Jackson, then we lost John Berecek and we replaced him with Denny Jackson. Al Twiss didn't actually leave the band, but I finally quit because the music, personality and attitude of the band had changed. The reason we'd done so well was because we played music the crowd could dance to and sing along with, and now the music was more psychedelic. The band wasn't playing that much anymore because people didn't like the music we were playing. When I quit, the band finally folded.

Tim Hogan tragically passed away in 1988 from an illness he picked up while volunteering at a medical facility in Arizona, Al Twiss moved to Peru for several years, and John Berecek became a top aerospace engineer at Timken Roller Bearing and now lives in Minerva, Ohio. Denny Jackson moved to Canada, and I'm sorry to say I lost track of Dave Jackson. John and I have stayed in touch and last year when Al Twiss was visiting him, we got together and played for an evening. It was really fun and brought back so many memories. Al has now moved to Arizona, so we talked about having a Chylds reunion show some time, but it's hard for me to schedule anything very far in advance because I'm so busy. But back in the '60's, I had nothing to go to after The Chylds days were over. I had no band, I was in college, and I didn't want be there.

For the next two years, life was really hard for me. I played with several bands and it was a very bleak time for my musical career after having so much success for nearly five years with The Chylds. I would never have quit The Chylds if things hadn't changed so radically, but if I hadn't quit, I would have missed a lot. It seemed like my career was falling apart, and although I couldn't see it and didn't realize it at the time, things were working out to take me to a whole new and better place. Sometimes life is like that.

I was still living in Canton when I first crossed paths with Joe Walsh at Moonlight Ballroom when he was playing there with The James Gang. I'd heard about this really great guitar player and I went to see him play. He and Rick Derringer were two of the best guitar players I had ever heard. I didn't get a chance to talk to Joe that night, but I could see his career was going places. Joe was living in Kent and there seemed to be quite a music scene happening there.

My mission was clear. I decided that I had to move to Kent, Ohio. Kent had become famous for rock & roll bands that played downtown in the clubs. The Chylds had even played there. I didn't go to my last exam at Walsh College, even though I'd spent almost all the money I'd made with The Chylds on tuition and books the two years I went there. My beautiful burgundy Mustang was now a white Plymouth station wagon so I could haul my drums around. I quit school, moved out of my parent's house, moved to Kent and met my future wife, Susie, all the same day.

CHAPTER FOUR

The Kent Days

I met Susie Swihart the first night I moved to Kent. She was having a party at her apartment and I went with some friends. She was really nice to me and we talked a little about that fact that we were both from Canton. I'm even in a picture she has from that night. It was June 30,1969. Susie and I became friends that night, and I started spending time with one of her friends who lived with her.

I'd joined a band out of Akron called The Lime, for a really short time. After I moved to Kent in 1969, I quit the Lime and joined The Measles. Joe Walsh had briefly been in The Measles a few years before. I didn't stay in The Measles very long, either. Then I joined Marblecake, which was named because we had four white guys and two black singers, Steve and Tiny, in the band. Alaina "Tiny" Reed Hall was an incredible singer, who eventually went on to have a successful career on Broadway acting and singing for the show "Hair," and has a flourishing career going today.

After Tiny left, the band was Steve Fultz, Bruce Rusin on keyboards, Glen "Big Luke" Lucas on bass, and me. Steve was an excellent singer and was perfect for the music we played, which was a lot of Motown, Sly and The Family Stone songs and material like Otis Redding's "Try a Little Tenderness," which Steve was famous for performing. Big Luke and Bruce were fantastic musicians and we all loved the music we were playing. Who didn't love Motown? I always did a lengthy drum solo at some point during the night...we all did solos during various songs. Sometimes Paul Bigby and Bernard Lawson would sing with us. The band was really tight and we had a lot regulars from the fraternity crowd who loved to dance.

That summer Marblecake got several months of work in Chicago, so I drove there with my drums in my station wagon, which wasn't such a good car by now. It broke down on the Ohio Turnpike, so I called my brother who came and got me. I took my suitcase, drums and the license plates and left the broken down car sitting along the road. My brother drove me and my drums to where I needed to go in Chicago. The band lived in a hotel, worked nights and slept days. We played six hours a night on Rush Street at two clubs called Rush Up and Rush Over. We also played at Mothers, which had great cheeseburgers and is still there, and at The Store and Barnaby's. We worked so much I lost forty pounds, really got in shape and learned to play better.

It was there that I first met Mike Finnigan, a star-quality B3 player and singer with The Surf's, who were playing at Barnaby's. Eventually, Mike and I would play together with Crosby, Stills and Nash for over thirty years. But, I'm getting ahead of myself. When the summer was over, Marblecake moved back to Kent and we started playing again at The Kove. The Kove was loud and smoky and the place was packed every night.

It was a golden time for music in Kent. One of the bars on the edge of town was The Fifth Quarter, a typical college dance club bar and the biggest place in Kent. It had a low ceiling, so it was always very loud, hot and smoky. Other bars like Walter's, JB's, and The Kove, where Marblecake played, were all downtown on Water Street.

Joe Walsh and the James Gang played next door to The Kove at JB's. I finally met Joe when he was playing there. He always said he played with the hippie band and I played with the greaser band, since Marblecake played funk and R&B. Eric Carmen and The Raspberries and Phil Keaggy and The Glass Harp also played at JB's and The

Fifth Quarter. Chrissie Hynde was hanging out in Kent trying to get into music. I think she was inspired by her older brother, Terry, who was a sax player in a group called, "15 16 75," which was later called The Numbers Band. They're still playing together.

Joe Walsh and I knew Chrissie, who was younger than we were and couldn't get into the bars, so we used to sneak her in. She wasn't interested in coming in and drinking, she was interested in hearing the music and seeing the bands. I remember her telling us that she was going to move to England and not come back until she was a star. She did it.

JB's was named after the bar's owner, Joe Buchak, who was a Polish guy who always wore the same sweater, or at least it seemed like it. He spoke in broken English and reminded me of the character Big Chuck played on Big Chuck and Hoolihan on WEWS channel 8 Friday nights. He didn't know anything about rock & roll. JB's sold 3.2 beer so kids 18 could buy it, and it became the place musicians hung out and played in Kent. It was always crowded, full of smoke and smelled like stale beer.

On the weekends, Water Street clubs and the sidewalks outside were always packed. One Friday night in early May we were off and I was over at Susie's. We heard all kinds of sirens and thought that there must have been a fire or an accident somewhere. We drove through the downtown the next day and it looked like a war zone. The strip with the clubs on Water Street was totally trashed. There were burned-out cars and broken plate glass windows everywhere. It looked like news footage of Beirut or something. It was really disturbing. We had never seen anything like it and we had no idea what had happened. The Kent riots had started.

The University wanted all the students to stay on the campus and away from town that Saturday night, so they invoked a curfew. Marblecake got a call to play at one of the large dorms, so the students would have something to do. Susie and I pulled up to the dorm in my station wagon, which was filled with my drums. An angry crowd surrounded my car. I had never had anything like that happen before and it was really scary. The crowd broke beer bottles on the pavement around the car and told me that if we played, they were coming in and trashing my equipment. My drums were my life. I wasn't playing!

So, instead of playing, we went over to Big Luke's apartment off campus and watched TV. We were laughing at the Alka Seltzer "spicy meatball" commercial when the station interrupted programming with what we now call "breaking news." The students were burning the ROTC building. Susie thought she'd better call her parents so they wouldn't worry. Her Mom answered the phone. "Hi Mom," she said, "it's Susie." Her Mom must have seen the reports on TV also and thought the worst. "You're in jail!" she said with an "oh, no!" sound in her voice. Susie assured her Mom that she was safe and wasn't in jail or anywhere near the burning building. Then we went outside and looked toward the campus. The sky was glowing orange.

The next day, Susie took her little instamatic camera and walked around the campus taking pictures. When I saw the pictures it looked surreal. There were several tanks on the campus and the National Guard and police were everywhere. The Guard guys were the same age we were. The Kent students weren't taking the situation seriously and the out-of-towners who had come to riot meant business. At that point, it was time to close the school and send the students home. They didn't.

By Sunday evening there was another curfew in Kent and no one was allowed outside. Kids were hiding in the bushes and scurrying from house to house to visit. It was like they were little kids playing cowboys and Indians. Still no one was taking this seriously. The telephones were dead because too many people were trying to use them. We had TV antennas back then, and the National Guard helicopters that were flying overhead all night destroyed the reception. Everyone I knew thought it was a game. I did, too.

I lived on River Street near the campus at that time. I went outside with my big flashlight and was watching the helicopters flying above me and waving to them. They were shining really bright lights down to the ground, so I thought I'd shine my light up. They shouted over their loudspeakers for me to get inside. We were idiots and thought it was really funny. They must have been so frustrated. They wanted everyone to stay inside, and I mean INSIDE…Joe Walsh was arrested just for sitting outside on his porch.

The following day, the students were shot. It was midterm week and although most of the students weren't involved in the riots, they still had to go to class to take their tests, so there were students all over the place. I was home and never went near the campus that day. Susie was student teaching in Ravenna. After the students were shot the University finally closed the campus, but it was too late. Years later when I had met Graham Nash, he told me that Neil Young heard about the students being shot, ran into the woods with his guitar and wrote the song "Ohio" in about an hour. The song was recorded with Neil, Graham, Stephen Stills, and David Crosby and rushed to vinyl. It was released in something like three days.

Kent was never quite the same after that, but after a while, things settled down and I continued with my music mission. I had decided that I needed to be able to play additional instruments to be more valuable to the bands I played in, so I bought a flute and practiced until I taught myself to play it. Besides vocals and drums, by now I could also play bass and keyboards. I needed to be able to play and sing everything myself so I could write songs. I started buying whatever equipment I could afford to start building a home studio.

I finally quit Marblecake because I wanted to work with a band who wanted to write and record original material. It was a risky step because Marblecake played all the time and we made good money. I started a new band and we called ourselves Voo Doo. That band was Phil Giallombardo, Tom Kriss, who was an original member of the James Gang, and keyboard player, Bruce Rusin from Marblecake. That band didn't do much. Then we got a new guitar player and put a band together called Sheriff. That band was Tom Kriss, Bruce Rusin, Paul Whittaker and me. That didn't do much either, but playing in it helped me get another step higher.

I'll never forget the time that The James Gang opened for Led Zepplin in Cleveland. After the show, Robert Plant and Jimmy Page came down to JB's. I was playing that night with Voo Doo, so they came up on stage and we jammed. Word quickly got around on the street that Led Zepplin was jamming at JB's, which only held about 250 people, so within an hour they had to turn people away. There was no room left to sit and people were packed even up the stairs. Joe Bujack had the biggest crowd and sold more beer that night than he had in his entire life. He didn't know who they were, so he went up to Jimmy Page and Robert Plant and asked them if they were available Thursdays. I love that story.

The guys I was living with wanted more room, so in the summer of 1970, we moved into a rat infested house in Brimfield which was just a few miles from Kent. The grounds were like a park. It had a pavilion and a pond in the back and could have been a really nice place. Joe Walsh lived a few houses away with his wife, Margie. I was hardly working. I set my drums up in the pavilion, which had no heat, and practiced my drums, even in the winter.

My career wasn't looking good and I was starting to lose hope. We had oil heating, ran out and didn't have enough money to buy more, so for a while that winter, we didn't have any heat in the house. Sometimes I only made $30 for the entire week. I had rocketed toward the top as a teenager, and now it was like I'd hit a brick wall. I often wondered if my career was going to stay like this. The house was in very bad shape. There were literally rats in the walls. Rats, as in more than one rat. You could hear them scratching around, and sometimes they'd peek their little noses out a hole they'd chewed in the wall. Their beady little eyes would be looking out at me sometimes. It was horrible going to sleep at night knowing that there were rats in the walls, but they never bothered us. It wasn't a good time in my life. There's an old musician joke that goes something like, "What do you call a musician without a girlfriend? Homeless." I'd had enough of the rats and the cold, so I called Susie and asked if I could move into her basement.

Susie had a teaching job and lived in a townhouse by herself with just her collie, so she let me move into her basement, and by the end of her lease there, she wanted more room for her collie, Karma, so she rented a large farm house. I put a studio in one room on the lower floor, and Susie took out a loan and bought me a beautiful antique upright piano so I could write songs.

Sometimes Phil Keaggy dropped by. Phil and I were very close friends and we spent a lot of time together. In fact, we used to say we were brothers. I recognized what an extraordinary musician and guitar player Phil was, and I think he respected my playing as well. I always wanted to play in a band with Phil, but The Glass Harp already had a drummer. Joe Walsh and Phil were starting to get some breaks, and I was still hoping and praying that I would get my big break someday, too. I was living with Susie and Karma at the farm house in Kent when I met Ted Nugent.

CHAPTER FIVE

Ted Nugent

In 1971, Kent was still a famous music town. Chip Killinger, The Glass Harp's manager, ran into Ted Nugent, who was playing in Cleveland at Public Hall. Somehow or other Chip got into a conversation with Ted, who said he needed to get a new drummer. I was playing at JB's with Sheriff, so Chip suggested that Ted come to Kent to hear me. Ted came to JB's to hear me play, but he didn't say anything to me that night and I didn't even know he was there.

Ted got my phone number from Chip and called me. At the time, Ted had a farm near Ann Arbor, Michigan, and lived there when he wasn't touring. When he called, Ted said he wanted to fly in and meet with me in Kent and asked if I would pick him up. I borrowed Susie's car and picked Ted up at The Akron Canton Airport. This is before there were jet ways there, so with his long hair blowing in the morning breezes, Ted emerged from the plane making a presidential entrance. Ted has always been a rock "god," a total character, and is high energy rock & roll 24/7. He arrived wearing a one piece black jump suit covered in shining silver studs and looked like he could have gone directly on stage. He looked like a wild man! I knew I was really going to have fun working with this nut.

I spent the day with Ted and he flew back to Detroit. He was going to be in New York and I was going to be there at Electric Ladyland Studios with Phil Keaggy, so we decided to meet there and jam before I was officially hired. I jammed with Ted and Al Pethal at the studio and Ted decided to hire me to play drums with his band. It was a major step for my career. After all of the struggle I

had been through since the Chylds, I'll never be able to explain how great a feeling that was for me. It was my first big break and I owe Chip and Ted so much for giving me the chance to get out of the night clubs and onto the concert stage touring America.

Ted is a wonderful American patriot. He loves this country and believes in the American dream. He doesn't drink or do drugs and is all about guitars, the outdoors and the troops. One of his records was, "Survival Of The Fittest" and that pretty much describes him. If we lost all modern conveniences, Ted would be just fine. He's an ace archer and I believe if he had gone to the Olympics he would have gotten a gold medal. But most of all, he's an incredible musician and entertainer. I went to one of his shows last year, and he's playing and singing better than ever. He's in fantastic shape, his stage show is awesome, and all I can say is when Ted walks out on the stage, you better put your seat belt on.

I played with Ted and The Amboy Dukes for about four months. The guys in the band were Ted, John Angelos, Rob DeLaGrange and me. Ted treated me with a lot of respect and as a peer, as an equal, and I really appreciated that. He had already been on the national scene for several years and had hits out, like "Journey to the Center of Your Mind," which came out when I was still in high school. I felt like I was finally on my way again, and the path was about to get wild.

When I arrived at Ted's farm, it looked like I was joining the army. He had an arsenal of bows and arrows, guns, knives and ammo. Everything you'd need to survive nuclear war. He had an entire archery target range set up in his back yard, and one day before rehearsal, he asked if I preferred him shooting a red or green apple off my head. With a complete serious face, he waited for my answer. As I stumbled for words, he broke into hysterical laughter. Thank God, he wasn't serious.

From my personal photo collection.

Ted was doing his own road management then, including driving the car...very fast, I might add. We had a truck that followed us with the gear. We played everywhere, including Canada. I'll never forget one of the shows, an outdoor Labor Day festival. Detroit type rock & roll fans are out of their minds, and in their enthusiasm, they started throwing beer bottles onto the stage. Ya gotta love 'em! It was like, "Here, have a beer with us," except the beer was still in the bottles. Then came the firecrackers. It was near the end of the show when someone threw an M-80 onto the stage. It went off near my bass drum and blew a hole in the head. The bass drum mic picked up the explosion and blew out the entire PA system. That was the end of the show. Tedmania! It was exciting…real rock & roll!

I had been through a lot of wardrobe changes with the bands I had played with so far. I started out with a suit, white shirt and tie with my Dad, matching outfits in the Echoes, the joker outfits in The Chylds, everyone in Kent played in jeans, and now I was with Ted playing Detroit rock & roll. I let my hair grow longer and started wearing red corduroy pants, lace shirts, velvet jackets, rhinestones, sequins, and platform shoes. It was an era of rock & roll stage clothes, and I miss that. I used to enjoy looking different on the stage than the audience at the shows. We really looked the part.

When we played in New York, Ted took us to this store called Granny Takes a Trip. It was nothing but rock & roll stage clothes. Before that, I had been buying women's clothes that were really shiny or fancy to wear on stage with Ted's band. Fortunately, on me, they didn't look like women's clothes. We didn't wear clothes like that walking around, but for the stage, it worked.

In contrast to the really wild clothes we wore on stage, off stage Ted was really an outdoorsman. If you played in Ted's band, you were also a hunter. I didn't have a lot of experience, having grown up in the city. I spent my weekends eating pasta at Nana's with the family and the only things I hunted were meatballs in the sauce. Well, Ted wanted to take us hunting. So, one day, we all got into his Jeep and brought the guns, bows and arrows and camouflage, and we went hunting. For me, it was like the hunting scene from "My Cousin Vinny." I didn't do so well in the wild of the outdoors. In fact, Ted commented on my outdoor skills in an interview he recently gave, even all these years later. I must have made quite an impression on him. He said I was making too much noise and I was scaring off all the animals. Hey, I'm a drummer. Noise is what I do.

Ted decided we'd go into the woods and hunt squirrels. Squirrels? At home, I feed my squirrels. They're like pets. When I was a kid, we had one named "Petey" that we were able to feed peanuts. So, now I was out in the woods hunting them with Ted. We didn't bring peanuts. Finally, despite my non-stealth hunting skills, we saw one on a tree. It was about five feet away.

Ted handed me his gun. The gun he gave me was called an "over under", which is a .22 caliber up top with a smaller barrel, and under that, there's a 20 gauge shotgun with a bigger barrel. There's a switch that changes it from one to the other. He goofed on me and handed me the gun with it switched on shotgun, and I was thinking that it was switched on .22. When I pulled the trigger, I expected a .22, which is loud but has no kick to it. Instead, it was on the 20 gauge shotgun. There was this big BOOM, a huge kick, and the squirrel was nothing but goo on a tree.

Fortunately, we were playing all the time and didn't have much time for hunting. One of the places where Ted played a lot was in Florida at The West Palm Beach Arena. At one particular show there were three bands playing. I think the admission was $5.00. The lineup was Bo Diddley, Ted Nugent and The Amboy Dukes, and The James Gang. By now I had known Joe Walsh for several years, we were friends, and I had gone to New York once with him.

For some reason, Bo Diddley never brought a band. He just figured he'd grab a couple of guys from the other bands playing, since everybody knew his music. I played drums and Ted Nugent played bass with him. We didn't rehearse or go over any songs. When it was time to start his show, Bo Diddley turned around and looked at me, nodding his head, and with his beautiful low voice, he said,

"You know my beat." It wasn't a question. He knew every musician knew his legendary songs and the signature beat he created. I have a photo of me and Bo Diddley that I took that night. It was fabulous playing with him.

Then I played our show with Ted, and Joe played his show with The James Gang. After that, Joe came up to me and said something like, "Hey, stop by my hotel, I want to talk to you." I hadn't seen Joe in about a year and I thought it would be great to catch up. So, I said, OK, and went over and met with him.

Joe said he was planning on leaving the James Gang later that year, and he was going to move to Colorado and put a new band together. He said he wanted me to be the drummer and asked if I'd be interested. I said I would, because I always did want to play with Joe, and all of the sudden the opportunity was staring me in the face. He said he wanted me to give Ted notice and move to Colorado and we'd put a band together. I said, "Are you sure about this?" and he said he was, so the next day I talked to Ted, who was really cool about it.

While I was in Florida with Ted, we recorded a few demos at Criteria Recording Studios in Miami. The songs have never come out on any albums, but I still have copies of the songs we recorded. Recording there was nothing like recording the records with The Chylds in Akron. I had no idea how important Criteria would eventually become for me, or that I would be recording at Criteria with other great bands in the future.

So, here I was. I finally got the break I'd waited for all my life and was out of the bars, clubs and local band circuit. I was on my first national big name group tour….and I was going to quit. We finished out the tour, Ted got someone else to start playing with him, and I came back to Kent. Now I had no job. Joe was supposed to call me. After weeks passed and Joe hadn't called, Susie drove over to his house and it was empty…he had moved!

Joe didn't call, didn't call, and it was nearing Christmas, which made it even worse. Joe still didn't call. Then New Year's came, and he still hadn't called. I was a wreck. I didn't have an address, phone number, nothing. I started getting really worried. Around Kent, there was an expression called, "Pulling a Joe Walsh." What it meant was, Joe would promise to call you or hang out or something, and then he just wouldn't show up. It became a common expression in town and was used even when Joe wasn't involved at all, like if a guy stood a girl up for a date or something, he was said to have "pulled a Joe Walsh." I was really freaking out by now.

All I wanted for Christmas was for Joe to call.

Finally, in January of 1972, the phone rang, and it was Joe. In his laid back voice he said something to the effect of, "Hey, are you gonna come to Colorado? I'm ready for you." I felt like, NOW you call? I've been going crazy for three months. Joe had just been moving his wife, Stefany, and baby daughter, Emma, out to Colorado and was getting settled. Susie gave me the money for my plane ticket. So, my drums, in their little fiber cases, and I, in my vinyl snakeskin jacket and platform shoes, got on a United Airlines flight to Denver in the dead cold of winter.

CHAPTER SIX

<u>Barnstorm</u>

I arrived in Denver, and Joe and his neighbor, Keith Bristow, picked me up in Keith's van. We went through Boulder and then headed up the mountain to Nederland, which is at about 8,000 feet above sea level. I thought Ohio's winter's were cold, but it was January and about minus twenty. We parked in front of Joe's house. I left the drums in the van and brought my suitcase into the house. We talked, Joe's wife, Stefany, made dinner and we went to bed. In the morning I went to get my drums, but we couldn't find the van, because about forty inches of snow had fallen. We ended up not getting the drums out until March.

While we were waiting for the snow to melt, I stayed at Joe's house. We wrote songs at the piano and I helped Joe build a small studio. Our original intention was to bring in producer Bill Szymczyk and record Joe's record at his home studio in Nederland. The studio consisted of a half-inch four-track Ampex recorder, a British recording board, a handful of outboard gear, a nice set of speakers, and a handful of mics.

The studio was finally together and we were excited to get started after all those weeks. Bill drove the sixty mile trip from his home south of Denver to Joe's mountain home and studio. That was when I first met legendary record producer Bill Szymczyk , whose nickname at the time was "Coach." All six foot four inches of Bill walked in, bursting with energy, with these giant eyes, black curly hair and a great big ornery smile that just beamed. I could tell he was a character. What an entrance! You had to look up to him, especially if you're my size.

We talked to Bill for a while and then the big moment. Joe said, "Let's go downstairs to the studio so we can play you some of the ideas we've been working on." Bill answered, "Well, let's record it!" We were thrilled. We went downstairs, hit the main power for the studio, and Joe's main power amps burst into flames. There was about a foot of snow on the ground outside the door. We grabbed the burning amps, ripped out the wires and threw them out into the snow, where they smoked and sizzled to their death. We all stood there speechless. It was very quiet. Bill broke the silence. "Let's go to LA."

Bill was so involved with the music, that although he wasn't a musician, he was like a member of the band. Bill had produced all The James Gang records, and had moved his family to Colorado to work with Joe. Bill and his partner, Larry Ray, had started a record label called Tumbleweed Records. Joe Walsh, at the time, was on ABC Dunhill Records, which was also the James Gang's label, so we made  the first Barnstorm album on that label.

Bill is another reason the early days I played with Joe are such good memories. Bill is an unbelievably funny guy. Really sharp witted. Although it was Joe who first came up with the saying, "The Smoker You Drink, The Player You Get," it was Bill who insisted that it be the title of Joe's second album. Not only was Bill really fun to work with, he was also brilliant. He got me countless opportunities to play and record with other artists and groups, and has immeasurably helped my career. Most importantly, he's been a friend for life.

And that brings me to Joe. I've always really enjoyed working with Joe. He has a dry sense of humor that I find really funny and he always makes me laugh. He was also always up to act crazy, which fit my personality really well. An instigator and accomplice. Musically, he has his own unique style of playing guitar and writing music and he's left his distinctive trademark sound in rock & roll history. More than that, even when our careers have kept us busy and we haven't spoken, sometimes for years, I've always considered him to be my friend.

Joe, Bill and I went to Studio A at The Record Plant in LA and recorded the first two songs for the Barnstorm album. First we recorded "Bird Call Morning," and since there were only two of us, Joe overdubbed the bass. Then we recorded a song called "Home," which we recorded with me, Joe and Chuck Rainey, the famous studio bass player. Bill Szymczyk had produced B.B. King's song "The Thrill Is Gone," so he was able to recruit top notch studio musicians to play with us.

Now, as I've said, I'm a city guy. I was stuck up there in the mountains, so whenever Stefany would take the Jeep and go down to Boulder to do the marketing or something, I'd go with her. "Are you going into town?" I'd ask desperately. "Take me," I'd beg. I wasn't good at living in the wilderness in the mountains. I needed to see people and cars and McDonald's. I slept downstairs in the studio under the grand piano at Joe and Stefany's those first few weeks.

I had to admit that it was really beautiful in the mountains, but the winters were brutal. Joe was a ham radio operator and put up a big tower, so he got fantastic reception. He loved being in the mountains. To me, it was like being on the moon. The city of Nederland had a reservoir, a gas station, the Pioneer Inn, which was like a saloon, and a general store. No McDonald's.

Joe was very at home in that Rocky Mountain environment, and had bought the Jeep to get around in the snow. One day, he needed to go down to Boulder to get some parts for his ham radio, and he asked me to go along. Leave the mountains for a few hours? Of course I would! We drove down the hill and I had two hours of civilization to look forward to…including getting a burger at Burger Chef. Oh, the excitement!

When we finished our errands, we headed back up the mountains. Although it was 35 degrees and sunny in Boulder, in the mountains it was February with twenty-two inches of snow, and we were glad we had a four wheel drive Jeep. We headed up Boulder Canyon Road towards Nederland. Joe lived slightly above the town, so there were a few hairpin turns to get to his house. In all of Joe's excitement to plug in all his new ham radio toys, we sped up the hill going way too fast and went into the first turn a little too hot. The back end of the Jeep started to fishtail and we slid right off the mountain, rolling the Jeep. It went over and over and over. Like most Jeeps, it had a roll bar, so we were protected. We weren't wearing our seatbelts, though, and I remember laughing all the way down as we flew around in the car. It doesn't seem so funny now, but back then, we were in our twenties and we feared nothing. When we finally came to a stop, the Jeep had settled on the driver's side, and I was kinda squashing Joe. He was laughing and yelling, "Get off me!" I was laughing and climbed straight up to get out of the passenger door. We were only about fifty yards from his house, but in that snow, it seemed like a mile. We got up to his house, still laughing, and got his neighbor to help us right the Jeep and drive it back to Joe's house. To this day, Joe still laughs about that story.

Eventually we started thinking about putting a band together and we needed a bass player, so we talked to Tommy Bolin, who was a local guitar hero in Boulder. Later, Tommy became the guitar player for Deep Purple, but back then, Joe found him in some club and started talking to him. Joe told him we needed a bass player, and Tommy said he knew somebody, but that he was playing in a jazz club in Canada. We called Kenny Passarelli, and he drove back to Colorado in his 1941 Chevy to play with us.

Kenny is a nut. We immediately hit it off and always got along extremely well. We cared about the same things and didn't care about the same things. He's half Italian, so we relate on a whole different level. He was this little Italian guy with dark framed round glasses, and he eventually got braces. He looked like a little teenager, a kid, but he was an extremely talented and valuable asset to the band. He has a really ornery smile and devilish laugh, great vibe. We still laugh a lot whenever we're together. I've got lots of stories about Kenny and me on the road.

So, here I was, a guy from Ohio, and I was in Colorado, where everyone wears parkas and work boots and looks like Eskimos. I showed up in stacked heels wearing my vinyl fake snakeskin coat. In one of the few pictures of the coat, Joe and I are in his Jeep at the top of a mountain when it was about ten degrees outside. I was freezing, but I loved that coat. To me, fresh out of Ted's band, that coat

Hey check out my cool coat!!

was pure rock & roll. To Joe and Kenny, it was a hideous nightmare. They hated that coat so much that one night they took it outside and burned it. Yeah, BURNED it. I had taken my coat off one day, and they threw it out into the snow, poured lighter fluid on it and burned it. Being vinyl, it really went up fast. Sometimes Joe and Kenny did spontaneously outrageous things like that. I related. We still laugh about that coat.

Last year in 2007 Kenny and I were on the road again playing with The Stephen Stills Blues Band, after not touring together for decades. I had so much fun with Kenny…more fun than I've had in a long time…I think because we've been through so much together, especially when we were just starting out. It really messed with our heads when we played back in Boulder, though. He's such a great guy and I feel like he's a brother to me. We go back so far, back to those original days of Barnstorm, when everything was new and exciting. I love playing with him, then and now.

In the early days of Barnstorm, I think that Joe found that Bill, Kenny and I became a team, and he could rely on us to come up with great ideas and input. All four of us are a bunch of comedians, and we were always making jokes and laughing. Making "Barnstorm," the first national album I was ever associated with, couldn't have been a better experience. Although the album "Barnstorm" was the least selling of all the albums we recorded, it's always talked about and receives the most critical acclaim.

In The James Gang, Joe wrote most the songs, and was the lead singer and guitar player. There was a lot of pressure on him to come up with all that. Now, and this is just my own opinion, I think what Joe was always looking for was to just be in a band. He called the first album "Barnstorm" and didn't even have his name on it. I don't think he really even wanted to be the leader. He used to say, "I just want to be the guitar player," but in a three piece band, you're the only guy out there except for the rhythm section.

What was initially really great about working with Joe was that he's an incredible guitar player. But later, it was recording with him and working with him that was also great. I think he really liked working with me, Kenny and Bill, and I really appreciated the respect he showed me. He would ask me for lots of advice and I was able to give tons of ideas for that record. He was open to my ideas, accepted them and the guys would always turn and ask what I thought, or what Kenny or Bill thought. We would try out the different ideas and see what worked. It was true teamwork, and that doesn't always happen with bands.

Kenny and I got an apartment together in Boulder, which was a college town below the foothills at the base of the mountain where Joe lived. The apartment building we lived in was like a dorm. Kenny and I shared a bedroom and bathroom and we had to share a kitchen with some other guy. I didn't even have a car. Kenny drove us wherever we needed to go. I was pretty broke at the time, so Susie sent me rent money. We weren't exactly living in luxury while we recorded up at Caribou Ranch, but I was starting to live my dream.

The picture of the beautiful old falling-down barn on the cover of the album was taken on the way to Caribou Ranch. I think Joe had in mind the kind of thing he wanted on the cover, but just hadn't seen it yet. Sometimes you just know it when you see it. Joe spotted the barn one day on the way to record up there, and stopped the car and said, "There it is, the cover of the album." The album was designed by Jimmy Wachtel and the photographer was Bob Jenkins.

It was a really great and comforting time of my life. Although Ted Nugent had been my big break from the bars to the national concert stage, I just played drums in his band. Ted was the star, and I was a back up musician. This seemed like I was going to get some involvement as a musician. I belonged to a band again and I enjoyed the respect and the music. I wrote and got songs on the first record. That's something when you're just joining up with someone for the first time. Kenny and I wrote "Mother Says" with Joe, and I had an instrumental called "Giant Bohemoth". I didn't even know what a Bohemoth was, but it sounded like a giant monster Godzilla might fight, so I used it.

Bill Szymczyk & Me at Caribou

Totally, the album, "Barnstorm," which was mostly recorded at Caribou Ranch, took about four months to make. We were the very first group to record there. What an honor! The owner of Caribou Ranch was the manager and producer of the group Chicago. His name was Jim Guercio and he was an Italian mogul from the city of Chicago. He had just built the studio and when we were recording there, they hadn't even finished the building that held the studio.

There were studs and dry wall showing, and the recording board in the studio was just temporary and wired up that way. We had to go to the bathroom outside. Since the cabins weren't finished, every night Joe had to drive twenty minutes to Nederland, Kenny and I had to drive forty minutes down to Boulder, but Bill and engineer Allan Blazek had to drive all the way past Denver to Englewood to get home. The picture on the inside of the album of Joe, Kenny and me sitting on the fence was taken outside at the ranch.

All along the Boulder Canyon road there were campers, and we were usually done about three in the morning. Kenny and I came down the mountain together every night at about the same time, so to entertain ourselves on the long ride home, we decided to greet the campers. Kenny would go really slow, and then we'd honk the horn and yell at all the campers to "WAKE UP!" and make all kinds of noise. After we did this every night for about a week, some of the campers stayed up and threw rocks at the car. You couldn't miss Kenny's '41 Chevy. After that, we decided to stop greeting them. We were really immature and thought everything we did like this was hilarious, but we never actually hurt anyone. OK, I still think it's funny.

Caribou Ranch became a famous recording studio. It was way up in the mountains in the middle of nowhere, and it was just like paradise. Elton John, Dan Fogelberg, the Beach Boys, Joe Walsh, John Lennon and Chicago are just a few of the groups that recorded there. Eventually, there were beautiful cabins to stay in while artists recorded. It's at 9,000 feet and the only problem was that doing vocals was very difficult due to the lack of oxygen. Unless you were like Dan Fogelberg, who was used to living up there in the high altitude, it was very tough to sing.

While the view outside at Caribou was spectacular, the inside became spectacular as well. The studio was state of the art and there was a kind of mess hall cafeteria place to eat. After the cabins were finished, when artists went up there to record, they moved in. Inside the beautiful three story barn, there were antler chandeliers and rustic chairs made with hides and horns of some kind, and a beautiful inlaid pool table. The barn was huge. The lower level had maintenance, the kitchen, and storage. The middle floor was the studio and the upper floor was the pool room. Pool as in pool table, not swimming pool. There was a second huge room upstairs next to the pool room that was fitted for film scoring. The room was so big that you could pull down the screen and put a full orchestra in there. Tragically, after such a stellar history, there was a fire in the '80's and the kitchen, control room and pool room burned, but the studio part of the building with most of the contents and the cabins are still there.

I had recorded in studios before with The Echoes, the Chylds, a few tracks at Criteria with Ted Nugent, and the first couple of songs with Joe in LA, but this was at a whole new level. This wasn't just putting down some demos. I wanted to learn everything about it, how the equipment worked, how to edit, produce…everything. We used two-inch recording tape back then, and everything was analog, so to edit, we had to physically cut the tape. It was nerve wracking to get out a razor blade and cut. Every time we edited, thousands of dollars were at stake. If we were off and we could hear the edit, we potentially could have ruined a master tape. Bill was the maestro of editing, and sometimes had sections of tape hanging all over the place. Then he'd rebuild the song and put the tape sections back together and we'd never hear the edits. He's unbelievable! That's who I learned from.

There also were very limited amounts of tracks to work with, and we couldn't correct pitch or tempo like we can now. We had to do what we called "punching in," which meant that if we needed to fix a small part of a track, we had to start playing or singing, and then the engineer would punch in "record" for the part we were repairing, and then punch out. It had to be exactly right. One time at Caribou we spent what seemed like hours on the second syllable of one lyric, "a-way."

Whenever we made a copy of the tape, we were putting wear on it, and second generations lacked the quality of the original master. Even playing the tapes too much could cause them to degrade in quality. Frequently we had to move the tapes from one studio to another if we recorded tracks in more than one location. Traveling with, sending or moving the master tapes was always risky, because the safety copies were just that, copies, and lacked the quality of the original masters. If the master tapes were lost or damaged it would have been a tragedy. The tapes from back then are fragile, and even with climate controlled storage, many are physically baked in an oven before they're transferred to digital. You usually can make one pass and the tape is shot. Today, you don't have to be a musician, singer or even talented to put out a record. Don't get me started.

When we weren't recording at Caribou, I always found lots to do. When we lived in Florida, my brother, Frank, and I used to build those little model airplanes that we held onto with a wire and they flew around us in a circle. I always loved building those little planes. There was a lot of down time in Boulder, so I started building those planes again. Joe Walsh really loved the whole thing and thought it was really cool, so I decided I'd build a BIG plane. I bought a kit and built one giant plane that took a couple of months. It had a lot of detailed work and I really spent a lot of hours carefully painting it. It was a beautiful plane when it was finished.

Joe came down and we took it out into the parking lot to fly it. In hindsight, a field with soft grass would have been a better plan, but the parking lot seemed more like a real runway. It was the maiden flight and I gave Joe the honor. It was so exciting. I proudly watched as the plane took off the pavement in the Colorado sunshine. All those months of work, and now it was in the air! It didn't even make it around one time until it crashed. I mean, it really crashed. It was debris.

I stared at the wreckage with my mouth hanging open. I didn't say much, and neither did Joe. He only said, "Oops." Then, it was very quiet. I know he thought it was really funny, but he didn't dare laugh out loud. He managed to hold back even the hint of a snicker. I'm sure it took everything in him to keep it inside, and he probably got in his car to drive home and lost it. I can just picture

him telling Bill the story. After that flight, Joe referred to the two of us as "The Wrong Brothers of Flight." The crash didn't diminish our interest in aeronautics, though, and we later turned to rockets. More dangerous and you expect wreckage.

Finally it was summer, and Susie moved to Colorado. We got an apartment in Boulder at the bottom of the canyon, and then at the end of the summer, we moved to Stratford Park Apartments. I actually put a studio in both apartments and the second one even had drums. I had a snare drum and I put foam around a mic and tapped it with my foot and that was my bass drum. At my little

nothing studio, I wrote "Giant Bohemoth," the middle part of "Mother Says," "Days Gone By," and "Bookends."

Susie eventually got a job teaching art with the Boulder school system, when one of the art teachers had a nervous breakdown from the kids. Now there's a job you want. Once we started touring I was gone most of the time, and left Susie to deal with the snow. It was the worst Boulder winter in forty years. According to Susie's calculations, it snowed 189 inches that year and was one of those continuing weather stories that ran on the nightly news

Meantime, I was working with Barnstorm. We wanted to go on the road and we knew we needed a keyboard player. Tommy Bolin's bass player said his cousin, Tom Stephenson, played keyboards. We called Tom, but he was busy, so he said we should call Rocke Grace. Yeah, that was his real name. The perfect rock & roll name. So, we called Rocke, who was living in South Dakota. We hired him and now we're a four piece band and ready to go on the road.

We needed PA equipment for our tour, so we called Bob Heil, who is known for his "Wall Of Sound PA Systems." Bob was like the mad scientist of sound, and was always thinking creatively. He designed and built great equipment and was a good man to know in the rock & roll business in the early '70's. He helped us decide what equipment to use live so we'd sound our best. I'm happy to say I'm still friends with Bob, who's still a sound genius, and run into him occasionally. Joe Walsh and Bob just designed a whole new line of microphones for the James Gang reunion tour in 2006. Barnstorm was fortunate to have Bob as part of our team from the start.

Mike Belkin, a manager out of Cleveland, had been The James Gang's and also Joe's manager, so he started booking our gigs. Our first warm up gig with Barnstorm was at The Draft House near Denver. Our first on the road show of our first tour was in New York City at The Bitter End in the Village. Over the following year, we played every nook and cranny in America. That's why everyone always asks me about Barnstorm, more than any group I've ever played with. We played cities that were thirty miles apart. We played big places, little places, clubs, theaters, bars…everywhere, and sometimes opened shows for other acts. We told Mike that we were a brand new band and all we wanted to do was work.

Throughout my career, I've met people who became very important to me in the most unplanned circumstances. Once, when we first started touring as Barnstorm, Joe said that this kid was going to ride along with us in the station wagon and play us some of his demo tapes. His name was Dan Fogelberg. He was from Peoria, Illinois and was still living there. He was really nice and brought along his little cassette player with his demos. His songs and singing were remarkable…so matured. It didn't seem like this voice and those songs could come out of this kid. He was friends with a booking agent, Irving Azoff, who wanted Joe to hear the songs in the hopes that Joe would produce Dan's record. Joe really liked the songs and eventually produced Dan's second album. So, that's how I first met Dan. I knew him before he ever made a record. Fame and fortune never changed him.

A lot of the time when we were just starting out, we flew to shows. Airport security was a lot different back then. If I were going to fly somewhere, Susie could actually get on the plane and sit there with me until it was time to leave. I had to fly back to Canton for some reason and stayed with my parents. My Mom and Nana thought I was too skinny, so when I left for Colorado, my Mom gave me a five gallon jar filled with meatballs and sauce. I actually had to carry it on the plane with me. There was no xray, security or anything at the time, none, so they just looked into the jar, thought it smelled fantastic and let me bring it on the plane. I had to sit with that thing all the way to Denver.

Barnstorm was doing pretty well, and we were doing a lot of interviews on the radio. One interviewer asked me about my gear, because I had an incredible stage set up. I had a double bass drum set, tympani, and a gong. I needed them because on the record we just made, I had used all this stuff and we wanted to sound like the record when we played live. So this radio interviewer asked me about the importance of having a gong. I went on about a twenty minute rap about gongs. I knew what I was talking about, but no one else did. Let's just say the train of thought occasionally strayed off the tracks.

We got a copy of the interview and we used to listen to it and laugh so hard we could hardly breathe. Joe Walsh told me that he still has a copy of it somewhere.

I had my most embarrassing moment on stage with my gong in the early days of Barnstorm gigs. As I said, my gong was part of my

set up and I used it as a giant, really dramatic finish at the end of "Turn to Stone." I would turn around, wind up and really nail that gong. So, we're playing a gig, and it's the end of "Turn to Stone." I stood up and turned around for the song's big dramatic finish, and the gong beater wasn't there. We're there in the middle of a show, playing a small venue, so the crowd could see us really well. If I didn't hit the gong, there was going to be a great big empty nothing ending. The seconds ticked away in slow motion. The moment was coming fast and I had to hit the gong or there was going to be a massive train wreck on stage. I desperately looked around for something to hit the gong with….and there was nothing.

They say necessity is the mother of invention. I think it's more like desperation. I reached down, ripped my shoe off and nailed that gong with the heel, right on time. The crowd thought it was part of the show and went wild, and the band just lost it. Walsh laughed so hard that I sometimes wondered if he was responsible for the missing gong beater. It sounded so good I considered switching to the shoe. Years later, Brett Tuggle, Fleetwood Mac and Stevie Nick's keyboard player, told me he was there that night at Tulagi's. He remembered that we were a really great band, but what he remembered most was the shoe. He thought it was really cool that I maintained my composure.

We were still flying to gigs at this time, so we had a lot of spare time between shows. Sometimes I clearly had too much time, and we were always playing pranks. Remember how much I love electronics? At one hotel, I took the face plate off the elevator buttons, and rewired them. If you'd push the lobby button you'd go to the fourth floor instead, push five and the elevator went to the tenth floor…things like that. I mixed up all the buttons and floors. I wrote down what I did, so everybody in the band knew which button to hit to get to the right floor. The hotel must have gotten a lot of complaints, because when we got up the next morning, it was fixed. I was young enough then that I didn't consider what would have happened if there had been an emergency. I just had too much time on my hands, a set of tools, and an active imagination. Sometimes, the tools really came in handy.

Rocke Grace, Joe Walsh, Kenny Passarelli, Joe Vitale

During the early Barnstorm years, Kenny had braces. I'm not sure how long he was supposed to wear them, but one night he was with a girl, and he called me up, because he knew I always had my tools on the road with me. "Do you have any pliers?" he asked. What a question to wake up to at 3:00 in the morning! I asked, "What the hell are you doing?" Kenny asked me to come over to his room and bring the pliers, so I got dressed and went. Hey, what are friends for?

Kenny, and the girl he was with had been making out. She had braces, too. The braces had gotten locked together and you should've witnessed the scene…me with the pliers, getting Kenny's braces to unbend, so the braces would unlock. It was really hard not to laugh. I knew if I started laughing, Kenny would, too, and we'd never get out of there. I carefully freed the girl, and then I had to bend Kenny's wire back. I didn't know the girl and she was really embarrassed.

It was really hard for someone Kenny's age to deal with having braces, and he really didn't like pictures of himself with his braces showing. In the picture inside The Smoker album, Kenny didn't smile very wide so you couldn't see them. Kenny also had very little patience, and I'm not sure when, but eventually, Kenny had just had it and one night he took the braces off himself. Amazingly, his teeth still look great.

Photos courtesy of Michael Stanley

Around this time, we went to Applewood Studios in Golden, Colorado, where they make Coors Beer, to record Michael Stanley's album "Friends and Legends." Bill Szymczyk had heard Michael Stanley's first group and thought he had a lot of talent, so he contacted Michael about producing an album for him. Bill had all kinds of contacts and had assembled an all star band to play on Michael's record… Joe Walsh, Paul Harris, Al Perkins, Kenny Passarelli, and me. I have to admit that my favorite song we recorded was "Funky is the Drummer."

When Bill Szymczyk was getting sounds in the studio, he'd ask us to play to get the engineering part set up. After he got a lot of that done, the guys would start playing and jamming just to warm up. We were all having a great time recording Michael's album. One day we were in the studio warming up and I started playing this funky beat and we started singing, "Funky is the drummer that plays the funky beat when he wants to." It was just a fun jam that became a song on his record, with all the musicians as writers. The album was fantastic and showed off Michael's talents really well.

Photo courtesy of Michael Stanley

Barnstorm went back on the road and was starting to make a name for itself. The fans really responded to our music. One time we were playing at Blossom Music Center opening up for The Guess Who. That historic show caused Blossom to shut down all rock & roll acts for a while. Here's what happened. Blossom was built for The Cleveland Orchestra to perform summer concerts. It was one of the very first outdoor amphitheaters in the country and still is, by far, one of the most beautiful ever built.

Eventually, Blossom started having rock & roll shows. I've always loved playing at Blossom. There are plenty of large dressing rooms downstairs and there's ample space for visiting with guests after the show. The concrete walls in the dining area have been softened by hanging huge quilts on the walls. The food is always excellent and the facility is top notch in every way. There was little or no security back then, so concert goers could bring coolers with food and beer to take out onto the lawn area. Sometimes it used to get pretty wild.

The show with The Guess Who and Barnstorm was sold out, so the place was packed.

The Guess Who was a bigger band than we were and they had more hits, but Joe had lived there and it was the first time since the James Gang that Joe had played back in Ohio. The crowd went crazy. We finished the show and were supposed to get off the stage, but the fans wanted us to play more and rioted. They were running up the sides of the building and started trashing the place. That ended the show. The police had to come to get things under control. I heard it was quite a while before any rock & roll band was allowed to play there again.

Since we were in town, my Mom wanted to have an Italian dinner for everyone. Both of my Nanas, Aunt Kate, Uncle Paul, my sister, Joanne and her friend Alice, my Mom and Dad, Joe, Kenny, Rocke, and I were there. My Mom served pasta with sauce and meatballs, peppers and sausage, salad and Norcia Italian bread. Then she brought out the

L to R: Joe Walsh, Kenny Passarelli, Nana Spataro, my mom Rose, Nana Vitale, Aunt Kate, Rocke Grace, Tom Stevenson, my sister Joanne. In front: My dad

green Jello, ice cream and Italian cookies. My Dad had a big barrel of homemade wine in the basement, and he and Joe started hitting the wine, toasting everything. In no time, they both were completely loaded. Then they brought out the instruments. Joe got out his guitar and my Dad got out his accordion and they started jamming downstairs

The Chylds at WHLO Appreciation Days at Chippewa Lake Park

Kent State University riot photos, Sunday, May 3rd, 1970. Approaching the intersection of Main and Lincoln, by the main campus arch over the KSU seal. A tank can be seen behind the squad car.

The still-smoldering ashes of the ROTC building, burned the previous night.

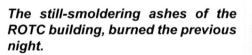

The ROTC building ruins, with the Kent State University Power Plant in the background.

As we climbed the hill on Summit Street, the armed National Guard soldiers watched us approacing. There are five soldiers in this photograph.

A tank guarded the back of the campus on Summit Street as a Jeep sped by.

A first aid center was set up across from the campus at University School on Summit Street.

Building my first mixing board.

My 21st birthday

Me & Phil Keaggy

Right: Susie & Karma at the farm house in Kent

Phil Keaggy in New York.

Leaving in the morning for my first tour with Ted Nugent.

Ted Nugent & The Amboy Dukes 1971. L to R: Rob DeLaGrange, Ted Nugent, Me, John Angelos

Me & Eddie Brigatti (The Young Rascals)

Rob, John, Me & Ted

Bo Diddley & Me

Bill Szymczyk

Los Angeles Record Plant

Kenny Passarelli, Me, Joe Walsh & Bill Szymczyk

Rocke Grace, Kenny Passarelli, Joe Walsh & Me - First Barntorm Gig

Joe Walsh & Bill Szymczyk

Kenny Passarelli & Joe Walsh

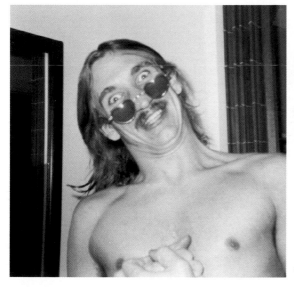

Joe Walsh

Joe Walsh eating corn and mashed potatoes.

Photo by: Rick Kohlmeyer - Backstagegallery.com

Photo by: Rick Kohlmeyer - Backstagegallery.com

Photo by: Rick Kohlmeyer - Backstagegallery.com

Me, Kenny Passarelli & Joe Walsh at Criteria Recording Studios, the day we wrote and recorded "Rocky Mountain Way."

Irving Azoff

Rocke Grace, Patrick Cullie, Kenny Passarelli & Tom Stephenson

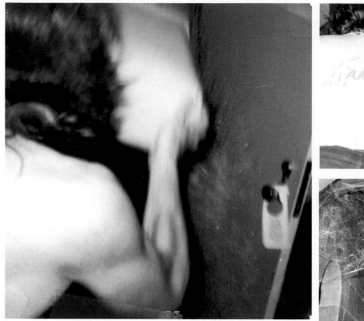

Water fight in hotel

Making spider webs for the Smoker album

L to R: Joe Walsh, Patrick Cullie, Kenny Passarelli, Tom Stephenson (In Back) Rocke Grace at the Sheraton Cadillac on the Detroit River.

My first gold album, "The Smoker You Drink, the Player You Get."

Patrick Cullie

Joe Masseria

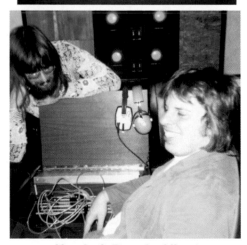

Howie & Ronnie Albert

I went deep sea fishing & caught a shark!

Me at Meyers Lake. Sad to say, the rollercoaster was being torn down.

Kenny Passarelli

Bob Webb

Tom Stephenson

Me

The Stage at the old Cleveland Stadium. My band, Madman, opened for The Rolling Stones.

Cleveland Stadium at full capacity... SOLD OUT!

Madman on stage

Dolby Duck

It was unbelievably hot that day.

Madman

Madman: Guille Garcia, Bruce Hall, Me, Bob Webb, Tom Stephenson.

Bill Szymczyk, Me & Jay Ferguson in the studio.

Stephen Stills & Chocolate Perry

Neil Young & Me   *Photo by: Julie McNulty*

Neil Young's Boat

Christopher Stills

Susie & Christopher

Neil Young & Chocolate Perry at Neil's Ranch

The outdoor stage at Neil's ranch

Chocolate & Me

Stills / Young Tour

Michael John Bowen, Guillermo, road tech and Elliot Roberts sing Stephen Stills most famous lyrics, "Do do do do do, do do, do do do do ," from "Suite: Judy Blue Eyes."

Stephen Stills with CSN logo on plane.

Our CSN baseball team, The San Francisco Hoovers

John Vanderslice, Armondo Hurley & David Crosby

Photo by: Jann Hendry

Stanley Sheldon, Bobby Mayo & Me

Stanley, Bobby, Me & Peter Frampton

Me & my son

Perth, Australia - Peter, Bobby, Stanley & Me

Below: Bobby Mayo, Stanley Sheldon, Peter Frampton & Me

in the basement. They played the blues, if you can imagine the blues on accordion. No matter what they played, the combination of guitar and accordion and seeing the two of them playing together made the whole scene bizarre and hysterical. What a sight! It was like some weird ridiculous dream you'd have after eating too much pizza late at night.

We had toured all over America as Barnstorm, and now it was time to record another album. In January of 1973 we went to Criteria Recording Studios in Florida to start the second album, the one that was called "The Smoker You Get, The Player You Drink." This is the album that had "Rocky Mountain Way" on it. That year, The Miami Dolphins had won every game and went to The Super Bowl and won that. I remember that we walked out of the studio and the streets were crazy, with cars blowing their horns, people hanging out windows,

Hey Walsh, stick to guitar!

yelling and drinking, because they had just won the Super Bowl after a perfect season. It was fun to see the celebrating first hand. We recorded most of The Smoker album there, some at Caribou Ranch, and a couple of the cuts in LA at The Record Plant.

Everybody always asks me about recording Rocky Mountain Way. Joe had just learned to play slide when Duane Allman, from the Allman Brothers, died. Duane was known for playing slide guitar and he was one of Joe's favorite players. In fact, Joe was a huge fan. When Duane died, I remember Joe saying he wanted to learn how to play slide in honor of him. Joe had started wood-shedding and practicing like crazy. He was already a fantastic guitar player, but slide is another animal. When he first started he was a little out of tune, his vibrato was a little fast, and it just didn't sound very good or mature. But he's a phenomenal guitar player, so it didn't take him very long to master it, and now he's one of the world's best.

He was really excited about this new talent of his, and he wanted to do a song that featured slide. Joe and I were jamming one time on a slow blues shuffle. He said, "This really needs slide." So, we went to Criteria in Florida, and one day when we were working on the "Smoker" album, Joe picked up his guitar and we started messing around with that slow shuffle again. I sat down at the piano and we wrote the song in about a half hour, because the song isn't that complicated.

Joe and I wrote the basic track and then we had Kenny come in and play bass and we cut the track three piece. We kept the second take. Then I played the piano part and Joe overdubbed the incredible slide part. It's the actual slide solo that he played for, I think, the first or second take. Joe was really excited because it was almost like being able to play a new instrument. After Joe's performance, everyone in the control room stood up and applauded...we were all impressed with his new talent.

We had this awesome, great-feeling, slow shuffle track. We left it at that and went back to Colorado to finish the record with Bill Szymczyk up at Caribou. There were no lyrics for it yet. Like many artists, for about 75 to 80 per cent of his tunes, Joe wrote and recorded some great track with kind of a melody in mind. Sometimes he had no melody at all, but he'd put a track down just because the music was so cool. We had recorded the track and we lived with it for about three or four weeks.

During that time Joe had started to sing and hum along with it to try to figure out vocals. So, here we were at Caribou, up in the middle of the beautiful Colorado Rocky Mountains. It was the perfect scenario and Joe just had to look around to get all this input from the view. Joe sat in the control room and maybe spent some time upstairs in the pool room that had windows all the way around it, and he put the lyrics down in less than an hour. He came down, went out and sang it.

Stephen Stills showed up at the studio that night just to hang out. He really liked Joe and our band and being around the music we were recording, so he sat in the control room while Joe sang "Rocky Mountain Way." I remember he made Joe and Bill a little nervous because he had an eight inch blade Bowie knife, and he was just sitting there flipping it. Here was Stephen Stills, one of the world's best acoustic guitar players, and we were afraid he was going to cut a finger off or something. I'm sure he was comfortable flipping the knife around, but for us it was really distracting. Bill or somebody finally asked him to stop. Stephen probably thought we were a bunch of sissies, but he stopped flipping it.

I really didn't know Stephen that well yet, but he was really kind and supportive, while he sat in the control room pushing talkback and encouraging Joe. I remember Stephen commenting on what a great job Joe did on the vocal when it was finished. It was just a great night. I was really glad that Stephen was there that night to witness part of recording "Rocky Mountain Way," which became such a classic rock song.

So, in one hour we had the vocals done and then Joe and I added the final touches. During the solo in the middle of the song I played a little synthesizer pulsing part and Joe went out and did the talk box solo. We did a couple hours work in Florida, a couple hours work in Colorado, and bingo...we're done. That simple song now has close to three million plays on the radio, TV and in movies, and was the first hit song out of Caribou.

Once "The Smoker" album was out, we realized we needed another keyboard player for all the synthesizer and keyboard parts, so we got Tom Stephenson, who was Stanley Sheldon's cousin. We were a five piece band then and we could play live all the parts we had recorded. Besides being a really good keyboard player, Tom had the right look and rock & roll attitude. It's funny what you think of when you remember someone. I remember Tom had really great rock & roll hair and he would always kind of flip his head to get it in place. He did that a lot, and he really hated for anyone to touch his hair. Tom completed the band, was a great guy and fit in easily since he already knew Rocke. Joe had moved down to Boulder from Nederland, and Tom, Kenny and Rocke lived in an apartment just across the parking lot from Susie and me.

When we were recording "The Smoker" album, we used this really  expensive British-made piece of equipment called a Melotron in the studio. It was a keyboard with a big box attached to it and inside the box there were tapes of real instruments. There were four sounds on the tapes; strings, voices, flutes and "ah-h-h's." When we pushed a key down, the tape would roll and it would play one of the sounds in that note. We could play chords of flutes, strings or voices. The Moody Blues were the first ones to use a Melotron on their records. We used it in the studio and the sound was on our record, so Joe bought one to take on the road with us for Tom to play live.

No one ever told us it had to ride right side up, and who bothers to read the manual? When we showed up at our very first gig with the Melotron, it came off the truck and when the crew opened up the case, it had been packed upside down. So what, right? But when we turned it on nothing happened, so we opened the box and all the tapes had come off the spools. It was just a big mess of tape and it looked like thousands of feet of unraveled recording tape had been thrown in a big box. That was the end of that. It was completely ruined and we had to use a synthesizer at the shows, which didn't sound nearly as good.

Joe's manager at the time was Mike Belkin, who had a management firm in Cleveland. The firm wasn't very happy with Joe for breaking up The James Gang, which was their biggest act, and moving to Colorado and starting Barnstorm. The relationship had kind of deteriorated, so Joe was looking for new management. It wasn't long before new management found him.

Photo by: Rick Kohlmeyer - Backstagegallery.com

We were playing five nights in a row at The Whiskey A Go Go in LA. All five nights, Irving Azoff came to the show. We never saw or spoke to him. He just came to the show and took it all in. The fifth night, Irving came up to the dressing rooms, which to this day are above the club. He was this young, short, confident guy with a beard, wearing a stocking-type hat, and he introduced himself to us as a booking agent. He said he was a big fan of Joe's and The James Gang, and wanted to manage Joe. Joe said something like, "Oh, sure," but Irving said he was serious.

Joe had no way of knowing what an incredible mogul Irving was going to turn into, so he started toying with him. Joe told Irving if he could get him out of his contract with Mike Belkin, he could manage him. It was like a joke. Now, this is before cell phones, email and fax machines. A short time later, Joe got a telegram or something from Mike Belkin, telling him he was released from his contract. To this day, I don't know how Irving did it.

So, all of the sudden, Irving was the manager. Even with a change in management, we continued working non-stop, and we had a lot of fun when we toured with other bands. We were opening shows for The J. Geils Band, and since he was the producer for both bands, Bill Szymczyk flew into New York City for the show. We had a day off and Bill, who was always generous and ready to party, wanted to take both bands out to dinner. We went to The House of Chan, one of New York City's better Chinese restaurants. There were probably about fifteen of us, and we all sat at a long table waiting for our dinner.

The servers brought some egg rolls on a serving dish and placed them on the table. Somebody from our band sitting at one end of the table wanted an egg roll, so someone from The J. Geils Band, who was sitting at the other end of the table, grabbed one and tossed it to him. He wasn't looking and the egg roll hit him in the head. It was an invitation to a gun fight. We got into one of the best food fights I've ever been in. By the time we were taking fists full of rice and putting them down the backs of shirts, the House of Chan asked us to leave. It looked like when people throw rice at weddings. We were still laughing when we got to the street.

That same night we were invited to go to The Atlantic Recording Studio, so we all got in cabs and went over to the studio to jam. Some of the Stones were in the studio next door, so Keith Richards and Bill Wyman came by and joined in jamming with us. We played for hours. They never mentioned that we were all wearing Chinese food. I'm sure those guys have seen worse. It was one of the most fun nights of my life. The following night we had a great show with The J. Geils Band. What a great weekend!

CHAPTER SEVEN

1973, Joe Walsh

Since "Rocky Mountain Way" had come out, the band had taken off. That one single opened the door to the kind of success we had dreamed of. We went from playing 3,000 seaters to selling out 10,000 seat halls. We also went from being "Barnstorm" to being "Joe Walsh and Barnstorm," to finally just "Joe Walsh."

We used to fly to the cities where we were playing, so I spent a lot of time in the air. It was a lot cheaper to fly back then, plus there were no security lines and fewer delays, so we could count on getting to the gig on time. Once we got to the city, we took cabs wherever we needed to go. There weren't tour buses for rock & roll bands yet, just for country or gospel bands. Things were really different then. Security? What security? If you bought an airline ticket with your name on it, you could give it to anybody and they could fly with it. If you missed your flight, you just scheduled another one with no penalty. You could even smoke cigarettes during the flight.

I loved flying. I had my airplane hobby growing up and thought that flying was wonderful. I was about to fall out of love. One day we took off on Frontier Airlines from Stapleton Airport in Denver on a 727, heading for Des Moines, Iowa. About a minute after takeoff, when the plane was really hauling and we hadn't gained much altitude, there was a huge explosion. Huge. The plane shook. People screamed. We blew the main center engine, which now had a hole in it. The plane immediately started nose down toward the ground. I have never been so terrified. I tightened my seat belt, clutched my arm rests and shoved my feet into the plane's floor in front of my seat like I was putting brakes on in a car, as though that would stop the plane from falling. We were going down. I took my wallet from my bag and put it in my pants pocket. I thought I was going to die, that this was going to be it, how my life would end. I closed my eyes and prayed that the plane wouldn't crash.

The plane was at about one thousand feet before the explosion, so the pilot had very little time to react before we would crash. He miraculously regained control of the plane and we leveled off. We circled around while they foamed the runway for our landing. It was horribly frightening to see the foam and the flashing lights on all the emergency vehicles, and know that I was flying on the plane it was for. The explosion had also disrupted the hydraulic system or something, so we had to land going really fast.

We were going so fast that we were unable to stop, so we ran off the runway into a ditch. Finally, the plane stopped moving and the cabin filled with fumes. We were all alive and unhurt, but still terrified. A woman near me was so shaken up that she lit up a cigarette. In the fume-filled plane. We all yelled at her to put it out. Normally, the door to a plane is about twelve feet off the ground, but the plane was buried so deep we got out at ground level. The airline brought us into a room in the terminal and gave us free drinks, which we all needed, and then put us right back on another flight. We didn't mind, because the odds of anything like that happening again were really small. At least that's what we thought.

About a month later, we were taking off, again from Stapleton on Frontier Airlines, this time on a 737 heading for St. Louis. We took off and flew halfway there, and then the pilot turned the plane around. I knew something was terribly wrong. The captain came on the PA system and said we were going back to the Denver airport because we were having a problem with the hydraulic system. We couldn't put the flaps down, so instead of landing at about 180 knots, we landed going about 400 knots. We were going so fast that the tires burned out and the plane ran off the runway. Again. We took the next flight out to St. Louis. Again, we were all OK, but flying was starting to get to me.

Then, we had a third incident about a month later, which finished me off. We were flying out of LaGuardia in New York on American Airlines. I always had a window seat back then, so I was looking out the window and I saw fire. Yeah, we're in the air, the engine was on fire, and I was watching it burn. You really don't ever want to see that. I figured that at any moment it would explode, the wing would fall off, and we were going down. Again. They extinguished the fire, but then we were flying with only one engine. So, we went through the third emergency landing in three months. This one really tore up the landing gear. My love for flying had now turned to fear. I never wanted to fly again, ever, and didn't for an entire year.

We were all pretty toasted from our three terrifying flights, and started driving. Sometimes we got a Winnebago, sometimes a rental car. Our tour manager, Joe Masseria, was usually the driver, but sometimes we drove ourselves. The gigs weren't close enough together to drive, so it didn't work out well and we were always tired. Tour buses were still not the norm for rock & roll bands.

We were always nervous about traveling the day of a show, in case we had car trouble or something. You have to be there, or there's no show. Being late is unthinkable. No matter what, you're there. However, one time Kenny, Rocke, Tom and I were in a van driving to somewhere in South Dakota the day of the show. It was about a four hour drive from where we started out. Joe was already there, and we were opening a great big show for The Beach Boys. This was the first time I had opened for them since I was in my band, The Chylds, back in Canton. I was so excited because I love The Beach Boys' music. I knew they'd listen to our show, and I really wanted to play well.

I started out driving for a while and I got tired, so Rocke said he'd drive. I thought that would be a good idea, because he grew up around there. We should have known better, from the time Rocke actually called down to the main desk at a hotel where we were staying and asked, "Where are we?"

But, I need a lot of energy to play drums for a show, and, as I said, I really wanted to play well. We were all tired because we had been driving so much over the past several weeks, so, better judgment aside, we all went to sleep, except Rocke, who was driving the van. I eventually woke up and saw a sign that said, "St. Louis, 35 miles." Rocke said, "Hey, guys, we're almost there!" He had no clue where we were going. He had made a left turn somewhere on the interstate.

So, it was 4:00 in the afternoon, and we're 200 miles from where we have to be for an 8:00 PM show. We about killed Rocke, who felt really bad about getting us so far off course, but we wouldn't let up. Remember, there were no cell phones, no tour itineraries, so we had no way of contacting Joe. We drove 100 miles an hour, got there frazzled and a nervous wreck, ten minutes late. Late. They were holding the show for us.

I can't explain to you how frightening that was for me. It was like one of those really bad nightmares where you're trying to get somewhere and you just can't make it. We had to drive all those hours and didn't know if we'd make it on time or not. All I could do was drive really, really fast. I gave no thought whatsoever to our safety. We can laugh about it now, but it wasn't funny at all at the time.

Sometimes when we were on the road, we wanted to visit the famous attractions in a city. We were on tour part of that summer with the band, Mott The Hoople. One night after the show when we were playing in Memphis, Kenny and I got into the limo with Mott The Hoople, and somebody said, "Hey, let's go over to Elvis's house." You have to understand that Elvis was still alive at this time, and he lived at Graceland…we thought he was probably at home. We drove over to Graceland and pulled up to the gate, which looks like a music staff with notes on it.

There's a guard's gate there, but for some reason, the guard wasn't on duty. There was an intercom box at the gate, and we could talk to the guard up at the house. The guys in Mott the Hoople were British, so one of the guys put on what we thought was this great Paul McCartney accent, and he said, "Hey Elvis, it's Paul McCartney, let's hang out!" The guard wasn't buying it. He kept saying, "You guys get on outta here." Finally, he came down to the gate and saw that we were in this great big stretch limo, but when we opened the window to talk to him, he could see it wasn't Paul McCartney. He kept saying to us, "There ain't no Elvis here. You boys get on outta here, or I'll be calling the police." Then he'd pretend to be calling the police. We finally left. I did eventually visit Elvis's home, but it was during the daytime, and it was a guided tour after he'd passed away.

Sometimes to pass the time on the long drives between gigs, we'd start making up names, like "Hugh Jass, Bill Fold, Pete Moss or Dan D'Lion." Then we'd all really laugh. Then it would be quiet for a minute, and then someone else would think of another one. For some reason, Rocke never quite got what we were doing. He'd say something like, "I know, Glove Compartment," and we'd say, "No, no, that's not how it works."

Our road stress needed an outlet beyond playing name games, and our on the road pranks escalated. As I said earlier, Joe was not only an accomplice, but an instigator. Here's the story of the ongoing water fights, which started one night and lasted for years. We were staying at a Holiday Inn and about 8:00 PM, there was a knock at my door. This door didn't have a peep hole, so I opened the door, and it was

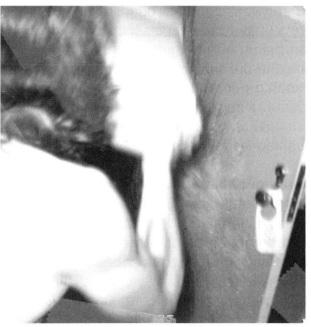

WATER FIGHT!!!!

Stefany Walsh, Joe's wife. She was holding a trash can and it was full of water. She totally drenched me with it, laughed and ran back to their room. I stood there in shock for a minute, thinking, "What just happened?" They weren't dealing with an amateur. I decided to get them back. I filled my trash can with water and knocked on Joe's door. They probably didn't think I was going to pay them back, so they just opened the door. Joe and Stefany were in there, and I soaked them both and ran back to my room. It was war!

Joe sent Stefany to both Kenny and Rocke's rooms and she soaked both of them. So, Kenny, Rocke and I decided to band together. We all filled buckets of water and knocked on the Joe's door. He knew what was going to happen this time, so when Joe and Stefany opened the door, they already had a bucket of water ready to go, and they soaked me again. But, Kenny and Rocke were right behind me, and they drenched Stefany and Joe. Some of the water splashed over into the TV and it blew up. We ran back to our rooms.

Joe and Stefany were roaming the halls, looking for us, and the fight went on for several hours. After a while, just throwing buckets of water wasn't good enough, so Joe got the fire hose. Back then, you didn't have to break glass, it was a little turn thing. He was drinking, had plenty of money to pay for damages, and just didn't care. He took the fire hose out, and dragged it to our door. I know he was laughing out loud while he did this, enjoying in advance what was about to happen and how we were going to react when we saw him with the fire hose. We heard a knock at our door and answered it. It was Joe with the fire hose. What a picture!

We didn't think he'd actually use it, so we laughed. We thought, "Yeah, right, he's got a fire hose." So, we opened the door all the way and WHOOOM! Those things are powerful! He broke the glass in the lamp, and tons of water went all over the place. It set off an alarm and the hotel manager came up and kicked us out, because there was so much water everywhere, and it was dripping down through the ceiling fixtures into the floor below us. The water fight had been going on for about four hours by now, so it was around midnight. We got into our van and went to another hotel. We left the road manager, Patrick Cullie, behind to pay for the damages and deal with the furious hotel manager. Water damages…an echo from my past.

These water fights went on for years. One night, about two weeks later, we were off and staying at The Sheraton Cadillac, right on the Detroit River. Patrick, our road manager, was wearing his new, really expensive, fringed suede jacket. We hated it because it looked like a hippie coat or something, and we really made fun of it. I knew from experience that Joe had a history with coats he didn't like. We were making a lot of noise and

The Sheraton Cadillac Hotel

the guests were complaining, so Patrick went downstairs to talk to the hotel manager.

Now, remember, we were a young, rowdy rock & roll band in the '70's. We knew Patrick had gone downstairs, and we knew that he had his new fringed jacét on. Before Patrick had gotten downstairs to try and smooth things over, the hotel manager had called the cops. Patrick talked to the manager, and called upstairs and said, "OK, I've straightened it out, but you have to shut up and keep it down or we're going to get thrown out of here. There's no place to go…all the area hotels are sold out." At this point we had only been making a lot of noise, and hadn't thrown any water yet.

It was really late by now, like 2:00 or 3:00 AM, and we knew Patrick was coming back upstairs on the elevator. So, all of us got water in our buckets, and gathered at the elevator doors. We were going to soak him, because we just hated that coat. The elevator doors opened, and all four of us tossed the water full bore at where we thought Patrick would be standing. It was like a tidal wave…huge splash…but instead of Patrick on the elevator, it was a cop with a dog.

The water hit the cop's pant leg and soaked the dog, which was one of those big German shepherds, standing there with his teeth showing. The dog wasn't smiling. Water was dripping off him and he looked like he wanted to kill us. Somehow Patrick, whose coat had escaped, managed to keep them from kicking us out of there, but we had to sign papers that we'd pay for any damages. The extent of the damages was just in the elevator area, because the water fight really was just getting started when it came to an abrupt end that night.

But that wasn't the end of the water fights. Oh, no. The water fights continued for years. We sometimes got into these water fights when it was a night off and we were bored. One of those nights, we got into a water fight and a lot of water was all over the carpet and everywhere. The hotel manager was getting a lot of complaints, so he got really mad, called the cops, and sent one upstairs. I shared a room with Kenny on this particular tour.

The cop knocked on the door really loud with his night stick. Boom, boom, boom! When he said he was a cop, we said innocently, "Just a minute, officer, we're in bed." I took some of my clothes off really fast, so I'd look like I was in bed, Kenny jumped in bed completely dressed and pulled the covers up over his wet clothes and shoes, and then I opened the door, trying to look like I had been asleep.

The cop demanded, "What's going on here? What's all this business about a water fight?" Faking concern, we answered, "Yeah, we heard all that noise, what the heck's going on?" As the cop walked into the room, his feet were squishing on the wet carpet. Yeah, we're really innocent. Then he said to Kenny, "You, sir, get out of bed, and I want to see your ID."

So, Kenny got out of bed with his wet clothes and shoes on. Well, that was an easy crime to solve. The cop let us go, and once again, we just had to pay for damages. Eventually, the water fights evolved to the point where there were rules. The water had to be luke warm,

96   JOE VITALE : BACKSTAGE PASS

since we didn't want anyone to get scalded and we were all singers, so we didn't want anyone to catch a cold. No soaking TV's, because they were too expensive, and we weren't allowed to use a dirty trash can.

Later that year, we were staying at the Lakeshore Drive Holiday Inn in Chicago. Kenny, who was staying in room 1901, got pretty loaded. Somebody knocked on his door, and when he went to answer it, he stumbled and hit his head on the door, leaving a gash in his forehead. He still has the scar, by the way. He had to go to the hospital and get four or five stitches. Kenny got really mad because we had the night off, he was partying, and all of the sudden he had to go to the hospital.

When Kenny got back to his room, he was so mad that he started throwing stuff around. He's half Italian...you know, just expressing himself. Finally, he threw something out the window. We were on the nineteenth floor above the parking lot. This was before suicide protectors were on the windows, so Kenny could open the window all the way. He enjoyed that and it made him laugh, so he started throwing everything that was loose in the room out the window...the bed, mattress, nightstand, dresser, drawers, lamps, blankets, towels, pillows...everything. The one thing he did wrong, besides all of it, was to throw the phone out, which had the room number on it. He went to jail for that one, but they let him out when he paid for the damages.

Some of the debris from the room hit a Mercedes down below in the parking lot, so Kenny had to pay for not only everything in the room, but also for the damages to the car. We were told that after this episode, the hotel manager put a note into the actual deed of that Holiday Inn that said Joe Walsh and his band were never allowed to stay there again until the end of time. The end of time? We still laugh about that. The water fights continued even through the Eagles tours.

Back then, we looked really different from everyone else, so if we went into a restaurant or someplace, people would come up to us and ask if we were in a band. Today, kids in bands just look like the audience. We had long hair and flashier clothes. I was still wearing the clothes I got when I played with Ted. I still wore the red pants, lace shirts, and platform shoes that I couldn't play drums in. Some promoter even gave us platform gym shoes and flip flops. I had several velvet coats. One was dark forest green and one was purple with embroidered pink music notes on it.

On the inside of The Smoker album there's a band picture and Kenny has on a gold suit. I can't talk, I had on a woman's sweater. You can see that Joe was going for a laid back Rocky Mountain look with the jeans, vest, and flannel shirt, and we looked like a Detroit rock & roll band. There's a publicity photo of us with Kenny in these giant platform shoes that look like extension  ladders. We must have been a bad influence on Joe, because eventually he got crazy with his clothes, too. In fact, in time, he went way beyond anything we ever wore. Way beyond.

We always wanted to look extra nice when we did TV shows. I gave Joe a black and silver shirt I bought, that was too big for me, to wear on Don Kirshner's Rock Concert. We loved TV and did a lot of shows once "The Smoker" album started getting really big. We did Don Kirshner's Rock Concert two times, once with Joe and once with Michael Stanley. We also did Midnight Special, where Richard Pryor introduced us as "The Barnstormers." Another time we were on ABC's "Rock & Roll Tonight." Susie had made these really cool airbrushed tee shirts with rhinestones that Joe and I both wore.

It was a really crazy time. Alice Cooper got into the goth thing, Elton John was wearing all the insane fancy clothes with giant rhinestone glasses, Rod Stewart had the bouffant hairdo and silk suits with scarves, things like that. It was part of the act. I've always said that Joe was born with one more bone than other humans, and that was a funny bone. Joe has a wonderful sense of humor and is so hilarious! He started getting into the whole clothes thing. He would wear the most idiotic combinations of things, like stupid big hats. People just loved it when we walked on stage. They had no idea what we'd be wearing that night.

I was still on the road most of the time. The more we worked, the more opportunities came our way. Because Bill Szymczyk had been producing Joe Walsh, a world famous rock & roll guitar player, Rick Derringer contacted him to produce his solo album "All American Boy," which had "Rock & Roll Hoochie Koo" on it. Rick entrusted Bill to get the band guys together, and he hired Joe Walsh, Kenny and me to play on it. We recorded it at Caribou Ranch.

I was praying that he didn't remember the suits we wore in The Chylds when we opened for The McCoys in Canton. Either he didn't, or he was too merciful to mention it. That was Rick's biggest album and single. The picture of Rick on the front is wild…pure rock & roll. I'm so honored I got to play my 1967 psychedelic red Ludwig drums on that album. I've heard that Elton John heard Rick's album and loved it so much that he started recording at Caribou.

The band was playing practically non-stop, and there was no way to plan a normal wedding and be able to count on me being there, so Susie and I got married in Boulder, Colorado, on August 7, 1973. We left Boulder the next morning, drove back to Ohio, and never did have a honeymoon. After we stayed in Ohio a couple of days, we met the band in New England for some gigs, and then drove back to Ohio where our parents had a reception for us. Susie stayed behind while I went back to Boulder for a week, then she drove back to Colorado alone. We met up for a day on her way back to Boulder in Kansas City, where I was doing a gig.

In the fall of 1973, it seemed like the Colorado music scene had peaked, and a lot of musicians started leaving. By September, Joe Walsh and Stephen Stills had decided to move to Los Angeles, and Bill Szymczyk moved to Florida. I was never home and Susie would be living alone in snowy Colorado, so we decided to move back to what she now called "balmy" Ohio.

We had started headlining shows and had Irving's acts like REO Speedwagon, Dan Fogelberg, Jimmy Buffett, and even the Eagles, opening shows for us. Yeah, The Eagles opened for us back then. We had started staying at nicer and nicer hotels. Irving was traveling on the road with us, and the water and food fights escalated. Joe and Irving got really close and Joe started spending most of his time with him. Joe also started carrying a chain saw on the road and he even got an anvil case made for it. The worst hotel thing that I know of that Joe ever did, was the infamous adjoining room incident.

Joe and Irving always got adjoining rooms. One time in Kansas City, there were no adjoining rooms available at the hotel, but Joe and Irving demanded adjoining rooms. The hotel said they were sorry, but they were sold out and none were available. You don't say no to Irving. So, later that night, I heard, "vroom, vroom, vroom!" Then I heard this screeching sound of sawing through of plasterboard, wires and wood. It didn't take long.

They made a hole about a six foot high in the wall. Then they said, "Now we have adjoining rooms!" Then they walked back and forth between the rooms, just like nothing was unusual. Joe literally did something like $8,000 damage, cutting a huge hole in the wall between the two rooms. He even did a music video for "I Can Play That Rock & Roll" with the chain saw in it, but this was real. Word started getting around. Imagine you're the hotel manager, and Joe Walsh shows up in your lobby, ready to check in, with a guitar and suitcase in one hand, and a chain saw in the other.

He had a lot of fun using the chain saw at hotels, but it was really noisy and it was expensive to pay for damages, so he switched to a Weedeater. I still have to laugh while I'm talking about this. He'd say he didn't like the curtains or they needed to be hemmed, like he cared, right? Then, he'd use the Weedeater to shorten the drapes or the dust ruffle on the bed. Then we'd all laugh really hard. It worked very well, by the way.

Another time, and there are pictures of this, Joe got a hot glue gun, and glued everything in his entire room to the ceiling. Upside down. Everything he could get up there....the dressers, mirrors, chairs, and all that. Put hot glue on the bottom of the chair legs, and you could just stick them up on the ceiling. He's a sensitive guy, into decorating. Most guitar players are endorsed by Gibson or Fender, he could have been endorsed by Sears or John Deere. Oh, man, what fun!

We were still into aeronautics, so sometimes we took the bedspreads or sheets, connected them to the room service containers and made parachutes out of them. Then we'd throw them out the window. I don't know what it was about us, but we had to throw things out the window.

It was never-ending. Sometimes we had pie fights. One time it was a crew guy's birthday and we were going to have him come out, sing happy birthday to him, and then throw pies at him. Somehow, it leaked to the crew, so it backfired on us. They took cream pies and put them by the stage lights so they'd get all warm and gooey. When Joe called him out  to the stage, the whole crew came out and pied us. Recently, I took apart a snare drum I have, and found dried pie stuck in it from thirty years ago. It also went into my flute, so I had to send it out to be cleaned. They got us so bad we didn't even try to retaliate.

We still had the same band members touring with Joe Walsh, except Rocke Grace was no longer with us. The music had changed, so the band had only one keyboard player and we had added Guille Garcia on percussion. We had the two albums out, and the next album we did was "So What."

Soul Pole Records

That year, Bill Szymczyk started putting out an album, called "Soul Pole Records." It was a collection of outtakes and great studio moments from the previous year. Each year, Bill only made a few of these 33 1/3 vinyl records. It was a really cool thing for Bill to put the records together for us, and we all LOVED to get our copies. One of my albums was marked "nine of fifty." I transferred them to cassette several years ago and got off hearing them all over again. The last Soul Pole Record of the five that I have from Bill was from 1982.

1974, Michael Stanley, "In Concert"

We were in LA finishing up Joe Walsh's album, "So What?" and Bill asked me if I could stick around for a couple weeks because he was putting something together for Michael Stanley. I said, "Sure, what're we doin?" Bill had arranged for all these amazing musicians to play with Michael Stanley on Don Kirshner's In Concert. We did a few days of rehearsal with the players he'd put together. Besides me on drums, check out this band….Michael Stanley, Joe Walsh, and Dan Fogelberg on guitar, Paul Harris on keyboards, Brian Garafalo on bass, Al Perkins on pedal steel guitar, and David Sanborn on sax. Bill Szymczyk always came through assembling the right guys for every project.

This was before many of us owned VCR's, so we only got to see the performance once. It got incredible reviews. We didn't know what had happened to that footage. Many years later, I got a call from Bill Szymczyk and Michael Stanley and they said they had a surprise for me. They referred to it as, "The Holy Grail." It was a DVD of that concert, which had surfaced with hundreds of other TV broadcasts of that era. The three of us sat and watched it and we were all blown away at how awesome it was. It had been thirty years since we'd seen it. We high-fived each other, and were mildly impressed with ourselves.

1974, The John Lennon Record Plant Jams

While I was in LA working on these different projects, John Lennon started having secret jam sessions at The Record Plant, engineered by John Stronach. They were three Sundays in a row, from about midnight till 6:00 AM. The lineup of rock royalty who dropped in to play was unbelievable...John Lennon, Ringo Starr, Keith Richards, Ron Wood, Bill Wyman, and Al Kooper, just to name a few. Joe Walsh and I were also invited to drop by and jam.

The first night we arrived, we walked into Studio C. It was filled with such rock royalty that I couldn't believe my eyes. Wow! There was John Lennon sitting at the piano with Ringo on drums. How cool was that? Although we were kind of new faces to this crowd, they treated us like we were one of them. They pointed to us and then motioned to some instruments, signaling us to sit in. So, within two minutes of our arrival, we were jammin' with these guys. There were a whole bunch of players there and they respectfully took turns playing and listening. The music was awesome. We played good old fashioned rock & roll, like Chuck Berry, Bo Diddley and Little Richard.

Out of all the great moments of the three Sunday nights, the most memorable moment was with Ringo. I was playing a tambourine and Ringo was playing drums, when he stood up, walked over to me, handed me his sticks and grabbed the tambourine. Imagine that! What a moment! Years later, Ringo came to one of our Stephen Stills gigs. Stephen asked him to join us on the stage and Ringo grabbed the tambourine and played, "For What It's Worth" with us. Then I stood up, walked over to Ringo, handed him my sticks and this time I grabbed the tambourine. I doubt that he remembered the same type of exchange at the John Lennon sessions, but I'll never forget that moment.

We were having so much fun none of us got tired, and when 6:00 AM rolled around, we weren't ready to quit. John and Yoko asked that we keep this under the radar for obvious reasons. We finished playing at the end of that third week, and walked outside as the sun was coming up.

The jams were going to last another week or two, but someone must have let it leak, because there were a few thousand fans waiting outside in the parking lot to get a glimpse of the superstars, John Lennon and his friends. It was scary and exciting at the same time. We went back inside and the studio personnel arranged for limos and police security to pick up the stars in the back alley behind the Record Plant. Unfortunately, that was the end of the John Lennon sessions. To this day, I'm not sure what they did with the tapes, but I'm sure someone has them, and I hope they surface someday.

CHAPTER EIGHT

1974, The Beach Boys

I had great song ideas in Colorado and now that we were back in Ohio, I bought a grand piano and started writing. I put together a little four track home studio and since we had a house instead of an apartment, I could use real drums. I was writing like crazy and I had made several demos.

The Beach Boys were playing in Wooster, Ohio, so I decided to take a break from writing and Susie and I drove over to hear them. I'd opened up for them at Memorial Auditorium in Canton years before and I also had opened shows for them with Barnstorm. They were and are one of my all-time favorite bands and I'm sure you can hear their influence in the songs I write. They're all really nice guys, and invited Susie and me into the dressing room after the show. We were sitting there beside the showers, talking to them when Mike Love just dropped his clothes and hopped in the shower. Yeah, what a surprise! There was no shower curtain, so Susie and I looked everywhere but in the shower. Hey, it was their dressing room.

I invited them over to our home in Canton. Carl Wilson, Ricky Fataar, and Billy Hinsche wanted to come, so we piled in our car and I drove us the thirty miles to our home. We played music and talked in my studio while Susie got together food and drinks for us. I couldn't believe that The Beach Boys were at my house and I was playing them my demos. Carl listened attentively to my song, "Falling," and said that it was one of the most complete songs he'd ever heard. What a compliment! I was amazed and humbled. I'll never get over that one.

We ate and had a great time, and then about three in the morning, we drove them all the way back to Wooster…and then we had to drive all the way back home to Canton. Susie and I always went to their shows whenever we could. Truly, forever, the All-American band.

Their music was a big part of my life, especially when I was in high school playing with The Echoes and Chylds. One of the most fun New Year's Eves Susie and I ever spent was in 1973 when Barnstorm opened for The Beach Boys in Long Beach, California, at The Arena. The band got to sit in with them and play "Fun Fun Fun." Me, playing drums with the actual Beach Boys singing and playing…a dream come true! At midnight all kinds of balloons and confetti dropped on everyone in the audience. After the show we stayed on The Queen Mary and celebrated New Year's Eve. What a great night!

1975, "Roller Coaster Weekend"

In 1974, after I had made a few demos, I talked to Mark Myerson, who was the Artist Relations person at Atlantic Records. He was interested in hearing my demos, so I took a trip to New York and went to Atlantic Records to try and get a record deal. I saw Mark and played him my four little demos, and he signed me. It didn't take a committee…that's how different things were back then. Atlantic had two studios that they used, and one of them was Criteria in Florida, where I had already recorded with Joe. The Eagles, Crosby, Stills and Nash, and The Bee Gees also recorded there, so I decided to go there, too. I recorded my album in Studio B, which had a fantastic piano.

Atlantic Records suggested that I use Ronnie and Howie Albert, who agreed to engineer and produce my album. They'd engineered and produced all the Stephen Stills Manassas records and solo projects. I'd already recorded demos of all the songs in my home studio in

Ohio, so all I needed to do was to go into the studio and reproduce the songs with better equipment. Ronnie and Howie were used to recording bands, not one guy playing most of the parts himself. When I said I was a solo artist, I really meant SOLO...I was the only guy on the basic tracks.

I recorded the songs for Roller Coaster Weekend the only way I knew how. Since I'm a basically a drummer, I'm most

Howie & Ronnie Albert

comfortable playing drums, but I also play keyboards, flute, bass and synthesizer. Usually when you're recording a track you play to some sort of click track or metronome, but they didn't have anything down there like that. I had a setting on my Arp synthesizer that made a sort of click and I could set the tempo, so I used that.

I recorded the tracks in a very non-traditional way. Usually when you make a "build a record," you play a piano or guitar part to a click track first, and then add the other parts to that. But I was most comfortable playing drums, and I knew the songs so well that I started with the drum parts first and added the other instruments and vocals to that. No one I know records like that. I had to play the drum track including every part and fill first, and as a result, the other instruments really followed the intensity and dynamics of the drums really well.

So, I'd go out into the studio and count off, and then play the entire drum track with stops, fills and dynamics to a click track without any music. The drums were the lead instrument. Then I'd record the piano part and add all the other instruments and vocals. There were no band tracks. Ronnie and Howie had never worked with anyone who recorded like that, but they were into it and let me record the way I was most comfortable. It usually took about an hour to get the click track, drums and piano down, then it was pretty clear sailing.

Within about three hours I'd have the entire track going. Then I'd put some vocals on it and we'd put it aside, knowing that eventually I'd bring in guitar players. Usually we record vocals last, but guitar was the last thing we did on the songs on my album. When the guitar players got there, all the tracks were finished including the vocals, so they really knew what the song was going to sound like and where there were empty spaces in the music.

Susie and I got a hotel room on the ocean and stayed for about six weeks. Joe Masseria was our road manager, Ronnie and Howie Albert engineered and co-produced with me, and Phil Keaggy, Joe Walsh and Rick Derringer eventually came down to play guitar. It was a really wonderful recording situation.

Rick Derringer is one of the greatest rock & roll guitar players and singers who's ever lived. He is Mr. Rock & Roll and has performed some of the very best classic rock & roll songs of all time. I knew Rick because of The McCoys and because I had played on his fantastic record "All American Boy." Bill Szymczyk helped me arrange for him to record on my album, so when the entire track of "Shoot 'Em Up" was done, Rick came down to overdub his guitar part. He arrived at the studio and we were ready to start. It wasn't necessary for Rick to go out in the big room at the studio…he just needed to put his amp out there, and he could stand in the control room with us and play. That's how we always did it, how everybody does it. Not Rick.

He listened to the song, plugged in and started getting some great guitar sounds. Then he started playing along to the song. I was really excited about what he was playing and thought it sounded fantastic. But Rick stopped playing and said, "I can't record like this. I need something to stand on, like a box!" Rick's about my height, about 5'5", so we got him a box, and he stepped up and stood on it like he was on stage. Then he turned the lights, which were pointing down towards the board, on to himself, and really rocked out.

I can't think of that time without shaking my head and smiling. Who does things like that? What a character...what a creative musician... supplying himself with the atmosphere he needed and giving it his all in the studio, as though he were playing for 20,000 fans. I was so lucky to have him on my record. What I would give to have a picture on him really getting into it while he was standing on that box with the lights shining on him...what a great moment for me...what a picture in my mind. I'll never forget it!

Atlantic released three 45 rpm vinyl singles from Roller Coaster Weekend, which included "Roller Coaster Weekend," "Shoot 'Em Up," and "Take a Chance on Love." For simplicity, at the time I didn't individually credit the guitar players for the songs they played on the album. I regretted that I did it that way, so here's who played on what. If I don't have a guitar player listed, then I did the entire track myself.

1. Roller Coaster Weekend (Joe Walsh)
2. (Do You Feel Like) Movin' (Rick Derringer)
3. Madman (Rick Derringer)
4. Take a Chance on Love (Phil Keaggy)
5. School Yard (Joe Walsh)
6 Shoot 'Em Up (Rick Derringer / lead - Joe Walsh / rhythm)
7. Feelings Gone Away (Phil Keaggy)
8. Two of Us
9. Falling
10. Interlude
11. Step on You

Buddy Miles was also recording at Criteria during the time I was down there recording my album. He walked by one day and heard me playing my blue Mosrite bass on "The Two of Us," and stopped and asked if he could come in. This was THE Buddy Miles, who had made a big name for himself with The Electric Flag and the Band of Gypsys with Jimi Hendrix. Buddy said he just loved the bass part I was playing. Wow, what a compliment! I was really flattered. He didn't know who I was or that I was a drummer, he just liked the music…my music. Buddy kept coming around and pretty soon we were friends.

He stopped by one day when I was working on this beautiful little instrumental synthesizer piece called "Interlude." I was inspired to write it after hearing Stevie Wonder's "Inner Visions." Buddy saw my drums sitting out in the room, and asked if he could play on my song. I really didn't intend to put drums on it, but I said, "OK."

Buddy was a big guy and had an even bigger Afro hairdo. He was known for it, and it was gigantic. Ronnie and Howie had the maintenance guy take apart a pair of headphones and add an extension piece to it…kinda like a seat belt extender on an airplane... so the headphones would fit around his hair. I initially wasn't that into Buddy playing drums on my song, but the more I thought about it, the more excited I got. Buddy was an unbelievable drummer and singer, and he wanted to play drums on my little "Interlude." I couldn't believe it and wondered what fantastic thing he was going to play. He went out to the drum set, sat down and put the headphones on. He took a deep breath. He was ready. I was so excited. Ronnie and Howie cued up my sensitive little instrumental piece and Buddy started to play.

It sounded like the drum solo Ginger Baker did in the song "Toad." I'd never heard so many drums and cymbals in my life. He kept playing. It sounded like the sham battle at the end of a fireworks display. He played like that the entire song and to my horror, I suddenly realized that I wanted to burst out laughing. Fortunately, the control room is soundproof, because the other people in the room did start laughing. They could hardly get their breath. Buddy could see me, though, and I struggled to keep a straight face. What in the heck was he playing? It was everything I could do to maintain, especially with the hysterical laughter all around me. Buddy finished playing. "How's that?" he asked.

How's that? Except for the awkwardness of that moment, that question would have brought on a whole new wave of laughter. It was totally silent in the control room. I didn't know what to say. Apparently no one else knew what to say either. Everyone was looking at the floor, trying really hard not to start laughing again.

Was he joking around or did he just have a wildly different impression of my song than I did? I wasn't sure, and I liked Buddy and had so much respect for him that I didn't want to offend him, so I just thanked him and with all the enthusiasm I could dig up and said, "Uh-h, great, man!" Then Buddy lost it. He started laughing really hard. He was a really big guy and even though he had a high voice, he had a huge laugh that filled the studio. I knew he got me. He laughed so hard that I thought he was going to cry. Finally, I could laugh, too, and we all really let loose. What a relief! The "Interlude" remained drum-less. I only wish I had a recording of Buddy playing on it.

It probably seems strange for a drummer to write such a delicate and beautiful song, but it was an expression of a dimension of songwriting that I really enjoyed. Joe Walsh also really liked the "Interlude" and for several albums down the road, including my second solo album, we included an instrumental piece. I'll explain in a later story how these instrumentals became labeled "Something Weirdos."

One day we decided to take a break from recording and go deep sea fishing. The ocean was like glass. Joe Masseria made fried egg and hot pepper sandwiches and brought beer. It was still morning. At first we were really enjoying being out on the ocean in the fishing boat after all the time we had spent in the dark stuffy  studio. After a while, it was really getting hot, and the sun started beating down on us. Susie was absolutely loving it and having a wonderful time, until she started feeling queasy.

Susie Before   *Susie After*

That didn't make any sense to us, because the ocean looked just like glass, but the waves were big, sickening swells. Pretty soon she was miserable and no matter what she did, she was still sick. Joe Masseria put on his best Italian eyes and looking as sincere as possible, said, "Well, we can all go back in, Susie, but you're the only one who's sick and we've already paid for the whole day. If we take you back in, it'll ruin it for everyone." He was Italian, and had perfected the craft of guilt-laying to an art form. I was so used to hearing Italian guilt-ridden logic that it seemed to make sense to me. So, Susie stuck it out. There's a picture of her sitting with her feet curled around a towel filled with ice. I caught a shark later, which the captain then shot and it bled all over the boat. The sandwiches, however, were delicious.

Ronnie and Howie Albert did an excellent job on my album and although it's not like we talk a lot, I'm still friends with them to this day. You get really close when you work together a project like that. They were really fun to work with and gave me a fantastic product that I'm still very proud of. The record is now a CD and is still selling over thirty years later!

We needed a cover for the album, which I had decided to call, "Roller Coaster Weekend," so Atlantic Records set up a shoot with a photographer, Armen Kachaturian, and flew me to New York. We went to an amusement park at Coney Island and did the shoot in the morning before the park opened on The Cyclone at Astroworld. It was such a big deal for me...my first solo album cover. I wore my favorite shirt, which Susie has since framed with a picture of the cover. It was a perfect day to take the pictures, and the white frame of the wooden roller coaster with the green metal cars with red seats really looked great in the pictures. The fact that we were going to take photos while we were riding on the coaster was really going to give us some exciting pictures. I have to tell you, I don't like to ride on roller coasters. I was in the second seat of the roller coaster and the photographer was in the first seat, sitting backwards, facing me. We weren't strapped in, like in coasters today.

Armen, who was a free lance photographer, had lots of equipment, including several cameras, lenses, film...all that. He took a few photos going up the first hill, but they didn't have my hair blowing, no excitement, they weren't any good. But after we started down the first hill, he never took another photo, because he was freaking out. His cameras were flying all over the place, the film was bouncing around in the car, and he couldn't focus. At one point, he almost fell out of the car because he was sitting backwards. So, we got to the end, and he hadn't taken any usable pictures.

We stopped and he reassessed the situation. He decided that he better take one camera with one lens on it, loaded with one roll of film. The manager of the park was really nice about it and said to go for it. He'd been keeping the entrance gates closed to the public until we were finished. We got back on the roller coaster...I hate riding on roller coasters...and started back up the first hill. Oh boy, another ride. I was really praying he'd get a good shot, since I didn't know how many times I could take riding on that thing.

We went down the terrifying first hill and we both held on for dear life. You always have to yell going down the first hill. No pictures were taken. We went back up the second hill and he started snapping pictures. I tried to look like I was having fun. Up, down, around and around we went as he snapped the pictures. We both agreed that the photograph that went on the album cover was the best one out of thirty six. The photographer told me that based on the picture's number on the slide, it was probably shot on the first turn after the second hill. The ride and shoot finally ended, except for a few still shots around the park.

The picture on the back of the album captured an interesting moment. No, the person isn't Susie. People always think that. The person standing on the ground was caught blowing a bubble gum bubble. It wasn't planned, just a coincidence. To this day, I get really great compliments from all around the world on this album and it really means a lot to me. The album was finished, the cover photo and design chosen, and I was back in Ohio. I needed a manager, so I called Mike Belkin, who had been Joe Walsh's manager. Mike was willing to manage me, so I started putting a band together.

Working with Joe was over for a while, and I knew the Barnstorm guys were looking for work. I also knew an excellent guitar player, Bob Webb, who was a friend of Joe's and mine from the Kent days, so I called him, too. We had worked together for a short while in a band called The Measles. I also hired Kenny Passarelli, Tom Stephenson and Guille Garcia. I  decided to call the band Madman, since that was one of the cuts on the album. I don't know that I'd ever name a band that again, but it was one of those things that seemed like a good idea at the time.

One of the promotional items Atlantic made up for the album was an ad that looked like a folded ten dollar bill. When you opened it, it was a picture and ad for my album. They looked real enough that everyone always would bend down to pick them up. We used to put them on escalators, just to make it a challenge. I only have a couple of them left. I'm not sure they sold any albums, but we had a lot of fun with them. I especially loved the ad Atlantic put in Rolling Stone. They used my album cover photo and had made my hair look like a greaser and it said something like, "Are you still listening to that greasy kid stuff? Get Vitale."

1975, Madman

Kenny Passarelli, Me, Tom Stevenson, Guille Garcia, Bob Webb

Just as we did with Barnstorm, we started playing Belkin shows. We opened for John Entwistle from the Who, with his band, John Entwistle's Ox, and also for The J. Geils Band. Our biggest show was for 70,000 people at the old Cleveland Stadium opening for The Rolling Stones. Here I was, opening a show for this world renowned band after being there at the Cleveland Stadium just a few years before watching the Beatles.

I still vividly remember how hot it was that day, and walking out on the stage to play. As I sat down at my drums, I looked out at over 70,000 cheering people, but this time it was my band and my songs they were cheering for. One of my dreams was coming true…it was a great moment and I'll never forget what it was like to be there that day.

When it was finally time for The Rolling Stones to play, they drove right up to the stage area in their limo, got out, climbed up the stairs and walked out onto the stage. They performed and did a fantastic show, walked back down the stairs, got into the limo and left. I never got near them, but I got to see them perform.

When you get that many people together for that many hours, a lot of people get sick from the heat of the sun, drugs or whatever. We have a few pictures of the concert and some of the ambulances that were taking people out of there. There were some teenagers who lived on our street who came over the next day and said, "Hey man, we were at the show in Cleveland." So, I said I hoped they liked the show, and they said, "We don't know, man, we were at the first aid tent, but it was really cool."

Madman was starting to open some big shows, but we weren't making very much money yet. Then Joe Walsh got Kenny a job with Elton John, and Kenny left in the middle of the night in the middle of our tour, and flew to Paris to audition. He even left his bass guitar behind. I saved it for him and gave it back several years later when we started speaking again. I really don't blame him. He had a great opportunity and it was going to take a long time to make it with Madman. We did try a new guy to fill in on bass, Bruce Hall,  who later went with REO Speedwagon. Bruce was a fantastic guy and bass player and he fit in really well, but Madman was struggling and it was time for all of us to bail.

Although the record never did as well as I hoped it would, as I said, you can still buy it on CD. It all came and went over a period of 18 months. We had felt it was OK to live in Ohio because I was in a major band and was gone all the time, but now Madman was over and I was out of work. Susie and I went out to LA and looked at places to rent. I needed to have my studio and we couldn't afford a place as big as I needed in a neighborhood where I felt my equipment would be safe. So, I came back to Ohio and I started making calls to let people know I was available for touring again.

CHAPTER NINE

1976, Bill Szymczyk / Jay Ferguson

Bill Szymczyk was one of the people I called, and he called me back to say he was going to do a record with Jay Ferguson. I owe Bill so much. He got me one great opportunity after another and helped my career more than I can ever tell you. He's a trusted friend to this day. Jay was the fantastic keyboard player and singer in two very well known bands, Jo Jo Gunne and Spirit, which had the song "I've Got a Line on You." He had gotten his own record deal with Elektra Asylum and Bill was going to produce it.

Bill said we were going to record Jay's album in Florida, because he'd folded up Tumbleweed Records and moved from Colorado to Florida when Joe Walsh left. He brought projects to Criteria like The Eagles and Joe Walsh and eventually opened up his own studio, Bayshore Recording Studio. Bill said, "I got some guys together and I want you to

Ed Mashell, Bill Szymczyk, Jay Ferguson

be the drummer for Jay Ferguson's album." It was called "All Alone in the End Zone."

One of the nights we were recording, Bill, Jay, Jage Jackson and I went out to eat. It was a New York style restaurant with the bar in the front and tables toward the back. We were just sitting there with our drinks waiting for our food and relaxing after a day in the studio, when someone burst into the restaurant and started firing a gun. That's the kind of thing

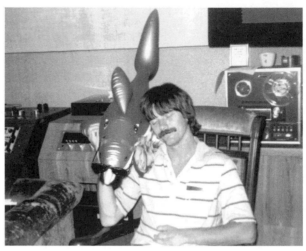

Jage Jackson

you'll never forget. We all sat there frozen in our chairs, staring in the direction of the gunfire with our mouths open. Bill had been in the Navy and his training kicked into gear. It only took a couple of seconds until Bill reacted...while we were all sitting there stunned, Bill was all action. In one swift move, Bill jumped up and flipped the two inch thick oak table over on it's side, knocking everything on the tabletop to the floor.

We all dove for the shelter of the table and crouched behind it. Other people in the restaurant saw what Bill had done and followed suit. It was all happening so fast, yet it seemed like it was in slow motion. Who was the guy with the gun? Were we gonna die? At least the table was between us and the gunman. We later found out the gunman's wife and a man she was having an affair with were sitting at the bar. A couple of big guys sitting nearby, who also wanted to live, grabbed the guy, knocked him to the floor and held him until the police came. We looked around us at the mess on the floor...drinks, ice, condiments, napkins...everything that had been on the table. We were still crouched behind the table when Bill looked up, raised his hand above the tabletop and said calmly, "Oh, waitress..."

The adrenalin from that incident made it easy for us to go back to the studio and work a few more hours. So, Bill not only helped my career countless times, but he also probably saved my life by keeping me from being hit by any stray bullets. What a producer!

Recording this album was the key to me working with my next big time band. When I worked on Jay's album, I met bass player, George "Chocolate" Perry, who was 19 and a regular session guy. Some of those sessions included

Jay, Bill & Joey Murcia

playing with Stephen Stills. He thought Chocolate was the greatest bass player he'd ever heard and started using him all the time. He even started to fly Chocolate wherever he was recording. So, I started playing drums, with Chocolate on bass, for Jay's album. It was remarkable playing with him, like no one I'd ever played with before, and I was blown away.

Stephen Stills

I wasn't the only one who was blown away by our rhythm section. Stephen Stills was in Florida recording demos at Criteria. I had first met Stephen when I lived in Colorado. Joe Walsh and I were driving up Boulder Canyon to Nederland in Joe's Jeep, and Stephen and Kenny were driving down to Boulder in Stephen's brand new Mercedes. We were going really slowly because it was winter and the roads were bad. There wasn't any traffic, so we both stopped in the middle of the road. Stephen lived way up in the mountains in Colorado at the time, a perfect place for him, since he was an ace skier. Kenny was already friends with him and Joe had met him some time ago, so I was introduced to him. Wow! Stephen Stills! How cool! We wore out so many Buffalo Springfield and CSN albums when I lived in Kent.

Stephen and Kenny were heading down to Boulder and then back up to Stephen's house. Stephen invited Joe and me to join him and Kenny later that night to jam, so we went over. Dallas Taylor was there, so I played drums and B3. We played songs like "Crossroads," "Red House," and other classic blues tunes. We had a great time and Joe and Stephen thought that this would be a great band, but Stephen was totally involved with his group, Manassas, and Joe, Kenny and I were with Barnstorm. Anyway, we all had gotten to know Stephen when we lived in Colorado. I could tell right off the bat that he was a really great guy, a real gentleman, and I immediately liked him. So, here we were running into each other again, in the small world of rock & roll, both working at Criteria. I had no idea how this get together with Stephen was going to affect my career for the next thirty-some years.

Graham Nash later told me that early in 1976, Neil Young had gone over to his house in San Francisco and played Graham a few new songs he'd been working on. He asked if David Crosby and Graham were interested in singing on them. Of course they would, Graham said. Graham had already known that Stephen and Neil were fooling around with some new music. At this point, I'm not sure if this invitation was to sing on a Stills/Young album, or if there were plans in Neil's mind for this to grow into a CSNY album. Who knows? It was Neil. Soon, working on Jay's album with Bill Szymczyk would make it possible for me to be involved with that project.

One night while Bill was doing playback at Criteria for Jay's album, he invited Stephen Stills to come over and listen. It appeared that Stephen loved what he heard. About two weeks later, we went to the L.A. Record Plant, Studio B, to finish up Jay's album. Chocolate called Stephen, who was also in LA, and asked him to come over to the studio. Stephen sat in the control room and listened for about an hour. He didn't say a word. He later said he was blown away by what Chocolate and I were doing.

At the end of that session, we were hanging out, kinda sitting around the piano. Stephen said, "I need a rhythm section like that." I said great, because I needed a job. Stephen was one song away from finishing his solo album and he thought it would be a great way to try out the new rhythm section. Chocolate and I recorded a track at Cherokee Studios with Stephen called "Circlin,'" which went on the album "Illegal Stills." These were exciting times. It got even better. That same night, Stephen said he wanted us to come to Florida to make another album with Neil Young. Now I was completely blown away. I wasn't sure what this meant...how many of the letters of CSNY were going to be part of this? It really didn't matter to me. What an amazing break!

1976, Bill Wyman, "Stone Alone"

Before I left for Florida to record, Joe Walsh called me and said that Bill Wyman wanted Joe and me to play on a couple of songs on his album, which was quite an honor, since he was The Rolling Stones bass player. Joe and I were both really excited so we spoke to Bill and said we'd love to do it. His people set up our travel and we flew to San Francisco. The Record Plant in Sausalito owned a home that bands could rent while they were recording, which was really close to the studio. It made travel easy and it was nice to stay together in a home instead of in a hotel for the three or four days we were recording. The band guys that stayed at the house were Joe Walsh, Bill Wyman, Ronnie Wood, Van Morrison, and me.

Sly Stone was also playing on the record and lived in the area, so he didn't stay with us at the home. Bill wanted Sly to play organ on a couple of cuts we were going to record. Sly arrived at The Record Plant with two huge body guards, which was kind of uncomfortable for all of us, since we were all musicians and friends. I mean, here were two Rolling Stones guys, plus Van Morrison and Joe Walsh, and they didn't have body guards. The body guards were standing out in the hallway and somebody in the control room spotted them and said, "Hey, do we really need the two refrigerators with heads?"

We got in the studio and started learning and recording the songs and the session was going really well. Sly's two big bodyguard guys were kinda hanging in the control room but they were cool, so we were all having a good time recording. In the middle of one song, we started hearing something like an oscillator tone, "Eeeeeeeeeee." It wouldn't stop and we were actually getting a really good take, so we were all getting frustrated, like, "Aw man, what is that sound?" The engineer was Gary Kjellgren, who was a big time L.A. engineer. He was working extra hard, trying to find out what this tone, this irritating noise we kept hearing, was, and where it was coming from. No matter what he tried, it wouldn't stop. "Eeeeeeeeeeeee."

This wasn't digital recording, this was real time, real analog recording. We were all professionals and tried to hang in as long as we could since the take was going so well, but it was driving us crazy. "Eeeeeeeeeeeee." We were recording in Studio D, which was known as "The Pit," because it was a weird room, an "in the round" bowl, and the control room was actually at the bottom of the pit. The tiers were at different levels, like shelves around this pit, so each musician was on a different level, using height to isolate each musician instead of using a sound booth. But the problem with that was, because we were physically isolated, we couldn't always see the other guys.

We finally all stopped playing, and the noise continued. "Eeeeeeeeeee." It had gotten to be like fingernails on a blackboard and we still had no idea where it was coming from. Finally, somebody noticed that Sly had passed out with his head on the B3 keys, and his head was playing that note, "Eeeeeeeeeeeeeeeeeeee." Unfortunately, it wasn't in the key of the song. After that, Sly and his body guards were gone.

We did about three cuts with several combinations of musicians working on the different tunes. Although all the guys we were working with were all big name stars and fabulous musicians, they were all fun, cooperative, and easy to work with. We had a great time with Bill, who was a wonderful bass player and an extremely funny guy with that dry British humor. It was so cool for me to be playing with The Rolling Stones bass player as the other half of the rhythm section. In fact, it was more than cool, it was fantastic!

1976, Stills/Young, "Long May You Run"

When I returned home from California, I had gone out and bought all the 8 track tapes that I could find…yeah, eight track tapes…with any combination of C, S, N, or Y, including solo projects. Our 1976 Cougar had a built in eight track player, and every time I drove for the next few weeks, I listened to nothing but their albums. I intently studied their music to make sure I'd have the right feel and dynamics for this wonderful opportunity. I finally felt confident that I was ready to meet this challenge.

I boarded a plane in Cleveland, and headed down to Criteria again to record. This was it, it was really happening. On the plane flight down to Florida, I was thinking back a few years when I had heard a song on the radio called "The Old Laughing Lady." It was an incredible song and I thought I recognized the voice, but I didn't know who the artist was. I liked it so much that I'd called the radio station and they told me it was Neil Young. Besides the Buffalo Springfield and CSN, I then became a huge Neil Young fan. As I reflected on this, I was excited about the upcoming project and actually being able to work with him.

We started recording the album at Criteria and Neil was exactly what I'd expected and more. He was creative, focused, non-stop energy, and was the kind of artist any band would want. The combined forces of Neil and Stephen were an incredible creative machine. I learned so much watching them work. Stephen was calling out bass parts, drum rhythms, and arrangements and I could imagine how great of a band The Buffalo Springfield was. The mutual respect between those two guys was totally evident.

Because there were a lot of familiar faces mixed in with new ones, I wasn't particularly nervous. The first few days were just Stephen, Neil and the band because David Crosby and Graham Nash hadn't arrived yet. We worked for a few days getting used to Stephen and Neil's material, and when David and Graham arrived, we immediately went to the studio. Stephen and Neil were really excited about playing David and Graham some of what we had worked on.

David and Graham really loved the material and without hesitation, Graham suggested that he and David go out and start singing. I was sitting in a chair in the corner of the control room and watched them. The four of them with acoustic guitars sat in a circle around a microphone and started working on a tune. The vocal blend was amazing. It already sounded great. The room was filled with talent…. CSNY! I sat there in the control room looking through the glass, and I thought back over my career and the path that had brought me to this moment. A few years earlier, I had been playing in Kent, broke, out of heating oil in the winter, and wondering if my career was over. Now, here I was, actually in the studio, playing and recording with these already legendary performers. For the next several days we worked on everyone's material doing tracks and vocals.

I wasn't sure where all this was headed, but the word floating around the studio at the time was that Stephen and Neil had discussed touring. The way everybody was getting along and the album was sounding, it seemed to me that this project was becoming a CSNY album and tour.

However, there was a serious conflict… David and Graham were in the middle of recording a Crosby/Nash album. There was no way they could break away from the focus and momentum of that project, do another album and tour with CSNY, and then try to get back to where they'd left off. I totally understood that. Although we started out with all four guys, soon David and Graham left and it became a Stills/Young album. I imagine they were all originally going to produce the album, but after David and Graham left, the album was produced by Stephen, Neil and Don Gehman.

Since it was no longer a CSNY album, Stephen and Neil had a dilemma as well. They had to use more of their own material, and had Chocolate, Joe Lala and me redo all the back up vocals. We weren't trying to match or beat what David and Graham did, we just went out and sang. The project had now become a whole new album. The blend was good and Stephen and Neil liked it.

The most nerve wracking night was when the three of us were out there in the studio singing some background parts, and sitting in the control room were Stephen Stills, Neil Young and "Flo and Eddie," whose names were Howard Kaylan and Mark Volman, two of The Turtles…all fantastic singers. Talk about pressure!  I'm glad I wasn't out there alone. We got a thumbs up from the control room, though, which made our night.

Neil has incredible versatility and can adapt to any new musical situation. We were in Florida, so he wrote songs about Florida and the ocean, as did Stephen, especially in the masterpiece "Black Coral." This was the first Stills/Young combo since the Buffalo Springfield days, and hearing them together reminded me of what a great band that was. This was the second album Chocolate and I had recorded together, and we'd become incredibly tight, both personally and musically. A happy rhythm section makes for great grooves.

I still hear the hit "Long May You Run" on the radio all the time, and it takes me back to the wonderful experience of recording it. Neil has a large and very tasteful car collection, and I read somewhere that he wrote that song about his first car, a 1948 Buick Roadmaster. I really don't know if that's true, since he never talked about it with us. He likes sparseness in his songs, as well as spontaneity and simplicity. He got all three when we recorded that track.

I used to smoke cigarettes, a great habit for a drummer who needs lots of wind, right? We were in the studio and Neil was warming up the guys, teaching them "Long May You Run." He was playing the song and singing and the guys were starting to play along. I was smoking a cigarette and had it in my left hand, and I thought I'd keep some time for them, so I started playing with my right hand, just some high hat and snare, and my bass drum. It was a 2/4 song, so I was just keeping time and they were running through it, playing and singing. About a third of the way through the song, I put my cigarette down and grabbed my other stick and started playing my full set. We finished the song, and Neil said, "Aw, that was great, guys, mark that as a take." I almost fell off my drum seat.

This was the first time I had played with percussionist Joe Lala, who, being a fellow Italian, quickly became a close friend. He's a fabulous percussionist and we ended up touring and recording together over the next several years. We became so close that he actually shared his Italian sausage recipe with my Dad. Once when my family had a dinner, Joe Fed Ex-ed homemade sausage he'd made, boxed in dry ice. In addition to being a percussionist, he went into acting and made a totally believable mobster character in several TV shows and movies, as well as doing voiceovers and touring with off Broadway shows.

This was also the first time I ever met Gerry Tolman who was working for Stephen. Gerry was a guitar player and song writer, and was doing odds and ends for Stephen, including being his guitar tech. I really got to like Gerry, who was part Italian, and we also became good friends. Eventually Gerry played guitar in The Stephen Stills Blues Band. He also came to my house and recorded some songs he'd written. Gerry worked really hard to do a good job for Stephen and wanted to make a go of it in the music business as a guitar player. Eventually, in about 1986, he changed course and became Stephen and Graham's manager.

While we were recording, we stayed in a "Home At Last" house. The Home At Last houses were beautiful old homes on the waterways in Miami that were rented to groups who were recording at Criteria. Each bedroom had it's own bathroom and the homes were completely furnished in an elaborate Las Vegas mobster kind of decor. They came complete with a maid and a cook, and if we were hungry for something, we just put it on the list and the maid picked it up that day when she went to the market. I loved getting up each day and making fresh squeezed orange juice. The homes usually had a beautiful pool and grounds landscaped with Florida's spectacular tropical plants. It was fabulous staying there.

The entire band would stay at these homes, which would make eating and transportation simple and easy, and since we all had huge private bedrooms, we could get away from everyone if we wanted. We ate dinners together and it was a really fantastic way to bond while we recorded. We could fish in the waterway right over the wall at the edge of the yard, and one night for dinner we had a big fish fry with all the different kinds of fish we'd caught.

Neil's boat

Although Neil thought that the Home At Last homes were luxurious and beautiful, he had his eye on the Intercoastal Waterway and decided to buy a boat. I don't know how old the boat was, but it looked like a 1940's or 50's yacht. It was beautiful and had lots of wood…very classy looking…and was perfect for Neil. It looked like a water version of the tour bus he uses today. Captain Young docked it on the edge of the property, had shore power and stayed on the boat. He immediately looked at home on that boat…it was a perfect fit.

Christopher Stills, Stephen's son, was there and being cared for by a nanny named Jean and her husband Red. Stephen makes beautiful children, and little Christopher was this angelic looking child with blonde hair and big blue eyes. He was eighteen months, and spent a lot of time with Susie while we were away at the studio. She instantly loved that little guy and said she wished she could bring him home with us. Today, Christopher Stills, who

Jean, Christopher & Stephen

looks just like Stephen, has a fantastic voice, plays guitar and has a music career of his own.

Eventually we finished recording the album and Stephen and Neil decided to go out on the road together for the summer. Just like recording the album, this was a combination they hadn't tried since The Buffalo Springfield. It was going to be an adventure.

<u>1976, Stills/Young Tour</u>

Unfortunately, this will be short, just like the tour. For rehearsal, Neil offered his ranch with his big beautiful outdoor stage. I remember arriving at this enchanted redwood forest…hundreds of acres in the middle of nowhere. It was absolutely beautiful. We could rehearse every day until about 5:00 PM. That's when the fog rolled in. At times, it was so thick we couldn't see twenty feet in front of us. All of the band and crew stayed at his guest house, which was a multi-room lodge, called "The White House." After meeting and working with Neil, it made complete sense that this ranch was his home. It was perfect.

There were horses, cattle, buffalo, peacocks, goats, turkeys, bob cats, and a full working ranch…it was like "Neil Young City." We all really appreciated his hospitality and being invited to stay on his private ranch. I noticed that from the deck on the back of the White

House, it looked like I was looking into a small canyon. I had an idea. I found some scraps of paper and Scotch tape, and made a glider. I launched it from the back porch. This was cool. Chocolate seemed interested in what I was doing. That's when I introduced him to aviation.

Until rehearsal started, most mornings were boring, so now we had something new to do. Chocolate and I immediately got into the building of all sorts of styles of airplanes. We continued to launch our fleet off Neil's deck. Of course, we intended to eventually pick up all the wreckage, but we didn't get to it fast enough. Neil stopped by the house one morning and was standing on the deck, wondering what all that "stuff" was

Chocolate & Me

down there in the back yard. Chocolate and I said we didn't know, but that we'd go down and get it. The next day we cleaned it up and decided we needed airplanes that would go further, so we went into town and bought a whole bunch of kits and raised the bar on our air force. These new planes flew great. When they hit the updraft near the edge of the canyon, they soared overtop the hill. We're not sure where they landed, and they're probably still there…vintage aircraft, just like Neil's cars.

We rehearsed at Neil's ranch for three weeks working on the new tunes from the album we'd just recorded. We also worked on material from The Buffalo Springfield, Stephen and Neil's solo albums, and some CSNY songs. I was looking forward to a full summer of gigs. There were supposed to be thirty dates booked that summer, but the eighth show in Buffalo, New York, was the last one. The band was Stephen, Neil, Chocolate, Jerry Aiello, Joe Lala and me.

We hadn't been out long when Neil asked me to ride on his bus for the trip between two of the cities. Stephen heard about the invitation and said, "How do you rate?" Apparently, Neil rarely had anyone ride on his bus. The bus was a cross between a space ship and The Spruce Goose. There was a spiral staircase which went down to the bus bay where luggage normally goes, but Neil had put a lounge down there for listening to music, reading, or just hanging out...and it had two portholes for windows. Everything inside the bus was made of beautiful, greatly detailed wood.

Neil also had mounted car sides and fenders on the outside of the bus...it was something to behold. That sucker had to weigh tons, but it looked really cool. We got on the bus and sat around and talked for a while after the show, had something to eat, and played a little bit of music. Neil had a Wurlitzer electric piano built into the bus, so he played acoustic guitar and I played piano. We jammed for about an hour. It was a very memorable night. He showed me the same hospitality on his bus as he did on his ranch. What a great time!

Even though I felt that the shows were going incredibly well and they were selling tons of tickets, for whatever reasons, Neil didn't want to continue, so after the gig in Buffalo, New York, we flew to Atlanta for the next show and Neil got on his bus and left, too. We didn't know it at the time, but when Neil got on his bus he headed west...the tour was over. When we arrived in

Neil, Stephen & Chocolate

Atlanta, Neil had sent telegrams to the band and Stephen. They read something like, "Funny how things that start spontaneously end that way. Eat a peach." We played the next two shows without Neil, but then the tour canceled. We had rehearsed for three weeks, and the tour only lasted for two. Only in rock 'n roll! I went back to Ohio, but I wasn't home for long…something always turned up.

1976, "You Can't Argue With A Sick Mind"

I got a call from Joe Walsh, who was putting together an all star band of musicians to record a live album. We played on the TV show In Concert, which was recorded and turned into Joe Walsh's live album "You Can't Argue with a Sick Mind," the album with the mirror ball on the front. Walsh recruited quite a task force for this performance.

He said that along with playing drums, he wanted me to be able to play keyboards including piano, organ, flute, percussion, and sing vocals, so he was getting a second drummer. I said that was great, because we could double drum, too. When he said he was getting Andy Newmark, I was thrilled because although I'd never met Andy, I knew all about him.

You know what it's like when you meet someone and you immediately hit it off? That's what it was like with Andy. I just love that guy. He has a very dry sense of humor, and I always find myself laughing out loud when I email or speak with him. He's totally hilarious and I really enjoy working with him…in fact, I'm also a big fan of his. He's a New York City guy and he's played with everyone in the world. He's been very inspirational to me…he says that about me, and I say that about him. He has a really great feel…what a fantastic drummer! He was able to show me grooves that he played that I'd never played, because he had a different style of drumming than I did. I'd listened to him on so many records, and I loved his playing. I knew recording this album was going to be an unbelievable experience.

Joe Walsh played guitar, keyboards and vocals, Andy Newmark and I were on drums and I also played keyboards, piano and organ, flute, percussion, and vocals. The phenomenal Willie Weeks was on bass, all stars Jay Ferguson and Dave Mason played keyboards, Rocky Dzidzonru was amazing on percussion, and Eagles Don Felder was on guitar with Don Henley and Glenn Frey singing backups. Yeah, the band was so great, that Joe had a couple of the Eagles singing backups. What an honor to play with all those legendary musicians.

We rehearsed for about a week, and then we played one night at the Santa Monica Civic. It was a really great concert and was broadcast live on TV, but it was also recorded and made into Joe's live album. The TV-show-turned-album was all live and stayed that way, without a single repair or overdub. The band was that perfect, that good. You can buy that show on DVD now. Many of the TV and live performances we recorded are also on YouTube.

Joe was already in the Eagles at this time, and they were working on "Hotel California." While I was there in LA working with Joe on the live album, he invited me over to his house one night and said something like, "Hey, I've got this piece of music I'm working on for the Eagles record." He really didn't have a title yet, just a verse. He didn't quite know where to go with it, but it sounded like a really pretty ballad, so we both sat down at the piano and I learned the song.

This was the same green antiqued grand piano I had slept under when I first went to Colorado to work with Joe in Nederland. I gotta tell you, I enjoyed sitting at it playing a lot more than sleeping under it. So, we sat there, and in about a half hour's time, I'd come up with a set of changes and a melody which seemed to work real well with what he'd written as the verse, and bingo, we had a song. He finished the lyrics and called it "Pretty Maids All in a Row." Don Henley and Glen Frey approved it and the Eagles cut it with Bill Szymczyk producing. They, of course, did an excellent job of recording it, so I ended up with a co-write with Walsh on one of the biggest selling albums of all time.

CHAPTER TEN

<u>1977, Crosby, Stills and Nash, "CSN"</u>

In January of 1977, I got a call from Stephen Stills. He said that Crosby, Stills and Nash were making a new album and that he wanted me and Chocolate to play on it. We were recording at Criteria and all stayed at a Home At Last house again. It took us a couple of days to move into studio B. Stephen loved that room. It had a wonderful Baldwin nine foot concert grand piano that sounded a lot like the old Steinway up at Caribou Ranch. It was a large room which made it very comfortable, and it was easy to isolate instruments.

The first couple of days, we set up all the instruments we could in various places in the studio and mic-ed up everything. Stephen liked the idea of having the ability to move around the room and play different instruments at a creative moment's notice, especially since all the musicians were multi-instrumental. We set up guitar amps, keyboards, drums, tympani, percussion, vibes…whatever we had or could get, we set up. That was a very good idea.

We had the studio booked, so we started recording a few things with Stephen and David before Graham, who I think was in England with his family, got there. It was great for me to witness the camaraderie of the band. Both Stephen and David had great ideas for each other's songs, and even the musicians in the band had some input, so it felt like a real band. We were all so excited that we couldn't wait to play Graham the new material and get his ideas and input.

The excitement level was like some young rock & roll musicians making their very first record, even though they'd all made so many successful albums before. When Graham finally got there, we played him what we'd done so far and he smiled and said, "Let's go to work!" That's the kind of energy he's always shown. This was the first time that I'd recorded with the three guys without Neil. They'd all brought fantastic material for the album, the room was filled with awesome musicians, and, I gotta tell you, I was unbelievably excited to be a part of this.

The musicians for the album "CSN," were David Crosby, Stephen Stills, Graham Nash, with Chocolate Perry, Gerald Johnson, Jimmy Haslip and Tim Drummond on bass, Mike Finnigan on organ, Craig Doerge on keyboards, Ray Barretto on percussion, Russ Kunkel on

We stayed at Home At Last again.

drums and percussion, and me on drums, percussion, keyboards and flute. It was produced by CSN with my friends, Ronnie and Howie Albert, who also engineered.

Obviously, with that amount of talent, we had a lot of input to choose from. Unbelievably for me, they also accepted input from me, and showed me a great deal of respect, giving me the freedom to bounce around the room playing all kinds of different instruments. Collectively, we all did whatever it took to make the songs sound great.

We recorded in Studio B, which was where I recorded my record, and the Bee Gees recorded in Studio C. It was so cool, because they were making the soundtrack album "Saturday Night Fever," which became a monstrously huge hit. I think Stephen and Joe Lala played on a couple of their tracks. So, here I was, just down the hall with CSN, while another legendary album was being recorded. It was exciting to be there, even though we had no idea at the time how big both "CSN" and "Saturday Night Fever" were going to be.

We recorded for about six weeks. We watched the Bee Gees record "Stayin' Alive" and a lot of the other hits. Both groups had a distinctive sound like no other group. The Bee Gees were really impressed by CSN, because they were also a three part vocal group and they appreciated the beauty of the vocals. I remember Don Henley, from The Eagles, always saying that Stephen was one of his favorite singers and that CSN was very influential on him. The Beach Boys also had commented to me on how inspirational the CSN sound was for them. Nobody has yet to match the blend and sound that CSN has perfected.

So, the Bee Gees would come and watch us record, and we'd go watch them record this new music they called "disco." Barry Gibb was just a genius in the studio. Criteria Recording Studios in Miami, Florida, was a very hot spot in rock & roll music back then, and everyone wanted to record there. Bill Szymczyk was also bringing a huge amount of groups in to record.

It was at that time that David first met Jan Dance. Harper Dance was the studio receptionist, and she had this cute little teenaged daughter who she brought to the studio to help out. Eventually, Jan met the guys and heard the music we were recording. When David and Jan met, it was love at first sight. They became inseparable and eventually got married, had their son, and are still happily married to this day. There's a whole book in that one sentence, but I'll let them tell their story.

After a lot of hard work and late nights, we finished up and polished off this gem of a record. Right out of the box, we had a hit single with Graham Nash's tune, "Just a Song Before I Go." To this day, I never get tired of hearing the story about someone he met at an airport somewhere, and this guy said, "Hey, you're Graham Nash, and you've got twenty minutes, why don't you write a song?" So, Graham did, and had a big hit. I love this business. We took a little time off and then started a huge tour.

1977, CSN Tour

As amazing as it was to record with CSN, now I was going to tour with them...the biggest tour of my career, so far. So, here I was, doing this enormous CSN tour only eight years after Woodstock. Night after night I got to play all those wonderful songs and hear those beautiful harmonies.

I was amazed at the response of the huge crowds. We worked really hard...about five shows a week, and the band got tighter and tighter as time went by. Because of the tympani work I did on the CSN album, I brought my two beautiful tympani on the road and played them live on tunes like "Cathedral." I couldn't ask for a better gig. With

Michael John Bowen, Craig Doerge, Stephen Stills & Graham Nash

the three distinct styles of CSN, we got to play every type of music and groove. You know, you never get tired of hearing the first few measures, those signature licks, of classic hit records. This band had lots of those. We played at least half the new album live, and then played an array of Crosby, Stills and Nash tunes.

I was on my very best behavior for this tour...no water fights, no food fights, nothing. This was particularly difficult for me and the strain became unbearable. Finally, I began to crumble. One of the songs we played every night was "Wind on the Water" by Crosby & Nash. While the band was playing, there was an incredibly moving film projected on a screen behind us about cruelty to whales.

While I had respect for the cause, I couldn't help but picture what it would look like if a few flashes of Charlie the Tuna would appear up on the screen. I waived the consequences of getting fired and offered John Vanderslice from the production crew $100 to add a few frames of Charlie to the film. This went on night after night…every night I made him the offer, and every night he refused. One night, I took a $100 dollar bill and taped it to the projector. Fortunately for both of us, John resisted the temptation and we both retained our jobs. To this day, whenever I see John, I mention it and tell him that with the cost of living, it's $1000 by now.

It was about that time that a long standing CSN tour joke was born regarding the food. When we travel, the band usually arrives at the venue about four o'clock in the afternoon. We do a sound check, and then we have a catered dinner for the band and crew, so we don't have to leave the venue, look for restaurants, or go back to the hotel. The catered dinners have improved over the years, and we usually have really healthy meals. The quality, however, isn't universal. One day Crosby said, "Have you guys ever noticed that when the food is really good, it seems like the show is bad, and if the food is really bad, it seems like the show is really good?" Yeah, we did notice it. It immediately became the daily joke.

As the tour progressed, we'd be heading in to have dinner and sometimes hear from band and crew members leaving the dining area, "Well, we're gonna have a bad show tonight." That meant dinner was really great. We'd all smile and say, "Alright!" But if we were heading into dinner and we heard, "We're gonna have a great show tonight," we knew that the food would be really bad. The worst thing I ever heard, however, was Crosby as he left the dining room at one of the shows. "Call management," he demanded sarcastically and with a completely straight face. "We should record the show tonight for a live album!"

The food joke isn't the only thing that was born that tour. I came back to Ohio for a break from the CSN tour on July 1, 1977. Susie and I were expecting a baby, and the due date was July 2nd. Her parents, Bev and Jim Swihart, drove up to the Cleveland airport and picked me up, since they didn't want her driving alone. Later that evening, Susie said she was having some pains. She decided to time them and they were no minutes apart, so she called the doctor and we left for Aultman Hospital. Five and a half hours later, my son, Joseph James Vitale, was born right on time on his due date. The perfect rock & roll wife, Susie had Joey during my break from touring with CSN that summer. I was able to stay home for about three weeks…and then I was back on the road again, this time with Peter Frampton.

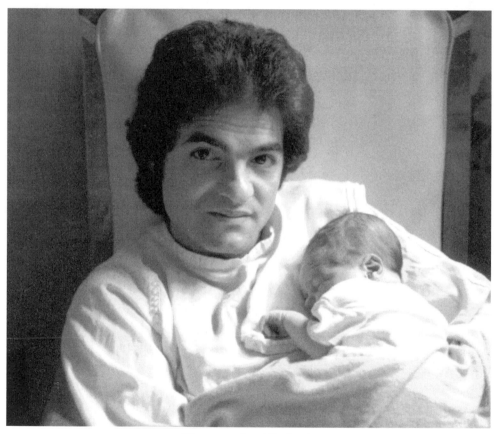

My son, Joe Vitale Jr.

CHAPTER ELEVEN

1977 & 78, Peter Frampton Tour

As I've said before, it was a small rock & roll world back then. When I lived in Colorado, there was a fantastic guitar player named Tommy Bolin, who I've mentioned earlier. Everybody knew who Tommy was, because he was such a great guitar player. He also had a great look…tall by my standards, he wore beautiful custom made stage shirts and had very long dark brown hair with colored streaks in it. If you remember, he was the one who got Kenny Passarelli, Rocke Grace and Tom Stevenson for Barnstorm.

His band's bass player was Stanley Sheldon. Stanley and I were friends from when I lived in Boulder, Colorado, and we jammed together a few times. Tommy went on to play with Deep Purple and tragically passed away at a very young age. Stanley went on to play with Peter Frampton when he started his solo career. Peter Frampton knew who I was, because Barnstorm opened up a lot of shows for Humble Pie when Peter was their lead guitar player. He always came out to listen to us play, because he wanted to hear Joe Walsh, so he'd heard me play drums. It was a very small rock 'n roll world.

Stanley was the bass player when Peter recorded his live album "Frampton Comes Alive," which eventually sold six million copies in the United States and sixteen million worldwide. In the midst of that incredible album sales phenomenon, Peter was getting ready to do a world tour. I'm not sure what the issue was with the drummer, but he left, and Peter had three huge shows booked in about three days...and I mean HUGE. The first show was for 52,000 people at Arrowhead Stadium in Kansas City, Missouri, on July 31st.

I had just finished up my tour with CSN, when I got a call in late July, the summer of 1977. It was Stanley. Now, I hadn't talked to Stanley for a couple of years, since we were both on the road. I'd moved back to Ohio and he'd moved to New York to play with Peter. He said, "Listen, you're the only guy I know who can pull this off. Would you be able to do a show with Peter Frampton three days from now if I send you a cassette of the show?" I knew Peter's music and I had his live album, so I said, "Well, OK!" I knew what a big star Peter was, so I knew it was probably going to be a big show. Then Stanley told me the first gig was a stadium show. Great.

Peter was as famous as The Beatles were at the time and his fans were crazy about him. He had long curly blonde hair and the girls screamed and would try to break into the dressing room to get to him. Sometimes they succeeded. They just loved him and he had to have a lot of security. It was exciting. The thing was that this was a stadium show which was an all day concert. There were multiple acts and that meant no sound check, so I didn't get to rehearse with the band, not even once. I just had the cassette that Stanley sent me, and I'd played drums to that cassette nonstop while I was at home. About three days later, I was at the stadium. I really didn't know Peter or Bobby Mayo yet, I just knew Stanley. Bobby played keyboards, guitar and sang. There were just the four of us...Peter, Stanley, Bobby and me. I've gotta tell you, it was one great band.

I was a nervous wreck envisioning all that could go wrong, but I was also confident in my abilities and young and cocky enough that I thought, "I can do this." I actually played pretty well and Peter seemed happy. I'll always remember that show which had a real "Spinal Tap" type moment. Steve Miller had been opening up for Peter on the tour, and he wanted to do something really special for the stadium show. He paid $10,000 for this psychedelic laser light show…but the show was in the daytime. It was hilarious. He made them do the light show anyway, since he paid for it, even though you couldn't see it.

So, I did the three shows and it was going really well. Peter came to me and said, "So, what are you doing for the next eighteen months? Do you want to do this?" I said, "Yeah," because everything about this gig was great… Peter, the guys, the music, everything. It was a fantastic world tour. We played in Canada, Japan, Australia, New Zealand, Hawaii on the way home, and all over the United States. On stage, Peter was not just a heart throb for the girl fans, but an unbelievable artist. The fans  loved him. Off stage, he was hilarious. The guys in the band were wonderful to play with on stage and really easy to get along with off stage. I was back wearing fancy rock & roll clothes again, which was really cool. It was a great time in my life.

Peter's fans' enthusiasm bordered on mania. We used to have to walk from the dressing room to the stage with four big guys carrying a four by eight sheet of plywood over Peter. He had to walk to the stage underneath it, because the fans used to throw things to Peter… not because they disliked him, but because they wanted something that they touched to touch him. They also wanted to throw him their panties, room keys and phone numbers. Unfortunately, sometimes they threw beer bottles, just like the Detroit fans did when I was with Ted Nugent.

It seems strange to think about that today, like smoking cigarettes on airplanes, but you could drink beer in bottles at concerts. Here's an example of why you can't do that anymore. One time, because Peter sold so many tickets, he sold out the arena in the round. That meant that he sold all the seats in an arena, even the seats behind the stage, which is usually curtained off. We always tried to turn around for the crowd behind us, I'd throw my sticks up to them, and we'd wave to them and try to make them feel like they were part of the show.

During the shows, the fans would always throw things up on the stage. They threw notes, flowers, panties, bras, shoes, everything. This era of throwing things also included "the quarter toss." The fans would throw quarters and try and hit the cymbals on my drum set. It really hurt if they hit me, and it happened about two or three times every show. One hit me in the forehead.

During one show, some enthusiastic fan decided he wanted to throw his beer bottle to Peter. He lobbed it from way up in the seats, but his arm wasn't quite strong enough. We were in the middle of one of Peter's longer songs, and it hit right beneath my drum seat. I felt something on the back of my heels and I looked down and saw that the drum platform was covered with all this amber broken glass. Then I saw a couple other

Bobby Mayo, Me, Peter Frampton

places where beer bottles had hit. That really scared me. If it had hit me in the head, I could've been killed, and so could any of the other guys on stage.

At Soldier's Field in Chicago, we had even more to think about while we were trying to perform. At that show, there was a rumor that Peter had a death threat. I remembered the dinner with Bill and Jay Ferguson when the gunman was firing bullets and how Bill provided us with cover behind the oak table, so I tilted my cymbals up so they made a wall of protection around me. That only gave the quarter toss fans a bigger target. Someone did throw a fifth of whiskey onto the stage that show, and it nearly hit Peter in the head. After a few years of this, venues got stricter, started searching the fans and banished all glass and plastic containers. So, if you go to a concert now and they search you and make you drink out of paper cups, I'm all for it. There's a long history of band abuse behind it.

<u>1978, Joe Walsh, "But Seriously Folks"</u>

During the end of 1977, I was just finishing up the first leg of the world tour with Peter Frampton, when I got a call from Joe Walsh and Bill Szymczyk. They asked me what I was going to be doing in 1978, and I said I was still going to be touring with Peter Frampton. They said that Joe wanted to do a solo album, which was going to be the first studio solo album since "So What?" in 1974. So, I checked with Peter Frampton on my scheduling and found that I had a nice slot of time open in the spring.

Bill had talked to Willie Weeks about playing bass and they also brought in Jay Ferguson on keyboards. We had a second guitar player, Joey Murcia, who was a well known Miami-based session guy, who's style was a little more R&B. Bill thought that he could add some guitar parts on some of the cuts. I played drums, keyboards, synthesizer and flute. After we set up a preliminary window of time, Bill called me one night and said, "Hey, ah, Joe had this idea to record on a boat." I remembered that Joe had always talked about that. It was some kind of creative thing he had floating around in his head...no pun intended. I said it'd be fine with me. At the time, I had no idea what that involved. I didn't know if he meant the whole album, one song, or what.

Basically, Bill and Joe had discussed putting together a four track Ampeg tape player, a nice little board, some microphones, a couple of power amps and limiters, ...a basic studio with four tracks. I don't think initially they were thinking, "Let's make this record on the boat." I think they were thinking we'd go out on the ocean and work through some songs instead of being in a studio, which can get boring.

What a difference learning the material, being creative and coming up with parts on the boat. That's how we used to make records...you came up with parts. The writer, artist or star would come in and play us a song on his guitar or piano or whatever, and we'd listen to it and come up with creative parts. What a great setting to be on a seventy-two foot yacht called "Endless Seas," out on the ocean with our gear. It was so relaxing and so much fun. It turned out to be one of the best recording experiences of my life.

First of all, we showed up at the pier in Coconut Grove, Florida, with Econoline vans full of our gear, and loaded it onto the yacht. All

the people around us were looking at us like, "OK, what are they smuggling?" Once everything was loaded, it took the better part of a day to travel down to Islaorada in the Florida Keys. We docked up at Plantation Harbor, which later became the name of my second album, because I loved it so much down there.

The yacht was beautiful. Spectacular. It had a captain's quarters for Captain John, who came with the yacht, a huge living room about twenty-five feet long and eighteen feet wide, and, as with all yachts, a partition with windows and then the back deck. We set up our gear in the living room and Bill set up his board and tape deck with all his cables and wires on the back deck, like it was a control room. I have a great picture of Bill underneath the table that had the board on it, wiring this whole thing together. It took a couple of days to get the whole thing set up. Joe and Bill had come up with an incredible idea.

We docked in the daytime and got supplies, and then we took the yacht, which ran on generators, out onto the ocean. At first we thought that all the amplifiers and recording equipment would have a serious hum because there was no ground on the ocean, but it was perfectly quiet. It was one of the most creative experiences in my life, and the album was musically one of Joe's best records, with the classic hit "Life's Been Good" on it.

Finally we were done setting up, the generators were on, and we flipped on a couple of old Fender and Vox amps that Joe had brought. I had my drum kit, Willie Weeks had a little bass amp, like an Ampeg B15 or B18, and Jay Ferguson had something like a Fender Rhodes keyboard. We had microphones, a tape deck, a board and Bill Szymczyk...we were ready to go.

We turned the equipment on once we got out on the water with the salty ocean breezes blowing through the open windows, and we plugged in and immediately started playing music. We were completely blown away at how cool it was to be where we were. For the next several days, we recorded both during the day and at night. We looked out the windows while we were playing music surrounded by the ocean, and Bill was recording it all. We went through all these songs of Joe's for the album and started coming up with parts.

We weren't really intending on recording masters for the album out there on the boat, because we were really limited by the equipment we had, although the Beatles made albums with four tracks. We worked for several days, and what we were doing was collecting ideas, parts, getting arrangements together, keys...it was fabulous, like brainstorming with music. It was so unique and wonderful.

When we'd pull into the Plantation Harbor Marina to dock up, we'd go to the only restaurant at the time and eat. I have a picture of all of us at the table in the restaurant. The local people referred to us as "those boat weirdos," so they made a sign for us that said, "Welcome Boat Weirdos," because they apparently thought we were really weird. Captain John had gas powered scooters which were fantastic, and when we weren't recording, we used to get on them at night and drive around the island on the little trails. We used them in the daytime to get down to the restaurant.

At night, the tide went out, it was shallow and there were a lot of little fish in the water, so the bigger fish came in to eat. I remembered this from growing up in Florida. I guess the local people thought we were weird because of some of the things they watched me do. I put on a full yellow slicker, tied a waterproof lantern to a fishing pole and lowered it into the water from the boat's deck. It was going down in the water and shining light all around, and I could see millions of fish, so I was yelling, "Hey fish!" All the guys came up on the deck, and I was showing them the fish. I wrote this "Hey, Fish" story that was inside my album cover when I did, "Plantation Harbor" in 1981. Like everything, we drove the "Hey Fish" saying into the ground. It seemed to me that all fishermen had a "fish story" to tell about some giant fish they'd caught. I hadn't had time for fishing, so I stayed up all night and wrote my own fish story in honor of all those fish I'd seen that night.

Here's how it goes:
Rita Calamari, the taxi crab diver, who lobster license in small clams court and for the halibut drove us drown Route One. Rita had a slight lox of herring so I had to trout at her. "Since it's abalone five-twenty tuna, we piranhably have enough time for a guppie coffee." "Bait idea," she refired, "besides my crab's nearly out of bass." So we pulled fin to what brooked like a dive-in restaurant, where aprawn we met some mufishians. "Are you guys in a grouper something?" I asked. "Dover a sole band, 'Killer Grass Fish and the Boat Weirdos.' Hey fish," I refried, "I pike it here." "Walleye don't sea why not," exclam'd Killer, "It's Plantation Harbor!"

We had a lot of fun on that yacht, but our main purpose for being there was to record. One night we were docked up, and Joe came upstairs from the galley and said, "Hey, you guys feel like playing?" We took the boat out on the ocean, Bill was taping, and we all started playing this little jam thing. It was a really

mellow piece of music…kinda tropical and peaceful and it sure fit our surroundings. In something like an hour, the song was all written and it was beautiful. That actual instrumental cut, which we all wrote and recorded on the boat, is on the record as the "Theme from Boat Weirdos."

We were on the boat for at least a week. We took this whole experience back to Coconut Grove, where Joe took the underwater picture for the album cover in the pool at the Coconut Grove Hotel, which was two doors down from the studio. We continued recording back at  Bill's studio, Bayshore Recording Studio. Bayshore was in Coconut Grove right across the street from the ocean, and it was absolutely beautiful. Coconut Grove was a little tropical community back then, and we could walk to and from the studio every day.

Bill Szymczyk had all these amazing production credentials, and he had worked in every major studio in New York, L.A., London, Nashville…you name it. When you had a producer like that, who had worked in that many studios…Caribou Ranch, The Hit Factory, The Record Plant, Criteria…all the major studios…you can imagine…he took every great idea he loved and put the very best features into his studio.

First of all, it was beautiful, and technically, it was state of the art. He even had a pool table and a kitchen, like up at Caribou. The studio had dark green carpet and a lot of tropical wood, and the gear was built into racks also made out of tropical woods. It not only looked fantastic, but everything also worked fantastically. The Eagles, Bob

Seger, Mickey Thomas, Jay Ferguson, Joe Walsh, David Sanborn, Marshall Tucker, Elvin Bishop, and I are just some of the artists who recorded there.

We started out on the yacht, and then went to Bill's studio. As always, Bill and Joe could pull in major talent to work on the album. On the beautiful song called "Tomorrow," which Joe wrote, we had Don Henley, Glenn Fry and Timothy Schmit from the Eagles sing the background vocals. Don Felder played some pedal steel guitar. We had such great players. On my first album "Roller Coaster Weekend," I had a song called "Falling," so we attached that to the end of his song "At The Station."

Then there's "Life's Been Good," the perfect Joe Walsh song. Here's the story behind that. There are several parts to "Life's Been Good." There's the opening, which is a kind of rugged guitar part with a perfect Joe Walsh lick, then it goes into an almost Jimmy Page-like classical guitar thing, then of all things it goes into a reggae part for the verses, then there's a very  cool synthesizer part for the middle, and the there's a Rolling Stones kinda part for the end. Well, this was about four or five individual ideas for different songs that Joe had brought. They really didn't go anywhere. So, we put the ideas down on the boat, and when we got back to Bayshore, Bill started talking to Joe about what he wanted to do with all those little bits and pieces.

We started recording for real in Bill's studio, and we recorded all those parts as individual songs. They were each about three minutes long and they came out great. We took the weekend off, but Bill, who's a brilliant producer, heard something in all these parts, and went into the studio over the weekend. He made copies of all the master song tapes on quarter inch two track, mixed them, and cut them up into a bunch of pieces, and then pieced them back together and created this eight minutes and four seconds long masterpiece of parts that turned into "Life's Been Good." If you listen to the song, you can hear all the individual parts.

On Monday, we went into the studio and he said, "Hey, I've got something to play for you guys." We sat down and he turned the volume for the speakers way up. It started with my drum part and moved from one part to the other while we sat there, stunned. We couldn't believe what he'd done. Bill was just beaming, because he could tell how much we loved what he'd done with all those pieces we recorded. The song that Bill built. There are so many things… there's a door slam in  the one part, and it was way before computers, so we had to get the right sounding slam of the door, and time it perfectly. It took us about two hours of slamming a big four inch thick studio door to overdub that part. Now that would take less than a minute to lay a door slam into the computer, and then you can change the sound and pitch. But the moment we finally got it right, we knew it. What a fabulous triumphant moment.

The material was coming out so well that we didn't want to stop working, and sometimes we had to make ourselves go back to the hotel to bed. When we got tired and wanted Bill Szymczyk to go home and go to bed, we had this reverb EMT plate, that's hung in a box in it's own room because you had to isolate the sound, and we'd beat on the side of it with our fist. It sounded like an atom bomb went off from the control room. When he wanted us to go home, he had Buddy Thornton, his head engineer, build a little box with LED lights that he'd turn on and it would blink, "GO HOME!"

As I said, it was one of the most creative recording experiences of my life...everything from Bill producing, Joe's ideas and songs, the incredible band personnel, Bayshore, and recording on the "Endless Seas"...everything was just perfect.

1978, Peter Frampton Tour

I went back out with Peter Frampton and continued the tour. I think the entire tour was sold out. I remember when we were playing in Canada that August, I was watching TV and the program was interrupted with the terrible news that they had found Elvis dead at his home. It was a really sad day. What a terrible loss. I imagine most Americans can tell you where they were when they heard the news.

We were playing gigantic shows...the biggest that I had ever experienced. All the acts I had played with to this point were big, but this was superstardom and fan mania. We had a great time on stage. One of the things the fans really loved was on the one long jam thing that we did, Peter, who's actually a really good drummer, came back and played drums and I played flute.

When we were traveling or had time off, Peter sometimes just wanted to be a regular person and do things with us. He couldn't go anywhere without being mobbed. He finally discovered that he could tuck his famous blonde curly hair up under a baseball cap and go out without being recognized most of the time. But if we were in a city where people knew that there was a Peter Frampton show that night and he was walking around town, they'd often recognize him, even with his hair under his hat and sunglasses on. He was that famous.

What we needed was a few more cameras...

The superstardom extended everywhere we went. This was the first time I'd ever gone to Japan. At the airport in Tokyo we had to get the police because there were so many fans waiting for Peter. Remember, it was before 9/11 and all the security, and fans could come right to the gate. We walked off the airplane, and there were something like 5,000 screaming fans. It was Frampton-mania! Playing for the Japanese people was wonderful, partly because they were aware of all the musicians and credits on albums. I signed records that I had forgotten I had even played on when I was in Japan. One of the things we did was take my film camera that recorded sound…called "the Talkies"…onto the streets and we interviewed people like we were from the news. Peter cranked up his British accent and said he was from the BBC. We asked them what they thought about rock & roll and things like that. Usually, they didn't understand what we were saying, but it was fun and the kids were so sweet. The girls always covered their mouths and giggled. Then we'd laugh.

If you're in rock & roll and you've worked in Japan, you know Mr. Udo, who was the promoter. He's a wonderful person and went with us to all the shows. We checked out the sights and had some great experiences. We got to ride the Bullet Train, which was a 140 mph train that went between cities. I remember I was so impressed at how

Peter taking my picture

smooth the ride was. We had traditional Japanese dinners sitting on cushions on the floor with our shoes off. But one of the most memorable things we did was all American in origin. Baseball.

Just like Americans, the Japanese are huge baseball fans and Mr. Udo had the American rock & roll bands that played shows for him play baseball with his team. We thought, hey, yeah, we'll play these guys. Little did we know, playing these guys was like playing pros. They had regular practices, were a team, had uniforms and did calisthenics before the game. They even had a dugout. We had long hair, which looked kind of stupid with baseball hats on and wore all different kinds of tee shirts. We had a fantastic time even though we were like a high school team playing in the World Series. The final score was 37-4.

After Japan, I got to play in Australia and New Zealand for the first time. We played at a soccer field that had something like 100,000 fans. All the shows we played were at huge venues and were sold out. It was really cool to be so far from home and see these places first hand. I never dreamed I'd be playing shows like this and I couldn't get over how beautiful the scenery was. I bought books and slides so I could show Susie when I got home.

One day when we were in Sydney, Australia, we all got to get on a beautiful one hundred year old 110 foot boat. We anchored the boat near the shore of a deserted island and had a picnic. We could either take little row boats, or we could just jump off the boat and swim to shore. Most of us just swam, because it was hot, the water was fantastic, and we weren't that far from the shore. It was really fun and we got to enjoy the day without any fans looking for Peter.

I was gone for six solid weeks, and it's the only time in my entire career that I've ever missed Thanksgiving, even though we did have a turkey dinner for the band. Since we had been gone so long, the guys in the band met our families in Hawaii on the way home. I wanted Susie and Joey, who was sixteen months, to meet me there. Joey had cried most of the flight, probably because of the air pressure and an ear infection which had developed. People were saying things like, "Throw that kid off the plane," when they were over the ocean. Susie arrived in Hawaii fried and with no sleep. I'd hired a limo to pick them up, but after I met them at the gate, I went to get the limo, couldn't find it and it took more than an hour to locate it. We finally got back to our room at the hotel and I was anxious to tell Susie all about the fabulous experiences I'd had during the last six weeks on the road. She put Joey down on the bed, snuggled up beside him, and immediately fell asleep. I mean, she was out.

The next morning Joey was still cranky and the doctor arranged for us to get an antibiotic for him. Unfortunately, the directions that came with the antibiotic said to stay out of the sun. Perfect for a vacation in Hawaii. I thought maybe some sightseeing would be fun, since the beach was out, so we loaded our movie camera with film and went to see a volcano. It was a beautiful view and I got some really great footage. When we got back to the room, I opened the camera to put a new can of film in, and the film popped out like one of those joke cans of snakes. Great. No movies.

Stanley & I take our brought families to see the volcano

We had adjoining rooms on about the fourteenth floor, so Joey would be able to sleep without us waking him. There were little patio balconies with sliding glass doors that opened facing the ocean. The second day we were there, Joey playfully ran into his room and slammed the adjoining door. We had a key, so no problem, right? But the door was pinned so our key wouldn't open it, and there was no way to open the door between the rooms. Susie called the desk and explained what was going on. She was pretty frantic, because neither of us could remember if the sliding glass doors were open. After an eternity, someone came to open the door. I mean, it had to have been a half hour. For the rest of the time we stayed there, we kept a towel thrown over the top of the adjoining door so it couldn't close.

By this time, I felt really bad for Susie, who was trying to get a tan sitting on the tiny wedge of a balcony near the sliding glass doors. She was probably thinking of jumping. I suggested that I'd watch Joey and she could go downstairs and sit beside the pool and get some sun. She immediately went downstairs, put on tanning lotion, leaned back in the chair and closed her eyes…and it started to rain. By this time, it was really getting funny.

We returned home at the end of our "Hawaiian trip from hell" flying on a 747. Joey's ears were still bothering him, so he was crying again. When it was time to eat, Susie said she'd entertain Joey and asked the stewardess if she could have her meal in about fifteen minutes. I ate and we finally got a stewardess again and asked her if she could bring Susie's meal. It had suddenly gotten very turbulent and the stewardess said that food service had been put away, so she never got to eat.

Joey cried and squirmed all the way to Chicago. All nine hours. We had a two hour layover, so Susie followed him back and forth and let him run around near the gate. We finally boarded our plane, took off and flew to the Akron Canton Airport. Joey fell asleep during the landing. Susie's Mom met us at the gate and said something like, "Oh, he's sleeping like a little angel. Did he sleep the whole time?" We were so tired, we just started laughing. What a trip! Susie said she wasn't taking Joey on the road again until he was six.

Playing that tour with Peter was an unbelievable experience, and I still count him as a friend. Some artists have meteoric success and then quickly burn out. Peter managed to weather the experiences of worldwide superstardom, and is still playing like a virtuoso in concerts today. He's not jaded at all, still loves to play, and won a Grammy for his last album. He's a great guy and has tremendous energy on and off stage. Touring with him was an amazing time in my life and I owe him so much for giving me such a great chapter in my career.

CHAPTER TWELVE

<u>March 1979, Havana Jam</u>

We went to Cuba for a musical foreign exchange concert, sponsored by CBS and called "The CBS All Stars." The artists were Billy Joel, Weather Report, Stephen Stills, and Kris Kristofferson and Rita Coolidge, who were married at the time. We also brought some Latin American bands. CBS brought some Cuban musicians up to New York to play a concert, and we went to Cuba. The record they made of the concert was called, "Havana Jam." We flew out of New York to Cuba on a chartered TWA jet.

We'd been given a sheet that said to bring our own toilet paper, soap and a towel. We also had these fliers that said, "Listen up. We're going to Cuba. DO NOT BRING DRUGS." So, we're on the plane, and we're getting near Cuba. The captain came on the PA and said if we looked down we could see Miami Beach. Then he said if we looked a little to the west, we could see Cuba. That was really frightening, seeing Miami and Cuba at the same time and how close they are to each other, since we all remembered the Cuban missile crises. We started our descent and all of the sudden, everyone got up and started heading to the bathroom. It had nothing to do with missiles. Then I started smelling pot and I thought, "What are you guys, crazy? We're going to Cuba."

Right before we landed at the Havana airport, two armed Russian Migs suddenly appeared and followed us down. As soon as we landed...ZOOM!...they were gone. While we were still sitting in our seats, a military security guard gave us a card and said, "Don't lose this card, or you'll never get home," so I put it in my wallet. I already felt really far from home.

Once we got off the plane in Cuba, there were a lot of rules to follow, and they meant business. They said we couldn't leave the premises unless we were with the group, and we weren't allowed to talk to any local people. There were guards everywhere. All these Cuban kids, who were the nicest kids in the world, would come up to us, and they'd want to see us, talk to us and ask how we were doing. We weren't supposed to talk to them, but we did anyway.

Stephen Stills & Joe Lala

A lot of us brought down a couple extra pairs of Levi's, and we gave them to the kids. They asked for Levi's, toilet paper and Adidas gym shoes, which were the hot gym shoe at the time. They got Miami radio stations and knew about jeans, shoes and rock & roll.

We played at The Karl Marx Theater in Havana. Honest, that's what it was called. Back then, wireless plug-ins were primitive and had a very short range. We were playing this one song of Stephen's and Stephen really got into it...he was playing a solo. It was a long solo, right? He decided to walk off the stage and into the crowd, because the front of the stage was only about two feet tall. The crowd went crazy. The place held about 5500 people and it was packed, but the lights were in our eyes, so we couldn't see past the tenth row.

Stephen disappeared into the crowd. He was playing and we heard him, but we were wondering what he was doing, because he wasn't allowed to get off the stage. So, all the sudden he's playing and we heard, "Eah…" and that's it. No more guitar solo. We didn't hear him anymore. We thought he was arrested and hauled away or something, but hey, we're professionals, so we just kept playing the song. About thirty LONG seconds went by and nothing, then he came back into range, the wireless unit picked him up and we could hear him playing again. We were so relieved when he got back up on the stage. Then it was funny.

Mike Finnigan, Jaco Pastorius, Gerry Tolman

Being there was pretty scary, though. I took a picture of a billboard that said, "Death to America" that had a missile on it. Hey, welcome to Cuba! The people tried their best to welcome us and make us feel at home. We stayed at a hotel with a beautiful beach, but the spigot where I brushed my teeth was salt water, and the shower was salt water, too. We had no phones and we couldn't call home. One of the weirdest things I saw was what had been a Ford Falcon, which had been repaired by putting new doors on it with regular house door hinges. Florida seemed really far away.

When we boarded the plane five LONG days later, there were two hundred and seventy of us, so the immigration official had to count two hundred and seventy cards. It was in the summertime and a tropical ninety-five degrees, the plane was packed, and the air wasn't on yet. It was so hot. We had to sit there sweltering while the guy counted and came up with two hundred and sixty-nine cards. So, everybody had to get off the plane, go to the belly and unload the bags.

Kris Kristofferson, Rita Coolidge and Bonnie Bramlett

They wouldn't touch the bags, we had to do it. Then we had to open up all the bags on the pavement by the plane. We found out that one of the musicians…well, you know how THEY are…had forgotten to give them his card. It took three or four hours to get through the crap they made us do before we were allowed to leave.

Although the people we met there were wonderful, I was never so glad to get off a plane and be back in America. It was so different in Cuba with all the military around, it sometimes seemed like we were in a bad movie. The trip was a really interesting experience, though, and it gave me a new appreciation of all that we have here in America.

Released 1981, John Entwistle, "Too Late The Hero"

Later in the spring of 1979, I was out west working with Stephen Stills and I got a call from John Entwistle. When I had my band, Madman, in 1976, we opened shows for John Entwistle's Ox, a great band, and we'd become really good friends. He always liked Joe Walsh and me a lot, so he called and asked us if we would be the rhythm section on his solo album. It was going to be a three piece band with John, Joe and me. We were thrilled. What a great opportunity!

Joe was off from the Eagles for a while, so we started working at a studio in L.A. called Crystal Recording. John had us staying at L'Hermitage, which was a very high-end hotel in Hollywood. John had a routine where we worked in the studio till all hours, and then we'd get something to eat at The Rainbow, a famous nightclub on Sunset Boulevard. He was there so much he had his own table. We did this for about a month. We did a lot of "cut out man," which was cutting pictures of people out of magazines and then putting them back together again so that they looked bizarre…like putting great big eyes on a regular sized head. I'll tell more about that later. That's also when I met his engineer who I still correspond with, Cy Langstrom. Cy's a British guy who's out of his mind funny and really ran a great session.

With John Entwistle being from the Who, you know those guys wrote the book on being ornery. They made us look like amateurs. So, John immediately got into the kinds of things Joe and I were doing when we'd stay up all night. At the hotel, they had really expensive artwork on the walls in the lobby and the halls, and we took magic markers and drew nose glasses on the people in them. In the morning, we heard this ruckus out in the hallways with people freaking out as they found the improvements we had made. Hey, everyone's a critic!

Joe must have really enjoyed our venture into the art world, because one time when he was visiting us in Ohio, he mentioned to Susie that he'd like to draw pterodactyls in magic marker on the original Marc Moon water color paintings we had hanging in the family room. Susie knew him well enough to know he just might do it, and was grateful that they were behind glass.

While we were working on John's album we got several opportunities to record with other artists. One day when Joe and I were working on John's album, Boz Scaggs' people came over, got my gear and I recorded the song "Do Like You Do In New York" on the Boz Skaggs album "Middle Man." On that cut, Ray Parker, Jr. played bass, James Newton-Howard played clavinet, David Paich played organ and synthesizers, and David Lasley, Bill Champlin, and Charles Irwin sang back up vocals. Also, during the time that we were recording with John, we recorded "In The City" for The Warriors movie soundtrack with Joe on guitar, Steve and Mike Procaro from Toto on bass and keyboards and Russ Kunkel and me playing double drums.

When Joe and I finished the tracks with John in LA, he went home to his castle in England, and we were going to join him a few days later. But on the way over there, we stopped in Miami, Florida, at Bill Szymczyk's beautiful Bayshore Recording Studio, and cut the song "All Night Long," with Paul Harris and Chocolate. Bill produced that song for the movie "Urban Cowboy."

Then Joe and I got on a plane and headed for London to finish the album with John Entwistle. Alan Rogan was Pete Townsend's and also Joe's guitar tech. He had been working with us in LA and was traveling with Joe and me back to London. Alan, who's a really good friend of mine, was in charge of getting our gear together and shipped over there, since he was from England and was aware of how to do this. So, Rogan thought it would be really funny to put panties, fishnet hose and one high heel in

Alan Rogan & Grandson

my trap case for when I went through customs at Heathrow Airport in London. While I waited, customs people were going through my cases, and called me over to ask if I was aware that I had lost one of my high heels. I was really embarrassed. Alan is a jokester, a prankster. We love him and get him back every chance we get.

A few years ago he emailed me a photograph of himself holding his first grandchild. My son, Joe, Photo Shopped John's face over the baby's face and we sent it back to him, telling him the baby looked just like him.

Joe and I arrived at The Who's studio to finish playing on John's album, and we stayed in London during the week while we recorded. But, on the weekends, we were off and went down to John's castle. It's a real castle from 1400 or 1500 AD and it's in "The Kids Are All Right" video. There are many stairways and hidden rooms and it's really amazing, this place. It's absolutely beautiful. He paid something like $100,000 for it around 1969 and it's worth millions today.

John had two cement statues of large wild cats at his doorway with nose glasses on them. One bedroom was about fourteen by fourteen feet square, and you couldn't even walk in there, because standing up, there was one bass after another. There were that many guitars. Remember, those guys were making records when I was in high school. It was around 1967 when "I Can See for Miles" came out and was a hit.

Downstairs there were ten or twelve foot ceilings and huge stones in the walls. It had everything but a moat. When you went upstairs you'd be in one room, and then you'd walk across that room and there would be another stairway downstairs, but it went into another part of the house. It was all crazy. Everybody had a bedroom and a bathroom. The room I was in was creepy enough already, but my bathroom also had a real bear rug on the floor, with a head and everything. I put a pillowcase over the head. I didn't want to look at that thing at night.

In the castle John had a bar that looked like a pub. Alan and I don't drink much, but John and Joe were getting pretty loaded. I had to go to the bathroom and the place was so big I didn't know where the bathrooms were, so I went upstairs to the bathroom in my bedroom. Joe and John didn't expect me to go in my bathroom until later when I went to bed, since there were bathrooms all over the downstairs. They all gathered around the bottom of the stairs, watching me go upstairs and listening. I went up one flight of stairs, and then another flight of stairs, and all of the sudden, they heard, "AAAEEE!" and they all laughed like fools.

Here's what they did to me. John had a real, full-sized human skeleton, and he sat it on my toilet with a magazine in one hand with the other hand on the toilet paper. It was pitch black up there, so I went into the room and turned the light on, and there it was! Oh, man, that scared me. Then I had to go back into that room and sleep there that night. That's when I put the cover over the bear head. Speaking of bear, John gave me one of those antique real black bear hats that the royal guards wear. The framework is actually wicker inside and it says, "Egypt." It's so cool and beautiful and it means a lot to me, especially since John has passed away. What a wonderful guy he was, and what great memories I have of him.

CHAPTER THIRTEEN

<u>1980, Graham Nash "Earth and Sky"</u>

Anyone who was around in the 1970's was aware of Skylab. Skylab was the first American space station and was launched in 1973. It was used for the next several years for manned space experiments, but it's orbit began decaying to the point that it needed to be lifted to a higher orbit. The original plan was to have the Space Shuttle do it, but it was unable to launch in time, so Skylab was doomed to enter the atmosphere and crash to Earth. No one could predict where the debris would land. At the time, it was a really big deal. It weighed something like 100 tons and when I saw a replica of it at the Air and Space Museum in Washington, D.C., it looked to me to be about as big as a couple of buses. Everyone was afraid Skylab was going to come crashing into their house, and it was all over the news for weeks. In 1979, Skylab came back into the atmosphere and the debris landed in the vicinity of the Indian Ocean and Western Australia, much to everyone's relief.

Graham had recorded a beautiful, bluesy kind of ballad for his solo album, "Earth and Sky" called, "Sky Child." It had these sensitive lyrics that, I think, were about his daughter, Nile. Graham took a break and went out to dinner for a couple of hours. I wanted to mess with Graham and write and record some new lyrics while he was gone. Stanley Johnson was engineering, so I asked him if he had any open tracks on a safety copy of the cut, so I wouldn't be recording on a master tape. He asked me what I wanted to do while Graham was gone, thinking I wanted to add some musical part, but I told him I wanted to do a vocal. I told him I had some new lyrics for Graham's song, and Stanley, who was always up for a joke, was in.

He set up a mic, got me headphones, and processed my voice, so it sounded more like Graham singing. When Graham came back to the studio later, I told him we'd worked on "Sky Child" a little. Graham totally trusted us and was always open to new things, so he enthusiastically asked what we'd done. We said we wanted to play it for him, so we all sat down to listen on the huge studio speakers. The song started to play the beautiful intro, and then, all of the sudden, the vocal started with me singing instead of Graham…I gotta tell ya', his eyes got wide…and then Graham began listening to my new lyrics. He started laughing so hard that he walked over and pushed stop on the machine so he could catch his breath. Then he rewound the tape and listened to the lyrics a second time. As a Las Vegas lounge singer might say, they went something like this…

"Sky Lab"

Sky Lab, on the day that we met,
You were fallin' on a restaurant, like a black burnin' vet,
David told me I'd be in trouble, if I dared to take a look,
I just got cooked by you.
Sky Lab, I looked up and said,
"Fly Lab, remember from the start,
You were always way up there, then you fell apart.
Well, you really made me nervous, you were aiming at my roof,
Right on target."
So I said, "Why Lab, why Lab?"
Yeah, go ahead David, play one for John Glenn.
(space ship sound effect)
Bye Lab, if you're ever back in town,
I don't know how you can miss me, I'm a Sky Lab beacon on the ground.
I'm takin' my pieces to San Francisco, where is my dough?
Fry Lab, I'll cook my own toast. Fry Lab.
Dry Lab, well you missed the ocean by a mile, Dry Lab.

I still have a cassette of the song with my lyrics and listened to it as I wrote this section of the book. I had to laugh. What sensitivity and talent! Some of my best work.

I wasn't the only one pulling practical jokes. We were recording late one night when we heard LOUD knocking on the studio door. It was Mike and Candy Finnigan. "Hey, keep it down!" they demanded with straight faces. "We can't get any sleep!" They'd driven all the way to the studio in their robes and pretended we were playing so loud that we were keeping them up..

<u>1979 & 80, Eagles tours</u>

The Eagles were in the studio around this time, recording an album called, "The Long Run." They finished it and realized that with all of the extra organ, guitar and percussion parts on the new album, there were a lot more parts on the new songs than they usually played. One of the many reasons that fans love to go to an Eagles concert is that the songs they play always sound exactly like they do on the record. They went out and did some shows and realized that they could use another set of hands playing drums when Don Henley sang, and extra keyboard parts on some of the new songs. Although Glenn and Joe Walsh played keyboards well, they and Felder were also the main guitar players at the time, so they wanted to stay up front.

They decided they needed what we call a utility guy. My main instrument was drums, but I played flute on this jam we did on "Turn to Stone," and I played keyboards on Eagles' and Joe Walsh tunes. Joe felt really comfortable with me playing drums on his music because I recorded those songs with him. Now that alone wouldn't have been enough for me to get the Eagles gig, because Don Henley did a terrific job playing my parts on Joe's songs like "Life's Been

Good" and "Rocky Mountain Way." I think the reason I got the job was because I played percussion, keyboards and flute, and I also think Joe wanted me in the band. I'll always be grateful to him for that and all the opportunities he got for me in my career. The Eagles still use a utility guy, and in fact, I think they have several guys now, including a horn section.

So, here's how I got the job. It was around September of 1979 and I was in bed, and about 3:00 o'clock in the morning the phone rang. It was Joe Walsh. Now, it wasn't unusual for Joe to call that time of night, because he knew that I usually stayed up pretty late. He asked, "Are you awake?" I said, "No." He said something like, "Good. Listen, you've gotta get on a plane tomorrow and come out. You're gonna be in the Eagles, 'cause we need an extra guy to play percussion, drums and keyboards. But you've gotta get on a plane TOMORROW and come out to rehearsal, cause we're gonna go to Japan."

I said, "Joe, why are you messing around with me? It's three o'clock in the morning. I wanna go back to sleep." So, I hung up the phone and he called me right back. He said, "Listen, I'm serious, you've gotta get on a plane tomorrow and get out here." OK, this was Joe Walsh, my partner in crime, my accomplice in pranks. I figured he was just screwing around with me, so I said, "Joe, if this is true, have Henley call me." The Eagles were already a huge band by now, and I knew that Glenn Frey or Don Henley was probably in charge of that kind of thing.

By now it was 3:30 in the morning, so I got off the phone and tried to go back to sleep. The phone rang again. I thought it was Joe running the joke into the ground. I picked up the phone and said, "WHAT?" This time it was Henley. I heard this really low voice say, "Joe Bob, it's Henley. You feel like coming out and practicing with us?" Now I knew this was for real, since I knew Henley wouldn't screw around with me. Suddenly, I was wide awake. "What time does the plane leave?" So they put someone else on the phone and made arrangements for a plane ticket to be at the airport in the morning. I packed up, went to the airport and got on the plane the next morning.

My first night there with the guys, I was introduced to "Eagles poker." When I first got there, the guys said innocently, "Hey, do you play cards?" and I said, "Sure, I love to play cards," and they said, "Do you play poker?" What a loaded question. I said, "I LOVE to play poker." They asked if I minded playing with money. I was such a sucker. I thought, "Hey, cool," cause I thought, hey, I was a good poker player and I'd win some money. Sure.

I asked what kind of poker they'd like to play and they said they had their own game, called "Eagles poker." Here's how it worked. It's initially a regular poker game. Let's say with an ante and a few bets, the pot was $10, and there were five guys playing. Say three of them folded, so now it's down to two guys. The winner of the game won the $10, but the other guy had to match the pot and put $10 in. The next game started with $10 in the pot. So then, you played another hand of cards, and at the end of the second round, there'd be something like $100 in the pot. The winner got $100, but the loser had to put $100 in the pot. The next game then started with a $100 pot. By the next round, we all had to ante up, there were a few bets, the pot had grown to $200 and now there'd be maybe three guys left in. One guy won, but the two who lose have to each put $200 in the pot. The next game started out with $400 in the pot. You can see how rapidly the pot grows.

Now, I lost every hand and was down $700. Whoa! This was the big time. This kind of poker was out of my league. They really laughed and in a show of pity and mercy for the new kid in town, they gave me my money back. Normally, it would have been, you lost, forget it, you dummy. I knew that getting my money back would never happen again, and I never, ever, played Eagles poker again.

We went to Japan and my basic job with the Eagles was to play percussion and keyboards. I had just been there with Frampton, and I felt really comfortable with the culture. There were no cell phones and we had to talk long distance while I was gone. I had Susie call me so we didn't have the hotel long distance fee added on to the phone bill, but the hotel personnel didn't speak English very well, so it cost a fortune just to get me on the line. The Eagles were pursued by their fans, so when we stayed at hotels, we used phony names.

I went under the name "Joe Bob," which the Eagles gave me when we picked out the names we were going to use at the hotels. They

Joe Jr. loved my cowboy hat.

also gave me a big ten gallon cowboy hat to wear, so I'd look more like a Joe Bob. When Susie called me, for some reason they always asked who was calling, so Susie had to say, "It's Mrs. Bob." The first month we got a phone bill for $2500 with a disconnection notice if it wasn't paid immediately.

I was really enjoying being in a band with Joe again. During the song, "The Best of My Love," I used to play drums and Henley would go out front with his guitar and sing. When we felt ornery, Joe and I would sing off mic, "You've got the best of Mike Love." Henley is a drummer just like me, and we play in sneakers. But when you're out in front of the band, sneakers look kinda funky. For me, at least, it's impossible to play drums in boots. Maybe there are some drummers who can play with boots on, but I'm not one of them. Henley would jump off the drum riser and I'd go up and play his drums. He's from Texas, so he used to have his cowboy boots underneath the drum riser and when he was on the way out front to get his acoustic guitar and do the song, he'd slip into his boots. The Eagles always made sure even the smallest details were perfect.

We spent three or four weeks in Japan, played everywhere, and had great shows. We had a lot of fun with the local culture, and I got to see Mr. Udo again. We wanted to learn Japanese, but only ridiculous phrases, so we talked to the Japanese crew guys and learned phrases like, "You have the face of a dog," and "You have the face of a monster." The word for monster was "bakemono" and it sounded like, "bakki moe no." We liked to say it to Japanese girls who would put their hand over their mouth, look down and giggle.

It was in Japan that Joe Walsh started a long running prank. We got into an elevator in Tokyo with about three or four Japanese people, and Joe turned to me and said something like, "Fifty bucks if you fart." I said I couldn't just fart, and he said, "Fifty bucks!" I couldn't. Then he upped the stakes. "Fifty bucks for each person on the elevator." I just couldn't do it. A couple days later, we were on an elevator again, and he just said, "Fifty bucks." I still couldn't. Finally, one time, there were about four Japanese people on the elevator with us, and Joe didn't even have to say anything. He just turned to me and gave me this look. So, I made $200 bucks that day. The other people on the elevator were appalled.

Another time we were in this really nice Japanese gift shop. We didn't see any clerks, so we thought we were the only two people in the place. Joe turned to me and said, "Fifty bucks." I challenged him and said, "I'll tell you what, I'll give you fifty bucks." He let off this huge one. All the sudden, we heard giggling and a little Japanese girl, who had been stooped down behind the counter putting stuff away, stood up and was red in the face from embarrassment and laughing. For the next several years, every time we were on an elevator, he'd just look over at me and say, "Fifty bucks."

On the way back from Japan, we spent a week in Honolulu and played in Aloha stadium. It was a huge gig. That's when I had a meeting with Don Henley. I really wasn't hired to do more shows than Japan, and I was wondering, "Now what?" The Eagles had a whole world tour ahead of them. Henley came to me and said it seemed to be working with me in the band and they liked having me out there with them, so I was hired for the rest of the tour. Then Joe spoke to Henley about me bringing my drum kit on the tour, because Joe has always liked having double drummers and he wanted Henley and me both to play on his tunes.

Besides being an excellent drummer, Don Henley's an incredible singer. It's remarkable how good he is, and I have to tell you, it's really difficult to sing lead and play drums. You already have your arms and legs doing four different things, and then to sing makes it even harder, because it also takes a lot of wind. But, it's REALLY hard to sing lead, play drums and play drum fills. When you do this, you're very busy. So, what I did was copy what Henley played, and then he'd play straight through and I'd play the fills. The three guys who are my favorites who can sing and play drums at the same time and do it really well, are Don Henley, Phil Collins and Levon Helm, from The Band.

What a great experience it was playing with the Eagles! People always ask me what it was like. As a whole, they're like no other band I ever played with. They're totally dedicated to their music and performance and put on a fantastic show every night. They're also an amazingly talented group of individuals. I'd been a fan of Don Henley's since they opened for Barnstorm. Don Henley is an incredible artist... singer, drummer, poet, lyricist, guitarist, communicator, performer and song writer. In hindsight, I can look back at Don's career and understand why he's such a big star. He's great at all aspects of what he does.

I can say the same thing about Glenn Frey...incredible singer, songwriter, guitar player, lyricist, and performer. I related to Don as a drummer, but I kinda related more as a person to Glenn Frey, because Glenn is from Michigan...he's a Midwest guy and I'm a Midwest guy. We both loved Bob Seger, who's a Detroit musician...Glenn and Bob are good friends, by the way. Ted Nugent was from Detroit and Joe Walsh spent a lot of time in the Midwest...we all had a lot in common because of growing up there.

I never really knew Timothy B. Schmit before I played with him in the Eagles, although I had listened to his work with Poco for years. When you're a drummer, your partner on the stage is the bass player, and it was great finally getting to meet and play with him. He's a fantastic songwriter and bass player, wonderful to play with, and has an angelic voice. He's also a very kind person and would  always go out of his way if anyone needed help with anything, and would patiently take whatever time was needed. He's one of those guys people always describe as, "one of the nicest people in the world." As an interesting side note, his wife, Jean, is the beautiful girl with long blonde hair near the beginning of the movie "Spinal Tap," who says something about becoming one with the band. I really love that movie, by the way.

Don Felder is one of the most under-rated guitar players in the world. In the, "it's a small world" category, I found out that Stephen Stills grew up in Florida with Don Felder, and when they were kids they were in a group together called "The Continentals," which was Stephen's first band . A couple of years ago I played with Stephen and Don for a benefit, and we said we should have a band name, so they said we should be called "The Incontinentals," since we were all in our 50's.

When I first met Don Felder, who I really admired as a guitar player, he and Joe Walsh in the Eagles reminded me of Jeff Beck and Eric Clapton or Jimmy Page and Eric Clapton, being two such phenomenal guitar players in one band. I had never met Don Felder before, but he knew who I was and I knew who he was, and when I met him, he mentioned that I was working with an old band mate of his. He's another really funny and great guy. He's also a fantastic singer and songwriter, and I really respect the depth of his talent.

In a band like the Eagles, where there are many stars, whoever was the songwriter was the band leader for that song. Crosby, Stills and Nash are like that, too. All the guys in the Eagles were always really nice to me and treated me with respect. They had nicknamed me "Joe Bob" during the days when The Eagles opened shows for Barnstorm, and always called me by that name. I felt very comfortable with them. On top of all the talent, they had the genius of Bill Szymczyk, who produced their albums, and the brilliant management of Irving Azoff.

I was coming from bands that were fairly loose about what I played and I didn't realize how strict the Eagles were about playing exact parts every night. I quickly came to find out that the Eagles are known for playing their songs live exactly like the record. Exactly. The vocals are always perfectly performed night after night. The fans who come to concerts don't want some new arrangement of the songs, they want to hear them performed just like the record. Eagles concert ticket buyers always get their money's worth. Well, one night

I got a little fancy on a drum fill in the song called "Those Shoes." It's an extremely funky song, and coming out of the talk box solo where Joe and Henley were doing dueling talk boxes, I did this really funky syncopated fill. The guitar players kinda turned around and gave me a nod and a smile, like they liked it. They really weren't smiling at me for that reason. They knew Henley a lot better than I did.

Later on at the hotel, Henley called and asked me to come over to his room for a second. So, I went over and knocked on the door. Henley, wearing the hotel robe, came to the door and opened it about six inches. He said something like, "Yeah, hey, you know that drum fill you played coming out of the solo in "Those Shoes?" So, there I was expecting to bask in this big compliment from Henley about my cool drum fill. I expectantly said, "Yeah....?" and he shook his head and said evenly, "Don't do that." Then he said, "Good night, Joe Bob," and closed the door.

Like I said, the guitar players knew Henley better than I did, and they knew he'd say something to me about the fill...and it wasn't going to be about how great it was. It made it even better for them since I was so pleased with myself for adding such a great part to the song. So, the next night at the gig, Glenn said, with a completely straight face, "So, Joe Bob, remember to play that fill." Then they all laughed.

Since Joe Walsh was in the band, I could count on the fact that we'd have water fights. Irving was as bad as Joe, maybe worse. One of the nights he was traveling with us, he started it. When the manager starts it, you know it's OK, because he's paying. We were playing in Birmingham, Alabama, at The Jefferson Civic Arena, which was across the street from a Hyatt Hotel. Just this past year, I stayed there again, although it's not a Hyatt anymore.

Anyway, the Eagles played a sold out show and we stayed across the street at that Hyatt. Irving started the water fight by soaking Joe. Joe immediately drenched him and then they decided to get me. I was an experienced water fighter, which was probably the real reason they hired me for the tour. By this time, the water fighting had escalated to tidal wave proportions. C'mon, the Eagles have to do everything big. So, everybody soaked everybody and water was everywhere. The cops came and kicked us out, so we had to move to another hotel around 3:00 in the morning.

I'm sure it wasn't because of the water fights that we were often required to give the hotel a credit card for each guy when we checked in. The problem was, we'd usually arrive late at night and we'd all be really tired. We really didn't feel like standing there at the hotel desk while they took down the information for each person in the band. There was one particular morning that we got to the hotel really late and I was especially tired. Sometimes when I get too tired, everything starts striking me as being funny.

I walked up to the desk and gave them my name. The clerk, who was getting the paperwork together for an entire band to check in, looked up at me and said, "I'll need an impression of a major credit card. Can you give me one?" I couldn't resist. "Why YES," I said, and stepped back. I turned my head to the side, showing him my Italian profile and brought my arms up around my head like I was making the letter "O." Perfect. Anyone would recognize it. "American Express," I explained, just in case he didn't get it. I thought my impression of the credit card was dead on. Although it's supposed to be a Viking in the original oval logo, to me the guy looked like a Roman soldier wearing a toga and cape with a helmet on. I'm sure he was originally Italian. "That's not funny, sir," he said, although I heard snickering in the line behind me. I really enjoyed my joke. Hey, it was late. It was the best impression of a credit card I could do.

This was The Long Run Tour, and we started getting used to staying up late. We had our own plane which was a Boeing 720, which was as big as a 707, with four engines. It was a gigantic party plane with two or three bars, seats, sleepers, a kitchen, lounge area...hey, it was amazing. With my flying history, though, if the weather was going to be bad, I'd occasionally fly commercial with the crew.

Since we had our own plane, sometimes we'd fly to the next city after the shows. Joe and I got into a bad habit, because most of the time, we'd be up all night. The show would end around 11:00 PM and by the time we'd get to the airport and take off it would be around 1:00 AM. Then we'd fly a couple hours, so it would be at least 4:00 or 5:00 AM by the time we'd get to the hotel. We'd be wired from traveling, and we couldn't just get to sleep, so we'd call

down to the front desk and ask them for a "go to bed" call. That would confuse them. They were used to being asked for "wake up" calls. They'd say, "Do you mean a wake up call?" and we'd say, "No, we're awake, we need a go to bed call." They'd laugh, and then we'd say that we were serious. So, we'd be in our rooms hangin' out and unwinding from the night, and the phone would ring at 6:00 AM and they'd say, "Hello, Mr. Vitale. It's 6:00 AM. It's time to go to bed." Sometimes we'd say, "Um, call back in an hour."

Again, since we had a plane we could hub out of one city, play a gig, and then fly back to the same city. That way we could stay in a really nice hotel and we didn't have to check in and out every day. We were hubbing out of New York City, and played a stadium show at The Yale Bowl at Yale University. The stadium held over 70,000 people at the time and it was packed. Inside the red "Eagles Live" album, there's a picture of our gig.

We were supposed to go up the day of the show, and because of the traffic and parking, management thought it would be a good idea if we went into New York City and took helicopters. So, we got on five Bell jet helicopters and flew to Yale, which only took about an hour. We were supposed to land in the parking lot, go in and play the show, and then come back out, get on the helicopters and fly back to New York.

I thought, oh great, helicopters, another flying experience. It was the first time I'd ever been on a helicopter and it was pretty amazing. We looked like something from M.A.S.H. I wish I had pictures of us, because it was really cool. On the way up, I flew with Joe Walsh, Smokey, who's Joe's road manager, and Glenn Frey. These were passenger helicopters, with a seat for the captain and one passenger up front, and four passengers in the back. We were flying at like 2,000 feet going 150 miles per hour, and Glenn accidentally bumped the door. It kinda got ajar, and the wind was really blowing in. OK, we had seat belts on and everything, but he was going to open the door and slam it shut again, like it was a car door or something, while we were flying. I just sat there for a second imagining all that could go wrong, and then I said desperately, "Glenn, don't touch anything." Everybody started laughing.

When we got there, we weren't allowed to fly over the stadium for safety reasons, but we flew in right next to it. When they announced to the crowd that the Eagles were arriving, you could hear the roar of the crowd even over the helicopters' engines. Great moment. Huge crowd. Packed, sold out stadium. Everyone cheering. What an experience. And what a dramatic entrance. Yeah, this was the future I had dreamed about when I was in high school.

We landed our five helicopters in the parking lot, played the show, and then got back on the helicopters for our flight back to New York. It was still Joe, Smokey, Glenn and I, but this time our sound man, Dave Reynolds, who was nicknamed "Snake," got into the captain's seat and the captain got into the front passenger seat. So, all the sudden the door shut, the engine revved up, the rotor blade started spinning and Snake started taking us off. I was pretty freaked out and said, "Hey, what's goin' on here?" Smokey turned over to me and

Loading the Endless Seas

Joe Walsh & Me

Hey Fish!

Tony Taibi

Bill Szymczyk

L to R: Jay Ferguson, Willie Weeks, Ed Michel, Jage Jackson, Me, Joe Walsh & Bill Szymczyk

Chocolate, Me, Gerry Tolman & Bonnie Bramlett   Photo by: Julie McNulty

Alan Rogan

Me, Don Felder, Joe Walsh, Glenn Frey, Timothy B. Schmit & Don Henley
Photo by: Tom Wright

Jean & Timothy

Joe Walsh

Don Henley

Glenn Frey

The Eagles 1980   *Photo by: Henry Diltz*

Photo by: Tom Wright

GLENN FREY

JOE WALSH

DON FELDER

WALSH / Vitale

POSSIBLE TOUR PASS PICTURES

Smokey Wendell

Our Boeing 720

Glenn Frey becoming Italian...

**Hey Glenn Frey...
That's-a so nice-a!**

The Eagles 1980   *Photo by: Rick Kohlmeyer - Backstagegallery.com*

Bill Szymczyk & Mickey Thomas

Tony Taibi, Me & Bill

Bill Szymczyk is officially Italian!

Joe Walsh, Me & my Dad

Russell Kunkel, Me, Chocolate Perry, Jay Ferguson and in front Joe Walsh

Joe Walsh in conductor hat.

How Ya Doin? Me & Bob Seger

Me & Joe Walsh

Rick Rosas, Joe Walsh & Me

Joe Walsh   *Photo by: Steve Jorgensen*

Photo by: Steve Jorgensen

Photo by: Steve Jorgensen

Photo by: Steve Jorgensen

Making of Plantation Harbor

Dr. Szymczyk   **And Mr. Hyde**

(Below) Photos at Bayshore Studio by: Jann Hendry

Kenny   *Photo by: Henry Diltz*   **Me**   *Photo by: Henry Diltz*

Byrd   *Photo by: Henry Diltz*   **Dan**   *Photo by: Henry Diltz*

Russ   **Photo by: Henry Diltz**

Photo by: Henry Diltz

Toast before the tour...   **Photo by: Henry Diltz**

Innocent Age Tour   L to R: Me, Mike Hanna, Dan Fogelberg, Mark Hallman,
Kenny Passarelli, Russell Kunkel, & Barry "Byrd" Burton.
Photo by Joe Meranti courtesy of Paul Neves

Kenny, Me & Byrd

Photo by Joe Meranti courtesy of Paul Neves

Waddy Wachtel, Me, Joe Walsh & Chocolate Perry

Space Age Whiz Kids Music Video

Waddy Wachtel, Joe Walsh, Chocolate Perry & Me on SCTV

Above: Me Left: Dan Fogelberg
Below: Dan & Kenny
Photo by Joe Meranti
courtesy of Paul Neves

Photo by: Steve Jorgensen

Above: Jessie Fernandez & Me
Left: Jessie & Charlie Fernandez

Dan Fogelberg, Dave Tolegian, Kenny Passarelli, Russ Kunkel, Byrd Burton
Photo by Joe Meranti courtesy of Paul Neves

Russ Kunkel, Dave Tolegian, Mike Hanna, Dan Fogelberg,
Kenny Passarelli, Byrd Burton & Me
Photo by Joe Meranti courtesy of Paul Neves

Dan Fogelberg, Snake Reynolds & Me

Charlie Fernandez at Dan's house

Dan Fogelberg's House

Dan shows me his paradise

Where Dan Fogelberg composed

The Buffalo Springfield Reunion

Bruce Palmer & Dewey Martin

Neil Young & Stephen Stills

Me, Doug Breidenbach, Neil Young

Dewey Martin

Neil Young & Richie Furay

Susan & Graham Nash   *Jan, David and Donovan Crosby*

Graham Nash   *Stephen Stills*   *David Crosby*

Bob Glaub   *Mike Finnigan*   *Joe Lala*

Doug Breidenbach   **Jan Crosby**   **Stephen & Gerry Tolman**

Jay Parti & John Vanderslice   **Joe Jr. and Me in New York**

Joe Jr. and Donovan Crosby   **David's birthday**

Neil Young's Ranch   **Stephen, Neil, Graham & David**

Photo by: Henry Diltz

"Joe overdubing"

Stephen Stills
at Second Plant
with Joe

Joe overdubs on
Stephens Guitar tracks

Dave cooking up
Joes Beak.

This is Hollywood
my Boy

Joe & Stanley mix
"Live it up"

Joe & his friends
(Joe is punching in)

JAN ASKS JOE TO
SIT ON HER SHOULDER

Joe Shows Craig
an Overdub for
Stephens Guitar Track

Ohio here I come!

Rance Caldwell

"Coach" Mike Sexton

Jan Crosby

Jorge Calderon

Kim Bullard

Michito Sanchez

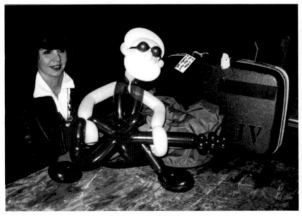
Susie with Jerry Garcia balloon

"Mouse" Danny De La Luz

said, "What? What's the matter?" He didn't know that I was the only one who didn't know that Snake had been an ace helicopter pilot in Vietnam. Flying us without having to dodge bullets and rockets was easy for him. He flew us back to New York and it was a beautiful ride. It was just a little exciting there for me, for a minute.

We had a lot of fun on that tour. One night after we played Glenn Frey's song "Take It Easy," Glenn came over to me, and since I was Italian, he said, "Hey...take it easy," like he was an Italian mob guy. So, we got into this "thing" then. If I saw Glenn and he was irritated about the hotel or the food or something that was bugging him, I'd say, "Hey, Glenn...take it easy." After a while, I said to him, "So, you like this Italian thing, huh? It's unfortunate that you're not Italian. Maybe we should have a ceremony and make you one."

Glenn overcome with emotion at my offer to make him Italian, gives me a hug. Hey... Take it easy!

One night, all the guys got together and we bought him a Stetson hat, a cigar and some kind of a greasy silk jacket and sunglasses, and I want to tell you, he looked good, he looked Italian...we pimped him out royally. We had an Italian dinner ceremony and then we all claimed that he was now officially an Italian. I don't think Henley appreciated that we'd made Glenn an Italian. He looked over at what Glenn was wearing...he looked like some kind of a gangster. Here's Henley's Eagles band partner looking like this mob boss, so he looked at Glenn in total disgust and said, "What are you doin'?" Glenn, who was now officially Italian, sitting there with his hat, cigar, sunglasses and silk jacket, squinted his now-Italian eyes, gestured with his hands, and with all this attitude, said, "Hey...take it easy."

The Eagles had a lot of friends and fans in show business, and sometimes they'd come to our gig. I don't think that I've ever met so many celebrities as I did the year I played with the Eagles. They were so respected, and everyone wanted to come to their shows, so of course, they would come back to say hello afterwards. It was really exciting for me to meet some of my favorite stars, like Jack Nicholson. Dan Akyroyd and John Belushi were also friends of the band, and were playing music themselves as The Blues Brothers. The Blues Brothers were a fantastic success on Saturday Night Live and it was the year they made their movie. I was a big fan, and I loved it when I saw them perform on TV. I think they wanted to travel with us so they could see what it was like, but touring with the Eagles wasn't like being on tour with any other band. At that time, the Eagles and Fleetwood Mac were the biggest acts in the world.

The road managers asked us if we minded having a couple of guests on the road with us for a while. We wanted to know who. They said it was Dan Akyroyd and John Belushi, and we said absolutely, yes, they could come. The Blues Brothers! How fun and cool was that? It was unbelievable to have them on the road with us for a while. They were on the plane with us, ate with us, and were on the side of the stage every night at the gig. We really got to know them and they weren't loud and crazy like you'd expect.

It was like they were invisible sometimes, because they didn't get in the way or try to make it all about them. They were just along on the road like any other guests would be. Keeping strictly to the show, the Eagles never had them come out on stage to jam or sit in during any of the shows we did while they were out with us. The shows were only Eagles songs, and again, the songs were performed just like they sound on the records. We tried to get Dan and John into a water fight with us one night, but they wouldn't do it. That's surprising, isn't it? They didn't want to get into any trouble or get any bad press, so they just blended in and we all had a tremendous time.

Later in the tour, we played some shows for Bill Graham, the famous promoter. Bill loved playing baseball, and he also was an ace ping pong player. Every time we worked for Bill when I was with Crosby, Stills and Nash, he and Graham would be playing ping pong. I'm not sure who won the most, but they really played a lot. Bill Graham also had a softball team made up of his staff, so when we played shows for him, we'd play his team. His team actually had practices and wore uniforms. When Crosby, Stills and Nash played Bill's team, they named our team the "San Francisco Hoovers." It was just like when we

Promoter Bill Graham

played Mr. Udo's baseball team when I was in Japan with Peter Frampton. When a team like that has practices and uniforms, they mean business.

The Eagles were playing that Saturday night for Bill at the old Cow Palace, which was a great big arena in San Francisco. That Saturday afternoon, we played his softball team. Around the fifth or sixth inning, I was up to bat, and since it had rained that morning there was a little bit of mud. I hit the ball and took off for first base. Near first base, I hit the mud, and not having uniforms or cleats like Bill's team, I slipped and fell, landing on my left thumb and breaking it. Oh, good. I had a show to play that night with a broken left thumb.

At first I just thought it was a really bad sprain and I could keep playing baseball, but I was supposed to wear my glove on my left hand and it hurt too much to put it on. Then my thumb started swelling. About an hour later it had gotten really huge, so I put ice on it. I went back to the hotel and it kept throbbing in pain, so I finally went to the emergency room. They took xrays and determined that it was broken, but just cracked, not like it was snapped off or anything. The doctor put a splint on it and wrapped it up, so that night when I played drums the crew duct-taped my drum stick to my hand. I played keyboards right handed and the stick had to stay taped to my left hand, so it just hung there. The crew also put a towel over the congas, so I could play those parts with two sticks instead of my hands. Every time I hit a back beat when I was playing my kit, it was like, hit, ouch, hit, ouch, hit, ouch.

Vitale at bat... right before I broke my thumb!

Fortunately, that was the last show before a two or three week break, so by the time I started playing again, I had gotten rid of the splint and just put an ace bandage on it. We resumed the tour in late summer and played in Philadelphia. Eagles management had been contacted by the Philadelphia Eagles football team management, who wanted to do a publicity thing promoted like, "The Eagles meet the Eagles." We played a show on Saturday night and all these great big Eagle football players came to our gig and sat on the side of the stage. They gave me a #1 jersey that was kicker Tony Franklin's, which I still have. He was huge. When I put the jersey on, it went all the way to the floor, like a dress.

The next day was Sunday, so we got to go to the locker room and hang out with the players before the game, and then they put us on the sidelines to watch the game. They warned us that if a running play came towards us, we were on our own. So, during that game, several times these refrigerator-sized guys would come running at us full bore and we had to scatter to get out of the way. The whole day was really great. We got to hang on the sidelines about five feet from the out of bounds line, right at the bench with the guys. It was fantastic! After the game, we went into the locker room and I gained a whole new respect for the football players. They were taking their gear and jerseys off, and they were all bruised, cut and beat up. Man! I can't believe what a brutal job they have. I never realized what a beating they take every week.

We had a wonderful two days with the team and were saying thanks and goodbye to everyone, when the coach came over to talk to us. OK, it was an honest mistake. He was a professional football coach and he didn't know that much about rock & roll. He very graciously tried to pay us a huge compliment. He turned to Glenn Frey and said with tremendous sincerity, "You know, Glenn, I want to thank you guys, because your music inspires our team." Glenn didn't know what he could possibly mean, so he asked, "How's that? How do we inspire your team?" The coach explained, "The first thing we do on Monday morning before practice to get the guys really going and wound up is to play "Fly Like An Eagle." We were speechless. The Eagles were used to everyone being familiar with all their songs. Finally we stammered a thank you, said goodbye and left. "Fly Like An Eagle" is by Steve Miller. An honest mistake, but another great moment.

A few times I'd mentioned that I wanted to rent a car while I was on the road, and I noticed that it wasn't received well. I'd hear, "Slowly I turn…" and then I'd hear "No car rentals." I couldn't figure this out…why they were against us renting cars. I finally asked Joe and I heard about the demolition derby. I eventually heard several versions of this story, so I don't know how embellished the story was when it got to me.

Apparently, from what I heard of the story, some of the guys were returning several rental cars at the same time, and someone accidentally backed into someone else in the parking lot at the rental place. That was all they needed. It quickly got out of hand and escalated into a demolition derby with several cars involved. I never got all the details, but I can understand why management didn't want to have to pay for damages to more rental cars. You just never knew what those guys were going to do.

We usually traveled to the shows in limos, and sometimes it was really hard for us to get into and out of a show. The fans would surround the car and in their excitement, sometimes they'd climb on it or try to get in. They'd swarm all around the car and wouldn't move away, and if we started driving, we were afraid someone would get run over or hurt. When we played in Cleveland, it was an enormous deal. Not only were the Eagles hugely popular in Ohio, but Joe and I were both from the area. We played two nights at The Coliseum in Richfield, and we left for the show from the Holiday Inn in Brecksville on Route 21.

Sometimes management would get creative with our transportation to try to avoid the crowds. Someone made arrangements for an ambulance to take us to and from the show, so Susie and I met the band at The Holiday Inn in Brecksville and got into the back of the ambulance. The guy sitting next to Susie politely introduced himself. It was Jackson Browne, who was in town and was going to the show with us. Even with the ambulance disguise, some of the fans didn't want to move, so the driver turned the lights on for a second. It worked really well and the crowd got out of the way.

After the show, we left the same way and went back to the hotel in Brecksville. The fans didn't follow the ambulance, so they couldn't follow the band to the hotel where we were staying. For some reason, local fans who knew where I lived thought that the Eagles would come over to my house after the show, and both nights lined the allotment streets with their cars. They must have been really disappointed when Susie and I were the only ones coming home.

To the fans, an Eagles show probably looks easy, because it's so perfect every night that it looks effortless. The Eagles treated every show as though it were the most important show. During the day, they each did whatever interested them, but when they got to the sound check, they totally focused in on making that night's show flawless. We called it "Putting your game face on." Every night, they gathered in a room before they went out and warmed up by singing together. When they walked out on the stage, they'd be totally warmed up and ready to perform.

Like all the other tours I'd been on, I always had my tools with me, and sometimes I'd get a call from one of the guys for some on the spot repair of something. On Peter Frampton's tour, we were all pretty boys, with pretty hair and clothes, so I had a lot of hair dryer repair. Henley knew I was "Mr. Fixit," so one night about three o'clock in the morning during the Eagles tour, I got a call and he said, "Joe Bob, you got your tools?" I said, "I've always got my tools." He said he couldn't sleep because there was this horrible in-house music, kinda like elevator music, playing really loud in the halls of the hotel where we were staying. It was kinda unusual to have music playing and it wasn't that loud, but it was loud enough that it was irritating and keeping Don awake.

So, I grabbed Don Henley's drum tech, Tony Taibi, and I got a chair to stand on. We saw that there were about six speakers in the ceiling of the hallway, so I'd get up on the chair, undo the grill that was covering the speaker, drop the speaker, take the wire off, and put it back up. It probably took us twenty minutes to disconnect all of them. Then it was totally quiet in the hallway. Fortunately it was before the days of video security cameras in hotels, so no one knew I did it. I saw Henley the next day and he thanked me for his good night's sleep.

The Long Run Tour lasted a year and we played every place under the sun. I think the Eagles sold out every show. I've gotta tell ya', it was a tremendous experience. I'm really glad we recorded the last few shows we played, because the band had really settled into a good place musically, and we sounded fantastic. The last few nights we worked at the Santa Monica Civic and the Long Beach Arena, which turned into the "Eagles Live" album released in 1980.

The Blues Brothers were no longer on tour with us and were playing at Universal. Joe and I were invited to the show and decided to dress like them, just to show our support. We stopped at a costume shop on the way and wore white shirts with ties, hats and sunglasses. We had backstage passes, so when we arrived in the limo it caused all kinds of confusion. Security looked at Joe and me with our costumes and backstage passes and said, "Don't tell us you're The Blues Brothers." We said, "We're not The Blues Brothers." They said, "Don't tell us that." They really got confused by the whole thing. John and Dan were surprised to see us in costume and thought it was really funny. We watched the show from the side of the stage but when they asked us to join them on stage and be Blues Brothers for the encore, we didn't have the nerve to go out. Joe always made everything we did a little crazy and a lot more fun.

Since it was the year of a United States Presidential election, Joe Walsh turned his attentions to yet another joke, and announced he was running for President. For his campaign, he promised free gas for everyone and to make "Life's Been Good" the National Anthem. The free gas platform would probably be a winner today! Fortunately for Joe, his career with the Eagles was more successful than his bid for the Presidency, although he did run for the Vice Presidency several years later.

The huge Eagles tour was now over and I had really been gone a lot. I didn't fully realize how much I had been away until I arrived back home in Ohio. Susie and I were adding onto our house, and several of the neighbors happened to have stopped over and were looking at the outside, when I pulled up in the limo. The driver got out to help me with my luggage, so we were both standing outside the car. Then, in front of the entire neighborhood, Joey ran up to the limo driver, threw his arms around his knees and shouted joyfully, "Daddy!"

<u>Santa</u>

I was home for Christmas that year and tried to shift gears from being on the road with The Eagles. Although by that time I was playing with and friends with a lot of world famous rock & roll stars, it meant nothing to my son, Joey. He would have been impressed with me knowing Big Bird or Grover. During this time, sometimes people recognized me when I was at home in Canton, Ohio, and out somewhere with Joey and Susie, and they'd want to say hello to me or ask for an autograph. I hadn't been home very much and time with my family was precious, but as long as people didn't want to talk to me for too long, I didn't mind and was even flattered. That year Susie and I took Joey to a special Christmas event that The Junior League held in Canton. It was always a big deal and this was the first year we took Joey.

We went through this winter wonderland North Pole thing they'd set up, with the glitter, cotton gauze snow, and paper snowflakes...the whole bit. At the end, the kids got their picture taken with Santa Claus. We walked through the entire maze of snowflakes and elves and were finally waiting for Joey to get to sit on Santa's lap. "Santa" looked up, saw me and forgot who he was supposed to be. Excitedly he said, "Hey Joe, remember me?" as though I'd be able to recognize someone in a full Santa suit with a huge fake white beard covering his face. Then Santa looked back down at Joey and blurted, "I went to high school with your Dad!" Joey's eyes got huge and he looked at me with enormous awe, wonder and respect. He was astonished. "Wow, Daddy! You went to high school with SANTA CLAUS?" He was totally blown away. It was fantastic.

CHAPTER FOURTEEN

1981, Mickey Thomas, "Alive Alone"

Once again, Bill got me the opportunity of recording another great album. This time it was Mickey Thomas's album "Alive Alone." Mickey Thomas sang "Fooled Around and Fell in Love" with Elvin Bishop and had just joined Jefferson Starship. "Alive Alone" was going to be a solo album, produced by Bill Szymczyk and Allan Blazek. I was hired

Mickey Thomas

to play drums, percussion, keyboards and some backup vocals. I enjoyed getting the chance to meet and record with artists who I admired and respected, because I really got to know them while we were working together in the studio.

I'll never forget the first time I met Mickey Thomas. What a character! I walked into the studio and when Bill introduced us Mickey was holding something and had to change hands to shake my hand. Then I noticed what he was holding. He was drinking Scotch but he couldn't find a glass, so he was drinking from the top of a rectangular clear glass butter dish. He even had ice in it. I could tell that this was one creative guy.

It was during the recording of Mickey's album that Tony Taibi and I decided to make Bill Szymczyk Italian. Tony Taibi is a drum tech and

Bill & Mickey

road manager, and was there working on Mickey's album. We had so much fun making Glenn Frey Italian that I think Bill was kinda jealous. He said, "Hey, when can I be made Italian?" Bill is Polish…gee, do ya think, with a no-vowel name like Szymczyk? However, making Bill Italian wasn't difficult at all, because except for his height, Bill already looked Italian. He could easily grow a mustache, slap on an accordion and completely blend in.

He also totally throws himself into anything he does, so I knew his accent and hand gestures were going to be impeccable. His broken English was superb. We started by giving him a new Italian name. Let's face it, a last name with no vowels is not going to cut it. We chose the name Guido Mondorano. It includes the classic Italian name of Guido, which isn't a name in any other nationality, and

Tony Taibi, Me & Guido Mondorano (Bill)

Mondorano's loaded with vowels and it ends in an "o." Perfect.

From living in Florida, Bill already had a swarthy tan, and his black curly hair and huge eyes were the perfect classic Italian look. Picture him in a black shirt, a white tie, suspenders and a black hat…the perfect cliché of a mob boss. We couldn't miss. We planned to hold the ceremony at a special Italian dinner…you have to have pasta to induct someone into Italian-ness. And gifts…we showered him with appropriate gifts for the occasion. We got him a switchblade that was a comb, a huge cigar, mob sunglasses, suspenders, a white tie, and a black hat. He was cool, and could do those squinted Italian eyes as well as I could. He was a natural. Yeah, Bill looked good…the perfect Italian. He's-a made me so proud!

1981, Joe Walsh, "There Goes The Neighborhood,"

Joe Walsh and I, "The Wrong Brothers of Flight," as he called us, had gotten into model rockets. I had started launching model rockets back in 1976 in the field behind my home in Ohio. I started out small and quickly escalated to bigger, more elaborate ones. I learned how to pack the engine and launch them so they'd parachute back to earth without crashing…well, most of the time. One of my earliest rockets crashed into the roof of a nearby house that was under construction, and stuck in it so it looked like bad special effects from a science fiction movie.

In the beginning I was lighting the fuse with matches, but I eventually made a launch pad with an electric start…it seemed like a better idea for someone who needs his fingers and hands. I launched a rocket for Joe when he came to visit for a few days. He LOVED them…the danger, the suspense, the noise, the launch…everything. As always, we became obsessed with rockets, so for a while, everything was rockets…bigger and bigger rockets.

The rockets still had to be constructed and painted and I really tried to make them look good for the launches. I had no sooner launched my latest rocket than I was back at the store looking for an even bigger one. Joe ended up being inspired to write the song "Rockets" for the "Neighborhood" album. We'd come a long way since the crash of my model airplane in the parking lot in Boulder back in the Barnstorm days.

Eventually we went into the studio to record Joe's album. There's a lot of down time in a studio and we couldn't bring rockets, so sometimes we got bored. Well, in a studio, you have razor blades, scissors, tape, and a whole bunch of magazines. In the beginning, we would go through them and cut out heads, and put them on different bodies and make weird pictures. Like, we might cut out the head of a football player and

Joe Astro-nut preparing rocket

put it on a ballerina. We called doing this "cut out man." We put large lips on small heads and other disproportionate body parts together. Then we'd tape the finished art up on the windows in the studio so everyone could see them.

That was the primitive version. We ended up pre-thinking what pose we wanted, and then we'd take Polaroid pictures of our heads in the perfect position and expression to go on our idiotic magazine photos. We got really good at carefully cutting out the head so it fit on the body, but we really liked the parts to be out of proportion. Chocolate always wanted to be a race car driver, so we'd take a picture of him and put it over the head of a guy in a race car. Some of them really looked real if we kept the proportion the same. Then we'd take a Polaroid picture of our "cut out man," so it looked like a real picture. Sometimes Chocolate showed his race car photo to girls and they thought he raced cars in his spare time.

We did this for a long time during several albums, so we got really skilled at it. Joe and I did cut out man when we were recording the John Entwistle album and got John doing it, too. He loved it so much he put some "cut out man" on his album cover.

1981, Joe Walsh Neighborhood Tour

The craziness of Joe and me touring together reached new heights with The Neighborhood Tour. The band was Joe Walsh, George "Chocolate" Perry on bass, Russell Kunkel on drums, Michael Murphy on keyboards and vocals, and me. The tour started in Japan and then came back to the United States.

One of the funniest things I remember from that tour was that Joe wanted us to dress up and look ridiculous. Joe didn't think we were doing a good enough job of it, so he came up with a plan where everybody wrote their clothes size down and we put all the names in a box. Then we'd have a drawing. So, let's say I picked Chocolate. I'd have his size for his shirt, coat, pants, shoes...everything, all his clothes. I'd go out that day and shop for him and he had to wear what I bought for him for the show that night. I also had to wear whatever the person who drew me had bought for me, no matter what they bought. You just didn't want Joe to pick your name. We did this about once a week for the whole tour, and ended up with an Anvil case full of these ridiculous clothes. Then every show we'd go to what we called "wardrobe," which was a

Me & Joe

case filled with our insane clothes and accessories, and get out something ridiculous to wear. I brought my outfits home with me at the end of the tour, and I still have them. That tour was Joe at his outrageous best.

When we played in Cleveland, we had a day off, so Joe came home with me after the show and we spent the next day launching rockets. The next gig was the following day in Chicago, so he thought it would be a lot more fun if we

Joe & Russell

took a train instead of flying. Management made the arrangements and a limo picked us up at my house early the next morning. We rode to the AMTRAK station in Cleveland, where we caught the train at about 9:30 AM. Joe immediately was into the whole thing and bought a conductor's hat. You can just picture it...he was suddenly the conductor. We went from car to car, moving from the back of the train toward the front, with Joe stopping to speak with the passengers,

Joe wearing conductor hat

wearing his hat. He'd ask them things like how their trip was going and if they liked traveling in the train so far. We went all the way to the front. I have to laugh just thinking about it.

Fortunately, we weren't allowed to go all the way to the engine. Once we got up front and Joe wasn't allowed to drive the train, we started back, with Joe stopping again to ask the same people if they were still enjoying their trip. Finally we had lunch. I have to admit the food was great. After lunch, we went back to our rooms for a while and took a nap, because we had a show that night.

That trip was one of the best memories I have from the road. Joe was, of course, being outrageous and crazy, but there was more to it than that. It was so relaxing to travel by train, we could walk around, there was a lot of room, and looking out of the train's windows, I could see a fantastic part of America…the backyards…the places normally not in view. There were barefoot children playing on swing sets who came to watch the train and smile and wave as we went by. Dogs barked and ran along the back fences, always successfully chasing the train away down the tracks. Some of the backyards had laundry drying in the sunshine on the clotheslines. American flags ruffled in the breezes. Families were cooking out and eating dinner together. Some children sat on the back porches eating Popcycles, while others were mowing the lawns or washing the family car. I saw kids playing baseball and shooting baskets. Neighbors visited over their back fences and looked up to see us passing by. Of course, there were those "two cats in the yard" CSN always sang about. I've always wanted to write a song about our trip that day. Someday, I will.

We played that night near the Chicago airport at an outdoor shed called Poplar Creek. A few shows before our Chicago gig, Russell ran out of sticks during "Funk #49," so I tossed a stick over to him while

we were playing and he caught it. The crowd went wild. Hey, anything for the audience, so we started throwing the sticks back and forth. They thought it was part of the act. Every time one of us would catch a stick, they'd cheer. The review in the paper the next day was all about us throwing the sticks. So, all the sudden, this was part of the act. We called it "stick toss." We'd start out throwing one stick at a time back and forth, and then we'd start throwing two sticks back and forth. People freaked out.

My stick toss partner, Russ Kunkel

Jim Keltner, who's a renowned drummer, had heard about the stick toss and came to the Chicago show just to see it. When we saw Jim was there, Russell and I really tried to play our best. We saw him after the show, and were hoping that he'd say something fantastic about our drumming, but all he talked about was the stick toss. For the next few tours when I was playing with Joe Walsh, we always had to include the stick toss, even if I was playing with another drummer. Of all the drummers I did stick toss with, Russell was definitely the best. Drummer Chad Cromwell was out with Joe during another tour and he wanted to do stick toss with me, but he wore glasses and it was hard for me to toss a stick at him, because I was afraid I'd hit him in the eye or break his glasses. For the next several tours when Joe would be looking for another drummer, part of the audition was, "How good are you at catching a drum stick?"

During that summer, the Major League Baseball teams were on strike, so during the show Joe used to say something like, "I know that you don't have a lot of baseball this summer, but we'll offer you some stick toss." Along with the stick toss, he also had a gigantic twenty-eight inch bass drum on the stage, leaning backwards. It was angled so that if he hit it with a ball it would fly out into the crowd. Then Joe would take tennis balls that he'd signed and throw them against the drum like he was pitching. Each ball would make this huge BOOM when the balls bounced off the drum head and then dropped into the crowd. The audience loved it and there was always a frenzy of people trying to grab the tennis balls, because they were autographed. The entire Neighborhood Tour was insanity and fun, as it always was when I was out with Joe. When it was over, I went back to Ohio and finished writing my second solo album "Plantation Harbor."

Chocolate, Me, Joe, Russell, Michael & Smokey (In Front)

CHAPTER FIFTEEN

1982, "Plantation Harbor"

I was signed by Asylum Records and returned to Florida to record my second solo album with Bill Szymczyk producing and engineering. Bill had a production deal with Asylum to produce three albums with the artists of his choice. Fortunately for me, I was one of the artists he chose. What an honor! Of course Joe Walsh was coming down to Florida, so Bill, Joe and I were going to be working together again... that's where the "asylum" part seemed to fit.

Photo by: Jann Hendry

I wanted to put something funny on my record and I thought a phone call bit with Joe Walsh would be good. I was still in Ohio at that point, but my demos were finished. I wanted to record a call with Joe and have him talk about having an idea for a part on one of the songs on the record. I called Joe and he was immediately all for it. He said,

"Let's not just record a phone call, let's use a real operator." Joe hung up and called right back, "person to person, collect." Remember that kind of call? If you do, you're about the same age I am! I don't think they even have that kind of call today.

On the record, the phone rang and then the operator said, "I have collect call for Joe Vitale. Is he there to accept charges?" I said, "Yes." She said, "Is this Joe Vitale?" I answered, "I think so." Then the operator said, "You should know something like that, sir." We could tell from her voice that she was starting to get uptight that we were fooling around. She seemed to be almost waiting for a prank call punchline. Then I said, "This is he," so she said, "OK, will you accept charges from Joe Walsh?" I said "Yes, I will," so she answered, "Go ahead." Then she put Joe on. He started telling me he had this idea for the song and explained his idea in complete gibberish. I brought that tape with my demos when I went to record with Bill. We decided to put the phone call at the end of "Lady On The Rock" going into "Bamboo Jungle." It had absolutely nothing to do with either song, but somehow, it works.

Bill still lived in Florida at the time, so Tony Taibi, Jage Jackson, Joe Walsh, and I stayed in a Home At Last house while I was recording. Somebody had a video camera and we started doing what we called "the bits." We saw a funny commercial on TV one night and Joe said, "Hey, let's make a commercial." We already had a camera, so we were immediately all on board to

Jage Jackson

tape. We decided to take it a step further and started taping our own commercials and routines like old time TV. Chocolate lived in Florida and heard about what we were doing. He wanted in on it, so he came over and taped some of the bits with us.

I think the best bit we taped was the one we made in the kitchen. There was a huge island in the center of the room with all kinds of pots and pans hanging down from it. Pots and pans! My heart be still! They were just begging to be played for our bit. Chocolate and I grabbed some kitchen utensils and started playing this beat, this groove, while we were walking around and around the island. We started playing faster and faster. We were kinda marching in time to what we were playing for about a minute and a half and then we walked out of the kitchen. For the ending, after about thirty silent seconds, Joe Walsh, who had been crouched in the cupboard with the door closed, swung the kitchen cabinet door open. He was covered with pots and pans, which crashed to the floor while he climbed out of the cupboard and walked out of the room. We thought our film was Oscar-worthy.

Bill still lived in Florida and had Bayshore Recording Studio, but he also had a summer home which was an A-frame cabin in the mountains in North Carolina. We recorded some of Plantation Harbor at Bayshore, and then Bill thought we should do some recording and overdubs at his cabin for a couple of weeks. We referred to recording at Bill's cabin as The Vinylrosa, like it was a regular studio. So, Bill, Buddy Thornton, James Geddes and I went up to the cabin to record at another beautiful location. Bill put together a little studio with a 24 track machine, a board, speakers, mics, cabling, and whatever else we needed. The time we spent at the cabin was very special. One of the nights Buddy Thornton went fishing and caught some trout and we had them for dinner. It was a lot like being out in the woods camping, just a LOT nicer.

The first night we arrived, Bill's neighbors had us over for dinner. We promised them we wouldn't make too much noise, but they said they wanted to listen and we should make all the noise we wanted. That night, Bill mentioned that he had a really great idea for the drum set. It was more than a great idea…it was ingenious.

I had brought my drum set and Bill decided that we should put them up on his back deck, which was really high off the ground. Talk about a drum riser! Since it was springtime, it was warm enough to wear a tee shirt and play outside. The view was spectacular. Bill really knows

what he's doing and is a totally creative genius. He took two U87 microphones and walked them out about a hundred yards into the field out in the valley, with Mount Mitchell in the distance. Then he put the mics about 50 yards apart and ran cable down to them, and that natural canyon was the echo for my drums. It was a brilliant idea.

He came back up to the cabin…winded, I might add…and went into the control room. The mics were so far away that after Bill left, some

Bill & mic

little critters that were floatin' around out there in the forest returned and started making noises, and we started picking them up in the mics. There was a little cardinal that landed on one of the mic's boom stands and started singing. You can hear him chirping right at the beginning of the recording and he sat out there on the boom stand and sang throughout the entire song. Bill had made the mics pretty hot, so you can really hear him.

Bill & I at the cabin cutting tracks.

Amazingly, he was singing in tune with the song, and the placement of his chirps fit right in...it sounds like we added him, but we didn't. We named him Harry the Cardinal and gave him credit on the album. Bill and I aren't real cosmic people or anything, but we decided that this was magical. We tried to find Harry to have him turn in a union session, but he flew the coop...well, you know how musicians are.

We finished that track and did some vocals, percussion, synthesizer and keyboard overdubs up there. Following our "Something Weirdos" theme, I called this one track we did up there "Theme from Cabin Weirdos." Then we went back to Bayshore in Florida to finish the tracks for the album. While we were recording there, we worked with Mickey Thomas and Ricky Washington, who was Chocolate's cousin, doing backup vocals on one of the cuts. They were some of the very best backup vocals I'd ever heard.

We also used Graham Nash's studio in L.A., Rudy Records, for overdubs and the string date for the album. We'd decided to use strings for "Laugh Laugh" and "I'm Flyin'" and had hired Jimmy Haskell as the arranger and conductor. He'd flown to Florida to meet with Bill and hear the material. We flew back to L.A. together and he wanted to sit with me and go over the charts and arrangements. We had cassette players with headphones back then, and he'd roughed in some string parts over the songs using a synthesizer. He got out the conductor's score and had it spread in front of him. He was going through the music one measure at a time, and had this little baton he was using like he was conducting. He was totally into it and oblivious to his surroundings...kinda smiling with a crazy look on his face, since he was really enjoying hearing what he'd written. No one else could hear the music, so it looked like he was conducting the back of the seat in front of him. I pretended I wasn't with him. Whatever he did to prepare, it worked, because he did a brilliant job on the strings.

Once we got to Rudy Records, we also recorded some of the overdubs with the Chicago Horns, including Jimmy Pankow on trombone, Walt Parazaider tenor sax, Marty Grebb tenor sax and sax solo, Stephen Stills, Graham Nash and Timothy B. Schmit on vocals, Don Felder on guitar, Paul Harris and Bobby Mayo on keyboards, and Joe Lala on percussion . I played drums, flute, electric piano, clavinet, organ, synthesizer, vibraphone and percussion on the album.

When the record was finished and it was time to have it mastered, Bill Szymczyk once again used his connections and got Ted Jensen from Sterling Sound to master the album. Ted is the Master of mastering and is probably the best on Earth. Ted's stellar credentials look like a history of major rock & roll acts right up to the present...totally impressive. I couldn't believe I was going to have Ted master my album. Bill made it happen.

I had decided to name my album "Plantation Harbor" because I had such a fantastic experience recording with Joe Walsh and Bill when we recorded in the city of Plantation Harbor on the Endless Seas. I had also written a song with that title for the album. Bill and everyone thought I should go down to the Keys and get a picture for the front cover. I would have liked to have had one with more action and not so posed. The cover photographer was Scherley Busch and the cover design was by Jimmy Wachtel. Susie eventually framed the shirt I wore with the cover from a CD. Asylum released three singles from the album, which were "Lady on the Rock," "Plantation Harbor" and "Man Gonna Love You."

Joe Walsh decided to do a second leg of the Neighborhood Tour, and generously allowed me to play a couple of the songs from my album each night, so I didn't get a band together on my own. With Russ Kunkel playing drums, I was able to play keyboards and sing on my tunes. Once again, the album didn't do as well as I'd hoped, but I'm really proud of it and you can still buy it on CD.

1982, Crosby, Stills and Nash, "Daylight Again"

Since I didn't have a band together for my album, after the Neighborhood Tour I moved on to my commitments with Crosby, Stills and Nash. We recorded "Daylight Again" at Rudy Records, Graham Nash's studio in L.A. It was a beautiful studio and I'd worked there a lot, so everything went really well…we got "Southern Cross" in about two takes, because it was so beautifully written. I'd heard that term before, but I never really knew what the Southern Cross was or what it looked like. It would be another twenty-five years until I saw it for myself during the CSN Australia/New Zealand tour in 2007. It was beautiful to see…no wonder Stephen wrote a song about it.

We recorded two more classic CSN hits for that album, which were "Wasted on the Way" and "Daylight Again."

1982, "Daylight Again" Tour

The band for the Daylight Again Tour was David Crosby, Stephen Stills, Graham Nash, Mike Finnigan on B3, keyboards and vocals, Chocolate on bass, Mike Sturgis on guitar, James Newton Howard on keyboards, Efrain Toro on percussion, and me.

I had just started the tour with CSN and I was at gig when I got a message that Phil Collins was trying to get in touch with me. The message said to call someone from Atlantic Records, who would then have Phil call me. I had been on Atlantic and so was Phil Collins, so that part made sense, but I immediately thought it was Joe Walsh playing yet another joke on me, because he knew how highly I thought of Phil. I figured when I called the number, it was going to be an escort service or something.

I called the number in the message I had, and the receptionist answered, "Atlantic Records," so I asked for the guy who was named in the message. He said, "Joe, would you let me know where Phil can call you?" I said, "Then this is on the level?" and he said, "Yes, Phil's in the country and he wants to hook up with you." He continued to say that when Phil heard what I did on the song "Rocky Mountain Way" and other tracks I'd recorded, he loved the pocket and groove and my feel so much that he wanted to work with me. Now a compliment like that is about as humbling and amazing as it gets! I'll never forget it.

Phil called me and said he wanted to come to a show and hear me play. We looked at our schedules. He was in Detroit and I was playing at Pine Knob, which is nearby, so Phil took a limo up to my gig and sat on the side of the stage about ten or fifteen feet from me and listened to the whole show. Afterwards, he came over, shook my hand and introduced himself. I said, "Phil, I think I'd know who you are!" He was just coming off his success with Genesis and had a huge solo record out at the time. After the first time I heard "Face Value," I listened to "In The Air Tonight" over and over, and just waited for the end with the huge drum fill. Phil's a keyboard player and singer as well as a drummer, so he thinks and plays drums melodically. I LOVE his playing.

Phil said he was putting a band together for his solo tour and asked me to be the drummer. It was amazing. A dream come true. I said, "I can't believe this is really happening…YES, of course I'll do it!" I was thinking it would take about six months to put together a tour. "When does rehearsal start?" I asked, and he answered, "In two weeks." NO! TWO weeks! I was shattered. I'd just started a three month tour with CSN and I'd given my word and commitment. There was just no way. I couldn't walk out on a tour. It would be totally unethical and unprofessional. Besides all that, Graham, David and Stephen were my friends. Overwhelmed with regret, I told Phil I couldn't do his tour. I was devastated, but Phil understood. With my professional integrity intact, I continued touring with CSN. Despite my disappointment over not being able to do Phil's tour, I was grateful to be working with CSN.

Flying... My favorite thing!

The summer seemed to be flying by…especially since we had our own plane, a Vickers Viscount, which had the CSN logo painted on it. Back then, people were calling the private planes bands were taking "party planes." After my several crash landing experiences, I wasn't too crazy about flying on a party plane, which referred to the decadence of having our own plane to fly us to gigs. I really didn't like what the name implied. I also don't like small planes because it's always something. One time we couldn't take off from New Jersey because there was smoke coming out from under the floor. Really nice. Made my day.

I did have one amazing and unusual experience that year, that almost made up for flying on a small plane. Almost. One night while we were in the air, I was looking out the window and I saw what looked like blue sparks flying off the wing. I thought, "Oh good. Now what?" Almost like he'd heard my thoughts, the pilot opened the cockpit door and said, "Hey, you guys need to see this." Then, probably for my benefit, the pilot quickly assured us that we weren't in any danger. He was really excited and wanted us to see an extremely rare and beautiful atmospheric phenomenon called 'St. Elmo's fire.' It was BEAUTIFUL.

It looked like one of those plasma balls from a science museum had engulfed the plane. Yellow, blue and red streaks of sparks were being discharged from what looked like a spider web surrounding the plane. What an extraordinary experience! It lasted about a half an hour, and I couldn't take my eyes off it the entire time. It looked like we were traveling through a force field in a science fiction movie. I loved it.

That wonderful experience in the Viscount hadn't won me over, though, and I continued to be relatively freaked out by flying. As I said, it's always something. Shortly after that, we had to fly over some mountains between Seattle, Washington, and San Francisco. The plane had a ceiling of 20,000 feet, which meant that it couldn't fly higher than that because of the air pressure. The Viscount was always bumpy because we had to fly through storms instead of above them. I didn't care how cool it looked with the CSN logo painted on it, I really hated flying on that plane. We weren't flying very high above the snow capped mountain tops and it was a little turbulent, when all of the sudden the pilot, not the copilot, the PILOT, came staggering back the aisle. At first, I thought he was drunk because he was staggering, but he was having an epileptic seizure.

Fortunately, Michael John Bowen, who was Stephen's manager at the time, had been a Vietnam Marine with a lot of medical training. The pilot fell down, so Michael John took care of the situation until the pilot's seizure had stopped. Also fortunately, there was a copilot, who then started flying the plane. Crosby, however, who had very little flying experience at the time but loved to fly, went up toward the front. I immediately knew why he was going up there. Can't you just picture Crosby up there smiling ear to ear while he flew the plane? I said, "NO!" It was all I could get out, "NO!" Then Chocolate said, "I can fly planes." Yeah, right, so I again said, "NO!" I was becoming a man of few words. What a nightmare. They both went up to the cockpit to tell the copilot they could fly the plane and offer their services. I could just picture us flying like those scenes in "It's A Mad, Mad World."

Now, Crosby really can fly small planes, but this was a big four engine Viscount. I'm sure the copilot really welcomed their offers to help fly it…yeah, right…but he was quite capable and we flew the rest of the way without incident. At that point, however, I decided that I was going to ride in the bus with the crew for the rest of the tour. I took a picture of the Viscount after we'd landed that day. It just seemed like if you've escaped death, you should photograph it. After a few extremely turbulent flights, the rest of the band became uncomfortable with the small plane, and we all started flying commercial again.

Speaking of aircraft, I think it was about this time that I found out that David Crosby was in "The Day the Earth Stood Still." Seriously. That's one of my favorite classic 50's science fiction movies about a space craft landing on Earth. David was around the film industry when he was growing up because his Dad, Floyd Crosby, was an academy award winning cinematographer, who worked on a diverse collection of films including, "Tabu," "High Noon," "The Pit and the Pendulum," "The Fall of the House of Usher," and "Beach Blanket Bingo."

David took acting lessons and was a boy at the time "The Day the Earth Stood Still" was filmed. He's in the crowd scene after the space ship has landed on the baseball field, and although I think I know which one he is, especially since I've seen his son Django at that age, he's never told me exactly which one of the extras he is. Over the years, David has occasionally been in films, like "Hook," where, with impeccable casting and very little additional makeup, he superbly played one of the pirates. He's also acted in several spots on Roseanne Barr's TV show. I'm personally glad he decided on a career in music rather than one being a professional pirate...like being in management, for example.

That tour Armando Hurley was David's road manager. Armando was the first African American clown with the Barnum & Bailey Ringling Brothers Circus and we loved hearing stories he'd tell about Clown College and being in the circus. He was a talented singer and wonderful person and I was really knocked out to see him again last year in Australia. He's a born performer and is making his living today singing in a band. Toward the end of the tour, HBO made a DVD called "Daylight Again" of our gig at the Universal Amphitheater

1981 & 1982, Dan Fogelberg & The Bar Codes
Inncocent Age Tour

Dan Fogelberg was probably the kindest and most down to earth person I ever met in the music business. He was a gentleman with a good heart, was always fair, and was an all around great guy. He was everything good he seemed to be. He was talented in art and music, a fantastic cook, loved the outdoors, and lived his dreams. He took the time to enjoy his Mountain Bird Ranch near Pagosa Springs in the Colorado mountains, his home in Santa Fe, and sailing in Maine. He had a dream of someday making a one man sailing trip from Maine to Ireland.

In 1981, Dan released The Innocent Age double album, which contained the hits "Leader of the Band," "Hard to Say," "Run for the Roses", and "Same Old Lang Syne." What a stellar album! He called me and asked me to be part of The Innocent Age tour, playing keyboards, percussion and flute. The band was Dan, Kenny Passarelli, Barry "Byrd" Burton, Russ Kunkel, Mike Hanna, Mark Hallman, and me. I'm really comfortable playing drums for anyone, but I have to tell you, I was pretty intimidated playing keyboards as my main instrument on his tour. I really put in the hours and practiced before I showed up for rehearsal. The music was unbelievably excellent, a masterpiece, and I was really excited about being on this tour playing any instrument.

We started the tour and it was quickly obvious that Dan had a hit album on his hands. The venues were sold out and the audiences loved him. Things were going great. The outdoor sheds always seemed like a perfect match for a Dan Fogelberg concert, so we played at a lot of them. We also played at theaters and auditoriums. We performed in New York City and had a gig the following night at Pine Knob Amphitheater, which is near Detroit, Michigan. We had our own plane for the tour and flew to Detroit after the show. All of us, that is, except for Kenny. Kenny had lived in New York for a while, and he decided to stay to hang out and party with some of his friends and then take a commercial flight to Detroit the day of the show. That's never a good idea, especially if you have one band member traveling alone. Especially if that band member is Kenny.

The next night no one had seen Kenny, and it was 7:50 PM. The show was supposed to start at 8:00 PM. He'd missed the soundcheck and this was way before cell phones and the Internet, so we had no way of getting in contact with him. Although Kenny and I had come close to missing that one show with Barnstorm, I'd never had this happen before. I couldn't believe it. Where was Kenny? Was he really going to miss the show? There was just no way to know.

When we play any show, we need to start as close to the advertised time as possible. The crowd usually gets to the venue early, and they've often waited a long time for the show to start. If it starts late, they start getting very frustrated and impatient. Every band I ever toured with always had the road manager walking around sticking his head in the dressing rooms several times during the last half hour to tell us how many minutes till show time. Then everyone makes their way to the stage so we can gather for a minute and then walk on stage at the same time.

We were running out of time and had to have a bass player, so Dan's guitar tech, Dan Murakami, who played guitar and knew all the songs, was all ready to play in Kenny's place. He was a nervous wreck backstage, waiting to go onstage at a large venue with no rehearsal. I gotta tell you, it was pretty tense back there. We held the show for a while, hoping Kenny would show up, and finally, right before we were gonna walk out on the stage, Kenny arrived. He'd gotten caught in traffic on the way to the airport and had missed his flight, so he'd taken one that landed in Detroit about 7:00 PM. It takes about an hour to get to Pine Knob from the airport with the traffic at that time of day, so he just made it before we walked out on the stage.

Dan and Kenny were friends and Dan didn't fire him, but Kenny had to have some payback. In addition to Dan's calm and refined demeanor, he was also one heck of a funny guy. He immediately came up with an idea to repay Kenny for what he'd put us through. The very next night we were playing at an arena in the Midwest. The venue was an older building with dressing rooms that were like locker rooms, because they were downstairs and had a lot of sinks with the pipes exposed.

After soundcheck, Dan had set it up for the security cops, who were real city cops, to grab Kenny and handcuff him to the sink. I don't know how Dan talked them into doing it, but he was a very persuasive guy. Kenny had to cooperate, because they were real cops with real handcuffs. It had to have provided Kenny with some adrenalin there for a little bit. OK, just the thought of that scene is making me laugh… Kenny handcuffed to the sink, and Dan saying he just didn't want to lose Kenny between soundcheck and the gig. We all had a big laugh

and eventually Dan had them unlock the handcuffs. Kenny was a good sport about it and it allowed all of us to have some fun getting even for what we'd gone through the night before.

That tour we had a show on Halloween, which was always great because we could dress up in costumes right along with the audience. Kenny, of course, dressed as the devil, and I wore Byrd's tee shirt, a tie and a belt with cowboy boots. It looked like I had a mini skirt on. I wore a wolf-man mask, so when I played the flute I had to lift the mask up to play. Byrd was a motorcycle greaser guy who looked like he was from the movie "The Wild Ones," and Dan, of course, was the Phantom of the Opera. The show was Halloween night, so a lot of the crowd also came dressed in costumes. Besides the Phantom, I figured Dan would have been  right at home dressed as a baseball player, too. He loved to have our band and crew guys play other teams on the road, even though we usually didn't win.

That tour, we had a game with a radio station that had a softball team. They had uniforms, regular practices and played games weekly… in short, we were no match for them. The radio station bought us matching shirts to wear so we'd look like a team, too. There's usually nine on a team and they had something like twelve. We had about thirty people, so we had way more players than we needed, and obviously, some of us weren't going to be able to play. I volunteered to sit out the game, but Fogelberg said, "No, no, Joe Bob, you can be the announcer." I said, "Can I do that?" and Dan said, "Sure!"

They had a regular booth with a PA system and their regular announcer from the radio station, but I was the announcer for our team. I named everyone "Sparky" because it's such an old-time baseball name. So we had Sparky Fogelberg, Sparky Kunkel, Sparky Hanna and so on. When they stepped up to bat, I'd say, "Up to bat is Sparky Hanna, with a batting average of nothing." It was going out over the PA, so I really got into it and had a fantastic time announcing. As usual when we played organized teams on the road, they beat the heck out of us. We were starting to figure out that if we went into a city and the team that wanted to play us had uniforms, we're gonna get pounded.

The band spent a huge amount of hours traveling together during The Innocent Age Tour, and we usually found something to do to pass the time. Byrd was a lot of fun on the road, and was the center of a game we used to play called "Stump the Byrd." He knew every signature guitar lick for every song that was ever recorded, so we could say "Please, Please Me," by the Beatles, and he'd play the lick, or we could say "Light My Fire," by The Doors, and he'd play the guitar lick. Then, to make it even harder, we'd say "Inna Gadda Divita," Iron Butterfly, in the key of G, and he'd play it. Byrd was remarkable. We never could stump him. No matter how weird the song or key was, he'd just smile and play it.

This past year, I heard from Byrd's sister that he'd passed away from cancer, just four months after Dan. Byrd was a great musician and person and I'm so grateful that I had the opportunity to tour with him. Byrd's second love was flying, and he finally made enough money to buy a small airplane. I always thought it was funny that someone named "Byrd" loved to fly. He's flying with the angels now.

Looking back, I'm so grateful to have been part of a tour for such a classic and legendary album even though I wasn't as comfortable playing keyboards as I was playing drums. Dan's musical talents were constantly growing, and every tour with him was a unique and exciting experience. Although I was looking forward to getting back to playing my drums, it was an extraordinary tour.

Dan, Byrd & Kenny   *Photo by: Henry Diltz*

CHAPTER SIXTEEN

<u>1983, Ringo Starr, "Old Wave"</u>

Joe Walsh had become friends with Ringo Starr and was producing and playing on an album for him called "Old Wave." Joe called me one night when they were recording at Santa Barbara Sound and said, "Listen, there's a song that Ringo wants me to work on, and you're the only guy I know who I think can pull this off." Ringo had recorded the ballad "As Far As We Can Go," but the music wasn't the quality it needed to be. The piano was bad and the song needed a new track, but the vocal was outstanding, so they wanted to keep it. Ringo's vocal on that song was one of the best vocal performances I'd ever heard him record, and he was really incredibly proud of it.

Joe and Ringo wanted me to play the grand piano part and replace some of the instruments on the track. If this problem would come up today with digital recording and computers, it'd be so easy to do. We would've just cut a new track and inserted the vocal. But that's now, and this was then, so it was very difficult. If you ever listen to the song, you'll hear that it's free form and doesn't have a set tempo, which made it even more difficult.

Joe had paid me quite a compliment when he told Ringo he knew only one guy who could fix the track. Since I wanted to live up to Joe's faith in me, I went and listened to the song. I knew it was really going to be hard, but we could do it. We decided to take the existing track and create a click track using a bass drum and a tambourine, so we could clearly hear the tempo and have something to play to that would hold the track together. That took a while, because the tempo drifted due to the nature of the song. It wasn't easy and took two days. Then I had to learn the song on piano and it wasn't an easy song, because there were times when the piano took the lead and other times it would lay back.

We pulled it off and Ringo was really happy. When he thanked me, Ringo had this big smile on his face, and said that it was the best vocal he'd ever done and that I'd made it possible for it to be on his record. I really don't think I was the only person who could have fixed it, and I certainly couldn't have done it without Joe, but I love Ringo and I was really glad that I was able to do it for him.

1983, Joe Walsh, "You Bought It, You Name It"

The summer of 1982 I was out with the Crosby, Stills and Nash Daylight Again Tour. I got a phone call from Joe Walsh and he wanted to know what my schedule looked like, because he wanted to do another solo album. I told him I was done at the end of August, and I could work with him after that. Joe called me back again around the end of the tour and we talked about what we were going to do.

Now, I have to give you some background information. In 1968, the group The Band recorded an album called, "Music from Big Pink." Big Pink was a big pink house where they recorded the album. At the time, this was a totally unconventional way to record, since everyone made albums in recording studios, and almost no one had professional level recording studios in their homes. Years ago when I first started working with Joe Walsh, he always loved the concept and idea of that style of recording...hence, "Theme from Boat Weirdos." I totally got what he was into. I understood...hence, "Theme from Cabin Weirdos." Bill Szymczyk, who was going to produce the album also understood and was fully into the concept.

If we were in a remote area recording, our creativity level changed. It excelled, amplified, and ideas were instigated and inspired by our surroundings. If you listen to "Theme from Boat Weirdos," the music is beautiful… it flows like a wave. When Joe called me to do his album, he said we were going to do this one a little differently, because we weren't going to have a keyboard player. If we needed keyboard parts, Joe

Joe, Waddy, Me & Chocolate

or I was going to play them. Instead, we were going to take an extra guitar player.

Joe decided the band was going to be Waddy Wachtel on guitar, Chocolate on bass, Joe and me. That makes a fantastic rock & roll band, 'cause Waddy brings the whole rebel, 60's, Rolling Stones rock & roll energy to a band. Waddy's a really famous guitarist who's played with just about everybody. He's well known for that great guitar lick he played in Stevie Nick's song, "Stand Back." As a side note, his brother, Jimmy, is the artist who's done a lot of great album cover designs, including several of Joe Walsh's albums and also my solo album, Plantation Harbor.

The next thing Joe said was that he had the idea to load the equipment onto the ferry that travels the twenty-six mile ocean trip from Long Beach to Catalina Island and record in the

Chocolate, Joe, Bill & Me

huge round landmark ballroom that's on the island. So, that October, we loaded the gear, brought the Record Plant truck from L.A., and headed for the island. The next day we set up in the round room above the ballroom and recorded the album using the recording truck, which

was parked outside. Bill Szymczyk and Jim Nipar were in the truck and had cables and wires running down the side of the building. We started every day around 2:00 in the afternoon and worked till about 7:00 PM, took a break for dinner, and went back to record until 10:00 or 11:00 PM.

Being on Catalina Island is something else. The sky is pitch black with a million stars at night. Because it's west of LA, the island air is clear and clean and smells like the ocean. It's just absolutely beautiful. We walked or rode on four electric golf carts, and immediately started

racing and playing chicken.   There were basically four things to do on the island besides recording…boating, fishing, eating and drinking. We went to the same bar to eat every night and became accepted as regulars after two or three days.

We recorded Joe's album "You Bought It, You Name It," there in the ballroom on Catalina Island. To continue our theme, we recorded "Theme from Island Weirdos." We used the real piano that belonged to the ballroom. Bill wanted to create the vibe and sound of the ballroom, so we set up on the stage and Bill put a couple Neumann mics out on the dance floor for room sound. There was something different and very special about it being recorded there. Really cool. Not so polished. Really human and alive.

Joe and Bill's plan was to only record tracks there and bring them back to Santa Barbara Sound, because with the truck downstairs there was no good scenario to record overdubs. The people who ran the ballroom let us have the building for two weeks for free, as long as we did a ninety minute concert and gave the money to the school system. We said, "Done." We had a great time doing the show and raised about $12,000 – $14,000 for their school.

What was really exciting was when we went back to Santa Barbara, took a few days off and then went into the studio and hit "play." We suddenly realized just how great an idea this had been and how fantastic it sounded. We did overdubs and a couple of new tracks. Joe and Bill were thrilled. We cut "I Can Play That Rock & Roll" on the island, and performed it on SCTV the following January while we were promoting the album.

We worked for about two weeks at Santa Barbara Sound and finished the project. The last night of recording, we worked till about 2:00 or 3:00 in the morning and I had 9:00 AM flight home from L.A. I was in Santa Barbara, which is about one hundred miles from the L.A. airport, I had a rental car to turn in, and my stuff was still at the hotel. I backtracked and figured I'd need to get to the airport at 7:30 AM…it's a two hour drive...so I needed to leave about 4:30 AM. I was used to staying up late, so I had a cup of coffee and left studio at about 3:30 AM, picked up my bags at the hotel, and was on road by 4:30 AM. I was really tired. I couldn't miss my flight, because I didn't want to have to stay up until the next one.

I arrived at the airport at 7:45 AM. In 1982 there wasn't the same amount of security as we have today, so there was no problem. I got my ticket and called Susie, told her I was at the L.A. airport, and that I'd see her in a few hours at the airport when she picked me up in Cleveland. Ticket in hand, I sat down at the gate…we were boarding in twenty minutes.

I fell totally, deeply asleep sitting at the gate, holding my ticket in my hand. I must have sat there sleeping for about four hours and never dropped the ticket. I mean, I was OUT. I woke up to the announcement that we were boarding. "Oh," I thought, "I nodded off for a second." I gave them my ticket and boarded the plane. I sat down in my seat, put my seat belt on, the plane took off, and I fell asleep again. I woke up to the stewardess's voice, "Sir, please put your seat back up, we're landing." "Oh boy, I'm home! Well, that flight went really fast," I thought.

I looked out the window. Hey, where's Lake Erie? I saw desert. What happened to Cleveland? Had something gone wrong with the plane and were we making an emergency landing? Where were we? Then the stewardess continued that we were landing in Phoenix. I was on wrong plane. The flight I wanted left at 9:00 AM…it was now 2:00 PM. Susie was at airport in Cleveland, along with my suitcase, which was going around and around on the luggage carousel. This was well before cell phones, so I couldn't call and have Susie paged until I landed in Phoenix. Then I had to buy my own full fare ticket home, since I was the one who'd messed up the flight.

For this to happen, two major things had to go wrong, besides staying up all night before my flight. First, the woman who took the ticket when I boarded the plane didn't look at it...it said Cleveland, not Phoenix. Secondly, the seat that I sat in on the flight to Phoenix wasn't reserved for anyone else, or they would have noticed at the gate in L.A. Then the worst thing was when I had to tell Joe and Bill what had happened. I think they hurt themselves laughing.

1983, John Candy, Second City TV

We had gone to Catalina Island and Santa Barbara Sound to make the Joe Walsh album "You Bought It, You Name It," in the fall of 1982. One of the singles and an MTV video was "I Can Play That Rock & Roll." So, to promote the album, in January of 1983, we went to Toronto, Canada, to do Second City TV. The band was Joe Walsh, Chocolate, Waddy Wachtel, and me. The cast on the program also had Eugene Levy, Martin Short, Joe Flaherty, Andrea Martin, and a lot of people who eventually went to Saturday Night Live.

John Candy's reoccurring bit as Gil Fischer called "The Fishin' Musician," from The Scuttlebutt Lodge, was a regular spot on the show. SCTV used this bit as a platform to have rock & roll acts on the show each week. John Candy was a real pleasure to work with...a real sweetheart...the nicest guy in the world. He was really into what he was doing and wanted to do a great bit with us. The plot of the script always was that the guest musicians played practical jokes on John Candy's character, Gil.

We flew into Toronto and the first night had dinner John Candy, Eugene Levy and a couple of the guys, and we kinda went over what we were going to do for the show. The following day we got up and went to the studio for a tour. Then we all jumped into vans and went out to the Scuttlebutt Lodge, which I believe SCTV owned. It was an actual outdoorsman's lodge way out in the country. Inside the building were enormous wooden beams showing and a fireplace made out of huge stones. The rooms had antlers and mounted fish hanging on the walls, and the whole fantastic place sat on about thirty acres of hilly land covered with Canadian forests.

We had lunch and again went over what we were supposed to do. The plot was that we were taking John Candy, as Gil Fischer, out into the woods on a "snipe" hunt. Of course, there's no such thing as a snipe. After we got him out into the woods on our hunt, we peeled off one at a time and went back to the lodge, leaving him alone in the woods all night, waiting to shoot a snipe which never appeared. When John finally came back to the lodge, he realized we had just fooled with him when he found us all sitting around the lodge cleaning our guns, with all this money on the table we were supposed to have bet on whether we could fool him.

Now remember, this was January in Canada. It was winter and it was FREEZING. The outdoor footage for the bit was actually shot outdoors that night and it was probably ten degrees in the woods. We were

all wearing outdoor hunting and fishing outfits from the wardrobe room. We could actually pick out and wear anything we wanted for the bit, and they had a ton of different things we could wear. I wore a hunter's brown and red flannel shirt and a brown hunting vest. Of course, Joe, being Joe, picked out his clothes to wear, and then he just kept putting things on…and piled on as much stuff as he could possibly wear. That's why he ended up with a duck on his head, a scuba diving mask, nose glasses, and a snorkel. He'd have probably worn fins if they'd had them.

They shot way more footage outside in the woods than they showed in the bit. For the one minute they used, they shot several angles of each of us  individually, and then of all of us in a group walking through the woods or sneaking off. They got close-ups and long shots and took footage of the owl, which was stuffed and wired up in the tree. We ended up being out there for at least an hour.

After we taped, we warmed up in front of the big fire they'd built in the fireplace and then had a barbequed dinner at the lodge. Then we went back to the hotel, went to bed, and got up the next morning around eight o'clock. We ate  breakfast and then went to the SCTV studio. The first thing we did was shoot the footage of us playing "I Can Play That Rock & Roll." It's pretty rough to play and sing at 9:30 in the morning, but Joe did a great job and we all looked like we were pretty awake. Then they sat us around in a circle with a microphone in the center, and played the edited footage they'd shot at the Scuttlebutt Lodge with no sound on it.

Chocolate

John Candy explained that we were doing the commentary or "voice over" on the footage. That was really kinda cool, because John wanted everyone to participate and say whatever we felt like saying while we were watching it. It was like if you were sitting around with your family watching old silent eight millimeter home movies, and everybody was talking about it and making comments, like, "Oh, I remember that," and everyone would laugh. He was trying to create the scenario so the dialog sounded real and natural.

He was a really great coach, which we needed because this was unfamiliar ground for us. He did comedy for a living and we were just musicians, so he tried to help the dialogue sound as though it were unrehearsed. He and Eugene Levy were very personable and nice to us, and everyone was incredibly helpful. What a team of people they had making those programs! There was absolutely no audience, just the lighting and sound guys and the crew when we shot the bit, but John made it appear that we were in front of a huge live audience. They used sound effects and canned laughter, which somehow made it even funnier to us. I loved the stuffed dog that he kept talking to like it was real throughout the bit.

When we shot the scene where we talked to John in front of the fireplace, they had told Joe to sit nearest to John, since he had the most lines. I sat up on the picnic table top and the other guys sat on the bench, so we would be closer together than normal without looking crowded. That part was pretty much improv…and John was really good at that. He set up scenarios to help us be funny during that part of the taping. We gave him a present, which was a tee shirt Joe had made up that read, "Joe, Joe and the Chocolate Waddy," whatever that meant, which was the joke name of our band at the time. It was such a treat to be on that show. If you liked Saturday Night Live, you'd also like that show.

John was an extremely funny person, and I was really sad when he passed away. He loved rock & roll music. I was so glad when I found out they'd released all the old SCTV shows, because I really wanted to have our episode on DVD. I watched it recently, and it really took me back to taping the show twenty-five years ago.

The next day Joe Walsh and I proceeded to fly to L.A. I stayed in a hotel for a few days while Joe went back home. Then Joe went over to the Channel Islands for the christening of his baby daughter, Lucy. I had the honor of being invited to be her godfather, so Joe arranged for me to be picked up at the hotel and taken to the Oxnard Airport to fly to the islands a few days later.

The Channel Islands are beautiful mountainous islands that you can see from the beaches at Oxnard, California. They're not very far off the coast, and I thought, "Oh, cool. We're going to fly over to The Channel Islands." I got into this little piper cub airplane, which I wasn't crazy about, but it was a beautiful day. We took off and flew probably no more than fifteen minutes. We were getting ready to land, and I said to the pilot, "Wow, this looks pretty desolate, like an uninhabited island. Do they have an airport here?" The pilot said, "Well, no." NO? So I said, "Wait a minute, where are we gonna land?" and he said, "Well, we've gotta circle here a couple more times and scare the cows away, and then we're gonna land in the cow pasture." I thought to myself, "Thanks, Joe."

We did a few fly-bys, and I'm talking about twenty feet off the ground, to scare the cows out of the part of the pasture where we were going to land. I thought it was going to be a really tense landing, but believe it or not, the plane had big spongy tires and although the landing was a little bumpy, it wasn't too bad. Then the pilot taxied down to the end of the field, where Joe had a guy in a Jeep pick me up.

We had dinner the first night and stayed in a beautiful guest house, and then the next day we had the christening in a picturesque old chapel that could seat about twelve people, although there were only about five or six people there. We had dinner again that night, and the next day the plane came back for me. I got on, we taxied up and down the field once to scare off the cows again, and

Lucy Walsh & Me

then we took off and flew back to Oxnard…and then I flew home. I wasn't going to be home for long, and was looking forward to touring with Joe that summer.

US Festival 1983

I was in L.A. to rehearse for the summer Joe Walsh tour where we would be opening up the show for Stevie Nicks. Our first gig was the US Festival. What a way to start out the summer! Anytime in rock & roll you have the word "festival" connected to an event, there are all kinds of bad connotations and elements that go along with that. When I hear the word "festival," I think of WAY too many people backstage, too many bands, too much equipment, no room to do anything, horrible dressing rooms, bad food, muddy conditions, bad weather, and the impossibility of having any guests. The promoter usually sets up this gigantic stage in the middle of a field somewhere and then brings in the masses. The security is usually overkill, there's overheating, people passed out, drunk or high, crowds crushing, and on and on. It's always something, because there are so many people. These, however, are the little things. The worst thing is running overtime.

When we're given a slot of time to perform and the first band runs over or starts late, the situation just snowballs. If we're a headlining band that's on later in the day, which we usually were, the festival can be running an hour and a half late by the time we'd play…or worse. So, we might have been there all day and then have to wait an additional hour and a half to play…and then they might tell us that we have to cut our set short. But, when I'm up on the stage and I look out and see 250,000 people there, it's suddenly all better.

The gig itself was fantastic. We drove from L.A. down to Glen Helen Park in San Bernadino County on Sunday, May 30th, which was Memorial Day weekend. It was the third day of a four day festival. We were dropped off at a hotel where we had day rooms and a little time to relax. Then the road manager called and said, "Time to go, guys." I was thinking we were going out in the parking lot to get in vans or limos or something, since we were only about 15 miles from the gig. Remember, there were about 250,000 people…a quarter of a million…that's a LOT of people. Woodstock had half a million. We were leaving about three hours before we were supposed to start. It all sounded good to me.

We were standing to the side of the parking lot when someone came over and said, "Step back, the helicopters are landing." All I could do was flash back to Glenn Frey in the helicopter wanting to open the door while we were in flight, and me saying, "Don't touch anything." Dave Reynolds, Snake, the pilot from Vietnam was with us, so I said, "Please don't fly the helicopter again!" We got in the four helicopters and flew towards the place, but we flew in on the side, and we could look down and see where we were going to play…it was really cool… we could see what looked like an ocean of people. There was an enormous stage with a roof on it, and behind that, the backstage area filled with all the Winnebagos for dressing rooms.

The promoter had set up a landing area in the field beside the stage, so it was a short walk to the backstage. Our scheduled slot was supposed to be at 5:00 PM. The lineup of stars for the festival was amazing. The Pretenders played right before us, and Stevie Nicks played right after us. The crowd was so huge that most of the people were really far from the stage, and the performers must have looked like they were an inch tall, if that. We didn't know they were going to be filming, but there were cameras taking shots of the bands that were playing, and they projected us up on the gigantic screens on either side of the stage so everybody could see us.

The footage they were taking for the big screens eventually turned into a DVD. The festival had so many acts, that I saw the DVD and a twelve CD box set being sold on the Internet. Twelve. I heard that the promoter lost millions of dollars, by the way, and I think it was the last festival he promoted. The backstage area was really run well, though, and we really got off playing for such a huge crowd. It turned out to be a fantastic experience!

1983 Joe Walsh / Stevie Nicks Tour

The US Festival launched our tour that summer opening shows for Stevie Nicks. This was the first tour I'd ever played where one of the bands had such an entourage of people...there were hair, makeup and wardrobe staff along, plus girl back up singers and dancers on the stage. Stevie was coming off a huge success with "Rumors" and was an enormous draw, so we played for large crowds every night. She was such a pro, great to work with, and really nice to us.

We thought Stevie and the girls she had with her on the road were up partying every night, because we'd hear all this noise and music coming from Stevie's suite till about 6:00 in the morning. It was like disco music or something and we thought these girls were absolute party monsters. Actually, Stevie was a night owl, so she had the girls who sang and danced in her show over in her room every night doing aerobics to music. We heard that they'd do aerobics and then go out for breakfast and get pancakes, but that might have just been a rumor. I've never been in a band that the band guys did aerobics at the hotel after the show, but it's a really hilarious thought.

One of the really great things about that tour was that my buddy, Liberty DeVito, played drums for Stevie's band. I'd met Liberty back in 1979 when we all went to Cuba for Havana Jam. He was Billy Joel's drummer for years and years, but Billy Joel wasn't touring this particular summer. That was great, because Liberty is my long time Italian friend and it was fantastic touring with him that summer.

One of the shows was at Meriweather Post in Columbia, Maryland, and we stayed at The Sheraton, with a night off. The guys from both bands went out to eat dinner and were hanging out together at a club. The club's house band was off that night, so we asked the bartender if we could play. Yeah, what do musicians do on a night off? Play music! He said we'd have to get permission from the guys who owned the equipment. We said that we'd already called them and they said, "Yeah, it's OK." The bartender said, "OK, great." I don't think he could've possibly believed us, but I'm sure he recognized Joe Walsh and I think he really wanted us to play.

The only problem was that all the microphones and cabling we needed were in a locked box. We didn't have sticks, guitar strings...nothing with us, but of course, we weren't going to let that stop us. We called Snake, because when he was in the military he was trained to pick locks and crack safes. He was the best at it...there wasn't a lock he couldn't pick. He was a really honest guy, though, so we told him that the bartender said we could play, but he needed Snake to open the box for us.

In less than a minute, the box was open and he started pulling out mics and setting up, because he was our PA guy. We played for about two hours and had a ball. We didn't play any Joe Walsh material, but played songs like "Midnight Hour," "Twist & Shout," "Wolley Bully," and "You Can't Do That"…if even half of the guys knew it, we played it. We even took requests.

Well, it's not hard to recognize Joe Walsh, so word got out that Joe and the band were playing in the club, and lots of people started showing up. It reminded me of the Kent days when Jimmy Page and Robert Plant came down and played at JB's. By the time we were done playing that night, the place was packed and the bartender had sold an ocean of beer. One of our tour guys left some money for the other band for the drum sticks we broke and the heads we used, because we didn't want to screw over fellow musicians.

Sometimes those kinds of situations are more fun than a real gig, because we were just fooling around with no pressure. The crowd can always tell when you're having fun and when you're not, and we were having fun! Night after night, concerts on a tour become a blur. It's very rare when you remember something unusual about a show. But nights like that I can remember in great detail. Once in a while, I run into someone who was on that tour, and they mention that night and we laugh about it.

CHAPTER SEVENTEEN

<u>1984, Dan Fogelberg, "Windows and Walls"</u>

I went to Caribou Ranch to cut the song "Language of Love" for Dan's album. I hadn't been up there for a long time, and it was really great to be back there to record. The only thing that had changed from the early days was that they'd added a bunch more cabins. My cabin happened to be about one hundred yards away, while Kenny Passarelli's was right across the dirt road from the studio. It had snowed and we saw bear tracks. Somebody at the studio mentioned that they'd seen a couple of black bears, which was normal up there. That wasn't normal for me.

About midnight we were done recording. I got as far as Kenny's cabin and slept on the couch...I didn't have to think twice about it...I wasn't about to walk another hundred yards alone at night in the mountains with bears around. Kenny was making fun of me, but I didn't see him going up to my cabin! The next morning I went through the snow up to my cabin, and I realized I'd done the right thing. There were fresh tracks in the snow, going right up to my front door, and they weren't from a pizza delivery guy. I'd had visitors. I love feeding animals, but I'm not into feeding them me.

Since "Language Of Love" was the hit from the album, Dan, Mike Hanna, Kenny and I recorded a video for it in L.A. These were the early days of music videos. The director came out to talk to Dan and said he envisioned the music video to be all white, as he felt love was pure and so the white should symbolize the purity of love. He got us a white grand piano, white drums with white heads, white guitars and told us we had to wear white clothes and shoes. I went out and bought a white jumpsuit and was getting worried that he was going to ask us to wear white bucks.

We wore white sneakers instead, and Dan wore what looked like white boots. Dan, being the star, got to wear blue jeans with his white dinner jacket. The floor and walls were also white…so white and bright that we sometimes disappear into the background during the video. You can see the video on You Tube…but wear sunglasses… it's really white.

1984, Dan Fogelberg, Tour Of America

We were at rehearsal in Boulder, Colorado, working out some of the new material for Dan Fogelberg's Tour of America. The band was Dan, Russ Kunkel on drums, Mike Hanna on piano, Kenny Passarelli on bass, Barry "Byrd" Burton on lead guitar, Mark Hallman on rhythm guitar and Dave Tolegian on horns. I was playing keyboards, flute and percussion. It was during our rehearsal for the Tour of America that I made the now infamous drum machine joke. Here's some background. In the early 1980's drum machines were invented and became popular in rock & roll music, and it seemed like they were suddenly on every song. I really hated the concept. They were putting drummers out of work and I wasn't sure how far the trend was going to go. There was speculation that all musical parts to a song could be triggered and played and musicians would become unnecessary.

The good thing was that there was a problem with that…electronic equipment wasn't always dependable. It could short out if anything was spilled on it, or malfunction if it was jiggled or dropped. That was a real possibility with all the rough treatment equipment goes through during traveling, set up, and tear down on the road. Road equipment has to be tough. You can't have an essential sound suddenly be unavailable during a gig. This made perfect sense to me, but drum machines were selling like crazy. Was this trend of electronic music going to grow and be the end of shows with live musicians?

There was a song we were going to do that had both flute and percussion on it, but the flute was more important, so I thought I should play that. Then Dan said why not get a drum machine to do the percussion part so I could play the flute, and we'd have both parts of the song covered. I was stunned. Dan Fogelberg, Mr. Natural, wanting to use a drum machine for his tour? When would this madness end?

I said, "Dan, you don't want to use a drum machine. You can't really depend on 'em. You need a person. Heck, you can pour a beer on me and I'll still play." Everyone really thought that was funny. It became the tour saying. Dan made an acoustic guitar reference to it as to why he liked playing acoustic guitar as opposed to electric. "Pour a beer on me and I'll still play." It got all around, because all musicians were anti drum machines. I heard from musicians from all over the country. They loved it. It expressed our musician value and probably our fears about being replaced by electronic machines. Russ Kunkel, being a fellow drummer, enjoyed it so much that he quoted me in David Crosby's book, "Since Then." I still feel the same about drum machines, but now I've included computers and hard drives as well...you can pour a beer on me, and I'll still play!

That summer, we played at Blossom Music Center in northeastern Ohio. It's a beautiful venue and I usually had friends and family come to the show, even my "Nana." That summer when we played there, I asked Dan if he'd be willing to do a TV interview with a close friend of Susie's. The friend was Suzie Ward Thomas, or "Sailin' Sooz,"

Nana Spataro rocks out at Blossom

who had a weekday children's TV show called The Funtimes Club, which was broadcast locally on WOAC channel 67. Sailin' Sooz had Susie do a weekly art spot on her show, and had even conned, I mean, *convinced* me, to appear on her show a couple of times teaching children about drums. Dan said, "Sure." Dan didn't ask for any details at the time, so I'm guessing he probably thought it was an interview with one of the network channels out of Cleveland.

Sailin' Sooz, who was about 8 months pregnant at the time and wore a sailor dress, showed up at Blossom with her camera crew which included her husband, Jim. They put some chairs for the interview out on the lawn backstage and set up the cameras. Dan came into the dressing room and said, "Hey, Joe Bob, there's a girl in a sailor suit out there to interview me. What the heck's goin' on?"

Fortunately for me and my job, Sailin' Sooz' had a degree in

television broadcasting and did an excellent job interviewing the band one person at a time. She asked Dan questions that children would be interested in, like, "Did you practice playing your guitar between your lessons?" When she asked him about his hobbies, he said he loved photography and liked to take pictures of things that didn't look like the original object. He liked to take extreme close-ups, and try different lighting or unusual angles of his subjects. No matter what he did, he was always thinking creatively.

Photo: Courtesy of Paul Neves

I talked to her recently when she lent me the video of the interview, and she said that what impressed her most about Dan was that when the interview was over, he stayed and talked to her and the crew for another ten minutes. We had a show to do. He could have just gone back inside, and was wonderful about doing an interview for a local children's TV show. She said what all of us who knew him already

Photo: Courtesy of Paul Neves

knew, that he was such a gentleman, so friendly, intelligent, kind and down to earth. At the time, I thought I was doing Suzie a favor, but Dan doing that interview was another great memory I have, that to me illustrates what kind of person he was.

<u>1985, Dan Fogelberg, Frankie and the Aliens Tour</u>

For normal tours, Dan's fans wanted to hear his hits, and he loved playing them, but Dan idolized Eric Clapton and BB King and loved the blues. One of his favorite guitars was a black Strat, just like Clapton's. So, in 1985, Dan called me and said he wanted to go out and play some gigs as a blues band, but he said he didn't want his name involved, because he wasn't going to play any Dan Fogelberg music. We were gonna play bars in and around the Colorado mountains. It was something he had always wanted to do.

Dan had two jokes that he loved about playing the blues, and I heard him repeat them many times during our tour that year. One was, "How do you make a million dollars with a blues album? Start with two million." The other was, "What's the difference between a blues artist and a jazz artist? The blues artist knows three chords and plays for millions of people, and the jazz artist knows millions of chords and plays for three people."

The band for this tour was Dan, Rick Rosas on bass, Paul Harris on piano, two fantastic players on harp and guitar whose names escape me, and me on drums. We all met up at Dan's ranch for rehearsal and we came up with a name for the band "Frankie and the Aliens." Perfect. We rehearsed in

the barn for a week and the last night we played our show for the ranch hands and the animals. We got a thumbs and hooves up.

The first gig was a dive in Pagosa Springs, Colorado, which was a small town forty minutes from Dan's ranch. During set up, a guy at the bar with a 30 caliber Winchester rifle yelled over to us, "Y'all better be good!" This tour was going to be interesting. The show was a ton of fun and we got to play a lot of great old blues standards. Dan had a blast. The bar was a small place, so we even took requests. We played everything from dives to saloons to old fashioned dance halls

on the tour. Maybe the most exciting part of the entire tour was going over Wolfe Pass in a full sized tour bus. Occasionally during that experience, we just closed our eyes.

The only time we left Colorado was to play a small rock & roll club in Santa Fe. I walked around downtown and I noticed that everybody had their weekend art exhibit out

on the street. The subject matter varied from realistic to abstract. So, hey, I've done art before. I'm a veteran cut out man artist. I can do that! I thought I could make some extra money like the other artists.

Hey, you should have seen the prices on some of that art work…a picture of nothing, and it would be $2,000. I was inspired.

I made little pencil drawings on small pieces of hotel stationary and put them on a piece of cardboard. OK, clearly, I have too much spare time on the road. I wanted to look the part, and I remember trying to find a scarf and beret, but I was unsuccessful. I needed a more dramatic name, so I considered both "Van Joe" and "Jobaub," and settled on "Jobaub" for my "Southwestern Series" drawings. I went outside in front of the hotel where there was a wall beside the sidewalk. Several other artists had leaned their art for sale up along the wall, so I leaned mine up right along with the others, and waited to make a sale. I think I was ahead of my time, for the other artists and shoppers didn't seem to appreciate my advanced vision of art.

My pencil stick figures on pieces of paper were like hearts with arms and legs, running down the beach with a spear, and I called that piece "Heart Attack", $250.00. Hey, it's an original drawing, not a print. I have one called "Wrist Band" which was a picture of

"Heart Attack" by Jobaub

a rock band drawn on a guy's wrist. People were coming along and looking at them and were getting all offended. They were appalled. I have to laugh, I really enjoyed doing that.

Of course, Fogelberg eventually came by, and he was embarrassed. He said, "Joe Bob, what are you doing out here?" I looked as sincere as possible, and trying to keep a straight face, I explained, "Hey, I'm just trying to make a living selling my art work." He came over and looked at my drawings, and, now remember, he lived there in Santa Fe sometimes, and he said, "Don't tell anyone you play with me!" It was especially funny because Dan was "The Renaissance Man" and actually did do artwork and paint besides his beautiful music and lyrics. I have all the original artwork I had for sale that day. For some reason, people looked but they didn't buy. Like I said, I'm just ahead of my time.

Our last gig of that tour was at a big place in Denver. Tickets for "Frankie and the Aliens," an unknown blues band, weren't selling well. Management let it leak that Frankie was, in fact, Dan. The place was packed. We had a few fans shout requests for Dan's hits, but in general, we felt that everybody enjoyed seeing that side of Dan. Besides being a great song writer, they were able to see him as a great guitar player. Frankie felt that this band had made it. It was a great way to end the tour.

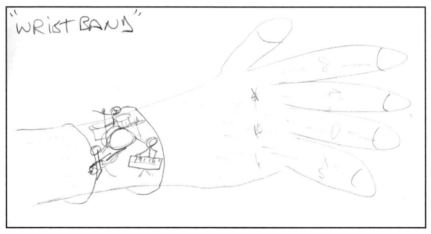

"Wrist Band" by Jobaub

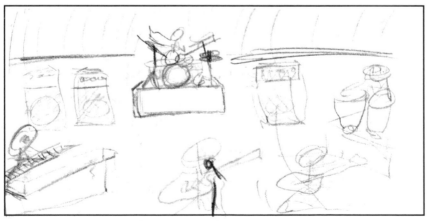

"Rock Group" by Jobaub

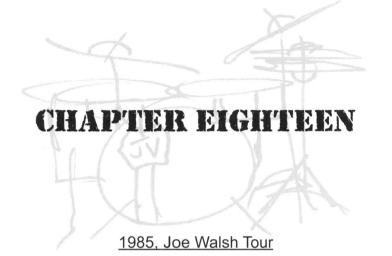

CHAPTER EIGHTEEN

1985, Joe Walsh Tour

It was around 1985 during a Joe Walsh tour that I said something which we drove into the ground for years. A really good friend of mine, J. D. Souther, was out on tour with us. J.D. is an incredible writer and wrote so many hits and memorable songs that the list would be as long as your arm. He really has a way with lyrics and melodies and wrote several of the songs the Eagles perform. He dabbles in every instrument from guitar to drums, and plays all of them well.

Like I've said, I'm one hundred per cent Italian and my heritage runs deep. J.D. and I were screwing around at the hotel before soundcheck one day, talking like old Italian guys speaking broken English. He thought that it was hilarious that we had made Glenn Frey into an Italian...and Glenn did make a fantastic Italian, I might add. J.D. said, "Hey, can I be Italian?" I said, "Well sure. The first thing you have to learn is how to say, "How ya' doin'?"
This is a direct result of my Italian upbringing...some of the first things I learned how to say were, "Ma-ma, Da-da, and how ya' doin'?"

He tried it and said, "Hey, how are you doing?" I said, "Not quite. It's like it's all one word, and you never put the "g" on the words. It's 'how ya' doin'?" J.D. practiced. I was an inspiring motivational coach and speech therapist...sort of like the professor in an Italian version of "My Fair Lady." I said it, he said it, I said it, he said it...eventually he mastered it...the face, the hands, the voice, the attitude. "How ya' doin'?"

J.D. was anxious to exercise his new speech skills and Italian-ness. When we got in the elevator, he was continuing to practice...it was, "How ya' doin'?" to everybody. "How ya' doin'?" in the elevator. "How ya' doin'?" in the lobby. We made our way to the street and climbed into the band van, where Joe was riding shotgun. J.D. looked at Joe and with an impeccable Italian inflection, said, "Hey, how ya' doin'?" I was so proud. He had learned so well. Joe said, "Heh?" and so J.D. said it again, "How ya' doin'?"

Walsh immediately wanted to play along and said, "I'm doin'. How ya doin'?" It was like with Mikey and the cereal. He liked it. A lot. Then Joe and the entire band started saying it. Joe was a natural and immediately got the inflection and accent perfectly. So, for the rest

of the tour...and his life...for Joe it was, "How ya doin'?" We all said it all the time. At the shows, on the radio, in interviews, on bumper stickers, to the crowd at shows, to the fans, it was "How ya' doin'?" Joe thought it was so funny that he continued saying it all these years and he eventually had it trade marked. It's even on his guitar picks. It's always the first thing out of his mouth. I'm-a so proud!

1986, Joe Walsh Kent Homecoming

Joe was invited back to Kent to play for Homecoming in 1986. We played a full show in the gymnasium at Kent State University's main campus. The band was Joe, Rick Rosas, a keyboard player, and me. Since Joe and I had played there in the late 1960's when we were just starting out, Kent held a lot of memories. Not all of them were good, but it was really fun to be back playing a gig.

The thing was, we had to rent gear for the show from a local music store. They didn't have a good drum set, and my gear was out west in the CSN locker, so we borrowed a beautiful drum set from a local drummer for the show. I could tell he really loved his kit. They were a set of vintage 1960 gold sparkle Gretsch drums. I understood that kind of love. When I got there and saw the drums I was going to play, I said, "All RIGHT!" They sounded fantastic. I was really careful to take good care of his kit while I was playing the show and I treated them exactly like I'd treat my own drums.

At the end of the show, we were playing "Rocky Mountain Way." To end the song, Joe always played one big chord, then another, and it got faster and faster....he'd jump up and down...faster, faster, faster...but that night, Joe turned around to me and yelled, "TRASH 'EM!" I yelled back, "NO!" I couldn't do that to another drummer's beautiful kit. It was a horrible moment. Joe kept yelling, "TRASH 'EM! TRASH 'EM!" I wouldn't do it. I was on a three foot drum riser, so Joe grabbed the front of the drum set and pulled them forward and down. I couldn't believe he did it. The kit went crashing down onto the stage with a huge amount of noise. I was in shock. Joe was laughing. I thought the poor guy who owned the set, who was standing on the side of the stage, was going to die right then and there. His beautiful vintage drums were in a pile of wreckage on the stage. I felt terrible about it. Joe kept laughing. The crowd loved it. Hey, rock 'n roll!

Unbelievably, because the stage was carpeted, there was no damage to the set except for a wee little scratch on the bottom of the bass drum that you'd never see. I was so relieved! A lesson to be learned here. Don't lend your equipment to a rock & roll band.

1987, Joe Walsh, "Got Any Gum?"

I was playing with CSN and didn't have any breaks to record with Joe Walsh, so although I have a couple of songs on Joe's album "Got Any Gum," I didn't play on it. I went over to Joe's apartment one night and Joe, Rick Rosas and I started listening to some songs for Joe's next album. We'd already done the song, "Fun," and we came up with the song "Got Any Gum," and "Malibu." That's when I got Rick Rosas and Joe working together. Who knew how fantastically well these two nuts were going to get along? After that, "Rick The Bass Player's" career grew to include playing not only with Joe for decades, but also with Neil Young and Crosby, Stills, Nash and Young.

1987, The Buffalo Springfield Reunion

Whenever a band has become legendary, fans always hold out the hope that someday there'll be a reunion. I was at Stephen's home in L.A. when I had the tremendous opportunity of witnessing a Buffalo Springfield reunion, even though it was just for an evening. All the original members were there…Stephen Stills, Neil Young, Richie Furay, Bruce Palmer and drummer Dewey Martin. They were actually talking about doing a reunion tour. I was playing keyboards for them and couldn't believe it. I was joking around, and I said in my best geeky sounding voice, "Hey, I'm in The Buffalo Springfield!" Stephen and Neil turned around and, still playing, said simultaneously, "Ah, no you're not." I shot back, "I am for tonight!" It would have been a fantastic tour, and I've never given up hope that it might happen some day.

Me, Doug Breidenbach & Neil Young

1987, Crosby, Stills & Nash Tour

The band that year was David Crosby, Stephen Stills, Graham Nash, Mike Finnigan on keyboards, Bob Glaub on bass, Joe Lala on percussion, and me on drums. In May of that year, David Crosby and Jan Dance got married in a double ceremony with already married Graham and Susan Nash. It was a beautiful wedding and eventually ended up with everyone in the wedding party jumping into the pool with their clothes on. Graham looked elegant, Susan and Jan looked beautiful and even Crosby cleaned up pretty good. We were all in a positive and enthusiastic frame of mind...it was like the sun had come out after a storm.

Everything on the tour that year was going great, but sometimes, the thing that nightmares are made of, suddenly happens. We were staying at The Hyatt in Kansas City. We were all up in our rooms and Graham must have just finished taking a shower after dinner. I think he was putting his room service tray out into the hallway or he was getting a paper or something. Anyway, he was completely naked, and walked out into the hall for just a second, when the door to his room closed and locked behind him. Hearing that door click shut must have been a horrible moment for Graham. I'm sure he must have uttered his favorite expletive.

When we play night after night in different cities, we have different room numbers every night. We have to have a room list each day that tells us what room number everyone has, and Graham didn't have the paper out in the hall with him. He didn't know what rooms had band members in them and what room numbers had regular hotel guests. He couldn't just go and knock on random doors, and at any moment people might come down that hallway. He was naked, no towel, no key, no list, no cell phone, no nothing...what should he do? It was like, panic city.

Graham's a really creative guy, OK? He definitely thinks outside the box. So, thinking at his creative best, Graham looked up and down the hallway and saw a big plant and a house phone near the elevator. It was an enormous risk to go over by the elevator in case anyone suddenly got off on that floor, but he had to do something...

and fast…so he went down the hall, grabbed the plant and held it in front of him with his back towards the hallway wall. Talk about Monty Python! Then he used the house phone to call downstairs, told them who he was, that he was locked out of his room, and asked if they'd send up a key. Hey, happens all the time in hotels, right? No big deal. Then he added, "Oh…and send up a MAN with the key." The following morning, all kinds of rumors were floating around and this was the story I heard. I thought Graham should have gotten some kind of award for fast thinking and creativity…or maybe we should have just gotten him a CSN robe.

Occasionally, nature makes a show a memorable experience in ways we'd like to forget. I always enjoyed playing outside at amphitheaters when the weather was good. It was always fun to see the crowd outside on a summer night enjoying the show. We were playing in Hershey, Pennsylvania, at their outdoor amphitheater. It was a beautiful summer day and after soundcheck, they gave us passes to go out into The Hershey Amusement Park. The park land is hilly and, at least then, had a lot of trees and shade, which made it have a whole different feel than most amusement parks. The

Graham's Bus

amphitheater stage was on the edge of the park by the factory, so we just walked through a gate into the park. The whole place smelled like chocolate and there were huge silos filled with cocoa beans.

I have no idea why…maybe crickets like chocolate…but during the concert that night there were thousands of crickets swarming the stage. It came to be called "The Night of the Crickets." They were probably attracted to the lights or maybe they thought the music we were playing was a mating call from a giant cricket from outer space. Whatever the reason, after we started to play, the stage area became covered with crickets. They were jumping around all over

Jim Wetherbee   *Joe Jr. & Me*   *Joe Jr. & Charlie*

Me & Jim Wetherbee   *Me & Astronauts*

Recording

Rick, Smokey, Joe, Al, Me & Chad

Bill & Al Kooper

Donnie

M1-A1 Tank

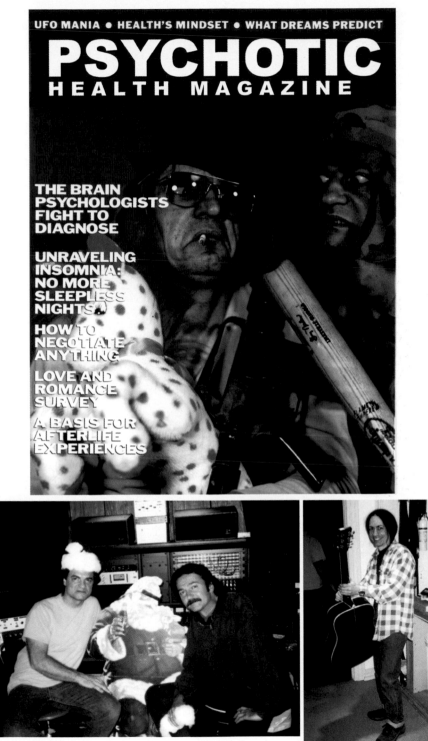

UFO MANIA • HEALTH'S MINDSET • WHAT DREAMS PREDICT

PSYCHOTIC
HEALTH MAGAZINE

THE BRAIN
PSYCHOLOGISTS
FIGHT TO
DIAGNOSE

UNRAVELING
INSOMNIA:
NO MORE
SLEEPLESS
NIGHTS

HOW TO
NEGOTIATE
ANYTHING

LOVE AND
ROMANCE
SURVEY

A BASIS FOR
AFTERLIFE
EXPERIENCES

Me, Santa, Father Guido Sarducci

Thom Lowry

Walsh meets with potential voter.   *Walsh gets the vote out...*

Joe Walsh, Zak Starkey, Me, Rick Rosas   *Me & Zak*

Animals from the Cincinnati Zoo   *Walsh as Noah*

Joe Walsh

Me

My photo of Henry Diltz

Glenn Frey

Concert photos by: Steve Jorgensen

Ohio State Fair perforamce with Joe Walsh

Joe Vitale Jr.

Big Beaver Road Exit 69

Steve, Joe, Ricky, Me & Chocolate
Photo by: Tami Jorgensen

My photos of Dan Fogelberg's ranch...

A double rainbow touches down.

Timothy B. Schmit, Robert McEntee & Dan Fogelberg

Dan, Timothy, Me & Robert   *Dan & his Grandma*

Dan Fogelberg crossing the finish line! Resort at Squaw Creek

Top the Rock Ceremony - Rock n' Roll Hall of Fame - 1994

Jerry Lee Lewis

Michael Stanley

Joe Vitale Jr.

Dale Peters

Stephen Stills - The Cool Party Tour - Toledo 1995

Front: Hoover, Christopher Stills and
Joe Vitale Jr. Back: Stephen Stills,
Mouse, Rance Caldwell, Denny Jones,
Gary Hartung & John Vanderslice

Susie & Joe Vitale Jr.

Stephen Stills - Singing the National Anthem
Jacob's Filed, Cleveland Indians Stadium - 1995

Captain Stills & Crew

Before White Water Canyon

After White Water Canyon

the place, and started jumping on David, Stephen and Graham while they were trying to sing and play guitar. It was like a bad horror movie. Every time they'd move...crunch...they'd step on a cricket. It was really distracting and annoying, but also started getting really funny. Stephen, being a creative musician, started stomping them in time to the beat of the song we were playing. David was singing one of his ballads where he has to hold a note really long and one jumped into his mouth and he swallowed it. It was like being in a plague.

We sent some stage hands out for bug spray, but that was really horrible, too. They sprayed all around and the fumes made it hard to breathe and we all started coughing. In honor of David's bug dinner during the show, we started making up cricket recipes on the bus on our way back to the hotel. Someone would say, "Cricket a la King," and we'd all really laugh. Then, "How about, Cricket Kabob?" and there'd be more laughing. After a few minutes of silence, someone would say, "Cricket Cacciatore." It went on all the way back to the hotel. We had a lot of fun with it.

I had a more serious problem with a bug later in the tour. The buses were always really clean and well taken care of...the drivers took pride in it. In about the middle of the buses are bunk beds, where we sleep on long hauls, sometimes all night if we have a long way to go. We can also sleep on the bus if we have time during the day at a show. I was asleep in the bus, and I felt a needle prick in my finger. It woke me up, but I didn't think much about it until about an hour later when my finger got about the size of a baseball bat. I mean, it had REALLY swelled up. The doctor at the show looked at it and determined that it was a spider bite. Then he gave me a shot of antihistamine or something.

He asked me where I'd been for the past twenty-four hours and I said I'd been sleeping on the bus. The bus driver searched the bus and found a black widow spider and killed it. I'd been bitten just a few hours before the show, and I could hardly even hold a drum stick because it was so swollen. It was also incredibly painful, so the doctor gave me something for pain. The shot took most of the swelling down and I used my left hand as little as possible during the show. I played most of the gig one handed, so there were no drum fills that night. By the next day, the swelling had gone all the way down and there was no pain, which was pretty incredible. I still don't know how a black widow spider got into my bunk on the bus…maybe the crickets sent it.

1987, HBO Welcome Home Vietnam Vets Concert

During the CSN tour that summer, we played for an all day festival for HBO, called the "Welcome Home Vietnam Vets Concert," which was broadcast on July 4, 1987. The show was wall to wall stars and included John Ritter, Ricardo Montalban, The Four Tops, John Voight, Neil Diamond, Linda Ronstadt, Crosby, Stills and Nash, Anita Baker, John Fogerty, James Ingram, Kris Kristofferson, James Brown, George Carlin, Ritchie Havens, Stevie Wonder, and many more. Martha Raye was there…yes, THE Martha Raye. It was really something to see her in person.

John Ritter and Ricardo Montalban were unbelievably wonderful to everyone, especially my son, Joe. It was so cool to see James Brown, The Godfather of Soul, on stage. That's when he was doing that song "Living in America." He walked in surrounded by his entourage with a girl on each arm and a couple more behind him. It was horribly hot backstage, but he had on a full three-piece suit and a fur coat draped over his shoulders like it was a cape. His band was so great. He always used two drummers…he worked them so hard, that one would play while the other one rested…they never played together. What a show and what a fantastic day, as one major star after another performed! I was totally in awe of the huge amount of legendary stars everywhere I looked. Although the backstage area was extremely hot and crowded, it was one of the most memorable concerts I've ever played and it was fantastic to be a part of it!

1987, Joe Walsh Tour

That summer I did a few dates with Joe Walsh. The gigs were all Six Flags Amusement Parks and several zoos. Perfect for Joe Walsh. They offered the concert as a package deal with regular admission. What a great time! First of all, it's always insanity playing with Joe. But playing at an amusement park or zoo was totally a bonus, because after the soundcheck, we could run around. Right off the bat, one of the things we spotted was something new to the parks...a karaoke booth.

Even though the person doing karaoke would be in a quiet little soundproof booth, they broadcast their singing through speakers out into the park. Some of the performers...well, let's just say, needed more lessons. It was hilarious. Not even close. I looked at Joe and Rick...we HAD to do it. So as not to judge the other "artists" too quickly, we went in to record. I looked at Joe and Rick again and knew how silly things were going to get...we were already cracking up. The engineer looked at us...and recognized Joe. Even though we were screwing around, I wondered if he thought we were going to do the songs like we were in a regular studio.

Before we walked into the isolation booth, Joe, Rick and I had looked through the song list. We picked three songs and the Six Flags engineer gave us the lyrics. We were all laughing now, because we knew it was going to be ridiculous and we'd have it on tape. The engineer put us in a booth, and we sang the songs to the track while he recorded us...and blasted our performances into the park. Joe picked "Raindrops Keep Falling on My Head" and sang it like Elmer Fudd..."Waindrowps Keep Faw-wing on my Head." Joe really outdid himself. He sounded just like Elmer. Then we all sang "Shout" together. On that one we took turns taking the lead. We improvised most the lyrics and Rick did an impressive bass vocal lead, while Joe and I did some really tight do-wop backups. We were awesomely horrible. For a fabulous finish, Joe did "My Way." What a rendition! Sinatra would be jealous. Joe sang it like a bad lounge singer trying too hard and singing completely out of tune with vibrato and a wavering tempo. The engineer in the control room was freaking out laughing. The best part was when we got to hear us during playback. We were falling all over ourselves laughing. Then for $10 studio time, we got cassettes of our brilliance. I've still got the cassettes and played them as I was writing this...they're hysterical. Beyond description. I've gotta send Walsh a copy.

CHAPTER NINETEEN

1988, Crosby, Stills, Nash & Young, "American Dream"

CSN was planning to record another album, and we went into a studio in L.A. called "Record One" to work on a couple of tunes. The band was Crosby, Stills, Nash, Bob Glaub on bass, and me. We were in the lobby and started hearing all this racket…it sounded like a beach party was going on, with incredibly loud surfer drums and music vibrating everything in the lobby. We had to know...what in the heck was going on in studio B?...so we went over to check it out. We opened the control room door and popped our heads in...and the music got even louder. The producer, who recognized the three CSN guys, motioned for us to come in. Pee Wee

Herman, one of my absolute all-time favorites, was out in the studio recording "Surfin' Bird" for the Frankie Avalon and Annette Funicello movie "Back To The Beach." He was out in the room singing his

lead, but he wasn't just standing there…he was dancing around like Pee Wee, totally into it, singing in his fabulous Pee Wee voice.

The studio was filled with the usual instruments and microphones… but there was more…a beach umbrella, an inflatable raft, flippers… Pee Wee was awesome…he knew how to create a mood and nailed the track. It was something to behold! The thing was, it looked totally surreal…here was the Pee Wee voice and dance moves, but they were coming out of Paul Reubens, who wasn't in costume or make up. We all HAD to get autographs and our pictures taken with him when he took a break.

It was about that time that I put together a studio for Graham Nash, and I found myself there writing with him almost every day. We started meshing well creatively and wrote some beautiful songs for the upcoming CSN album, like "Shadowland," "Soldiers of Peace," and "Don't Say Goodbye." Little did I know that the three guys and Neil had discussed the possibility of a CSNY album. They played the demos they'd all done for Neil and he loved them, so they decided that what started as a CSN album would become a CSNY album.

We recorded the Crosby, Stills, Nash and Young album "American Dream" in 1988 at Neil Young's ranch. The core band was Crosby, Stills, Nash, Young, Bob Glaub on bass, and me. It took about seven weeks to record it and we stayed on the ranch during that time.

To get to Neil's ranch, we had to drive about thirty or forty minutes on this bumpy dirt and gravel road that's one lane with huge drop-offs down the mountainside on one side of the road. It was a real treacherous drive way deep in the mountains and we really didn't like going up and down that road, especially at night. The ranch was wild and beautiful. There were gigantic redwood trees on his property that were something like fifteen feet across. Parts of the ranch were so spectacularly beautiful that they looked like a movie set.

If you drove into Neil's ranch, you'd never know that a rock star lived there, because it was a full working ranch. It had horses, long-horned cattle, regular cattle, buffalo, goats, chickens, turkeys, and peacocks, that made a kind of scream that sounded like, "NEEIL!" We kept saying that Neil must have trained them to say his name. The place was enormous and part of the land was leased to farmers, so there were crops in the fields and tractors and machinery working on the land. Neil has a deep love and respect for farmers and because of that, he's done all the Farm Aid concerts.

Neil, of course, had dogs. One was a wonderful bloodhound named "Elvis" that rode with Neil in his Jeep. The Jeep was Elvis's territory, and if any of us went near it, the dog did "teeth" against the glass window. There were several buildings and barns on the ranch, and one building was Neil's personal recording studio. There were a bunch of us, so to give us more room, we brought a Record Plant truck from LA, parked it outside the beautiful storage barn, ran cabling in for all the microphones and set up a little stage inside.

If you pull the sleeve out of the vinyl album, there's a picture taken at Neil's ranch of the four guys in the barn with some "gobos" around them. Gobos are room dividers that we used to deaden the sound. We could see that we needed some, so Stephen's guitar tech and my good friend, Doug Breidenbach, and I built them when we were just starting to record in the barn. Doug and I later referred to ourselves as the "Bunion Brothers."

The first tune we cut had a real 50's flavor, so we all greased our hair back and that's the way we played and recorded that day. It was a great way to start recording and it helped us get the right attitude for the song…and I'm right at home looking like that. We all looked pretty greasy, so I had someone take a picture of us. The song never made it to the record, but we all had a great time being a 1950's group for a day.

Since we were there for so many weeks, the guys in the band would drive up from L.A., and then they'd go home for the weekends. The band again stayed at the house on the ranch Neil called The White House and he provided us with a guy who was a really great cook. Every morning, he made us fresh eggs gathered from Neil's chickens, and almost every night, Neil would come down and eat with us. We'd talk about whatever song we were working on, and it was a really great band atmosphere. Graham talked Neil into getting a satellite dish at The White House, and I think Graham paid for it, since he knew we needed to watch TV during down time. We had all the luxuries of home.

Some of the guys had their cars at the ranch, and remember they're rock stars, so they have rock star cars. Crosby had his big beautiful BMW there, Stephen had his Mercedes, Graham had his Mercedes and they all parked those beautiful cars outside the barn. One of the cars was a Mercedes convertible, and the top was usually down. We were recording in the barn and there were always goats running around outside. One day we were taking a break and walked outside to find the goats at play. The goats, who love to climb on things, had started scaling the cars. They'd created a game on Crosby's car where they climbed up on the back of the car, onto the roof, slid down the windshield on their little hooves, and tap danced across the hood…probably because it was hot. Then they'd jump to the ground from the front of the car and go around to the back and start all over again.

While the one set of goats were working Crosby's car over, another group was enjoying the Mercedes. They looked like a gang of vandals. They had eaten some of the beautiful leather mesh strapping that went around the steering wheel, and it was all frayed and unraveled. Some of the goats were sitting in the seats looking around like they were passengers. A couple sampled the fine leather interior and apparently found it to be delicious. The goats thought that the cars were their new playground and were really having a spectacular time. The guys stopped parking their cars there, but I got some great pictures of the goats playing on some of the other cars.

The turkeys, however, caused the most trouble. The barn where we recorded was on the ground level, but it had a room underneath it

that opened out into the pasture. That's where the turkeys lived. Picture a split level house on a hillside…that's what it looked like. The turkeys responded to sound and they were gobbling a lot. I had to do this. I went down and sat among the turkeys so I was at their level, which was kinda freaky, because they're really big and there were probably sixty of them. I waited until they were all quiet, and then I went, "Gobble, gobble, gobble" and they all gobble, gobble, gobbled. It was hilarious.

The turkeys could really gobble loud and there were a lot of them, which made them even louder. OK, now, this is just sick. Crosby had spent a lot of time writing a song, which was very personal, called "Compass." He went into singing about the years he was involved with drugs and how he had wasted all that time of his life and career. It says how he's glad to be clean and sober now, among the living and doing well. It's a beautiful, sensitive, very personal song and he bares his soul. It's very slow, and there are spaces in between the lines of lyrics. I recorded this song with Cros in the main barn, just me and him, with Neil off to the side playing a beautiful harmonica part while Stephen and Graham were in the truck with engineer Niko Bolas, producing it. Crosby had to be in a certain mood to do this song, because it was so personal to him and it took a lot of mental and emotional energy to perform it.

It was warm that day and the windows in the barn were open. It's very peaceful and quiet at the ranch and the fresh air really felt good. Now, I'm not quoting the exact lyrics, but you can get the picture. So, we started the song, and as soon as Cros sang something like, "I have spent…" the turkeys went, "Gobble gobble gobble gobble!" "…so many years," "Gobble gobble gobble gobble!" "…being blinded," "Gobble gobble gobble."

Niko pushed talkback from the control room in the truck...and as soon as he pushed it, we could hear hysterical laughter. He could hardly talk. "Unless you want the turkeys on the track, you're going to have to start over," he said. Stephen chimed in, "Do we have to pay the turkeys union scale?" Neil, who was upstairs with us, said, "Aw-w-w, just leave it." Crosby looked over at him and grinned.

Niko Bolas

It wasn't a happy grin. Neil saw the look and said, "Well...or not..."

Every time he paused, it was like the turkeys were backup singers and they were testifying with Crosby. We stopped and started, stopped and started. Finally, we closed the windows…duh! Crosby is a really powerful singer, and he really projects when he sings, so we started again with the windows closed, and he sang, "I have spent…" and we heard this muffled, "Gobble gobble gobble!" like when you put your hand over your mouth and talk. He put his guitar down in frustration and we decided to work on another song. I imagine they were gobbling the whole time we were recording there, but remember, we're a rock & roll band and we play loud and couldn't hear them. I honestly don't remember how we tricked the turkeys into being quiet when we finally recorded "Compass," but it's one of Crosby's best and most moving songs.

Even now when Crosby plays "Compass" at gigs, he gets really upset if the crowd is making noise and not paying attention, because he's making himself vulnerable and confiding a very personal and private story about himself to the audience. Sometimes during the quiet times in a show, fans, in their enthusiasm, will yell out, "Where's Neil?" or song titles, as though we don't have a rehearsed show and set list. Do they actually think we take requests? I'm sure, however, that the turkeys' gobbling enthusiasm was a shout out in support of Cros's moral victory. As I said, they were just testifying.

One night during the time we were there recording, there was a full moon. Neil has a thing about recording when there's a full moon, so when we got there he said to find out when there was going to be one, and whenever that was, to expect a call in the middle of the night to go up to the barn. One night we didn't know it was going to be a full moon and we all went to bed. The phone rang in the middle of the night and, all of the sudden, somebody was walking around in the White House, knocking on all the doors, saying, "Get up! I've got the coffee on! We're going to the studio." It was about 2:00 AM. We went up and cut a song for the album and it was fantastic. We went back to the White House when the sun was coming up and went back to bed. We got up again about 2:00 or 3:00 in the afternoon and got right back to work up at the studio.

Neil has a great energy and when he's recording...he's totally into it. He has a really interesting way of checking the feel of a song after it's recorded. He has an extensive car collection that he keeps in a car barn on the ranch. The cars are rare, in beautiful condition and very classy. Neil used to grab a cassette of whatever we were working on, get one of his beautiful older cars, and drive around the ranch listening to it. I did this a couple of times with him. He'd listen to what we did the night before and judge whether he liked what he heard and decide if we needed to cut it again. It was really nice to go for a ride in a classic car through the beautiful countryside on his ranch and listen to the music. It's such a cool way to do it. Your head is completely clear and you're really able to focus and listen and see if you got it.

Neil's ranch is an amazing world where he's lived some of his dreams. When I was a little boy, I loved to play with my Lionel train set. Neil loved trains, too. He still has them. Several years ago, Neil bought the business "Lionel Trains," and he actually bought an entire box car and caboose and he has them on tracks on the ranch. He uses them for the office of Lionel Trains. I have no idea how he managed to get them over that road to the ranch. He has an incredible layout of Lionel Trains in a room about forty feet square, filled with his trains. It's like the mother of all train layouts. He's an interesting guy and has made quite a life for himself up there.

After a short break, we recorded some more in L.A. to finish up the album. Recording the American Dream album was really special for me because I got to co-write four of the songs. I co-wrote "Don't Say Goodby" and "Shadowland" with Graham Nash, "That Girl" with Stephen Stills and "Soldiers of Peace" with Graham Nash and Craig Doergy. "Soldiers of Peace" has beautiful string parts on it. When we recorded it, we used synthesized ones, but then we started talking about using real strings.

"Soldiers of Peace," is a very beautiful, majestic production kind of song. We did the demo at Graham's studio and I played piano, drums and the string parts. Then we recorded the track at Neil's ranch. It was coming out really well, the guys loved it and all four of them put fantastic vocals on it. Graham said, "You know what, we've gotta have real strings on this," and everyone agreed, except for Cros.

I understood Cros's position, because he was right in being conscious of the fact that it was going to cost something like $40,000 to use real strings. Stephen was neutral about it. He had used real strings in the past and really appreciated the idea and the cost wasn't an issue for him. Graham and Neil were for it. But Crosby was still a little concerned and questioned if it was worth $40,000 for some strings on this one particular song. It was a valid concern. We had a major budget for this record, but he didn't want to waste money. But, he was outvoted in the democracy that was CSNY, which has worked for them for years.

There's nothing more beautiful than a real string date, a real orchestra, on a record. Nothing more beautiful. It's awesome to hear, and it's awesome to watch. It's also an awesome price tag, because there's at least sixty musicians out there. They're union musicians and they're very aware of double tracking, so if you double them, you have to pay them double scale. It was so expensive to hire them.

A string date in the studio is usually a very costly, stressful day. You hire a conductor who's also very expensive and he writes the charts, gathers the players, and directs the orchestra. With the dawn of synthesizers, we've been able to make records and get away with synthesized string sounds on tracks with proper engineering, EQ, production and mastering, but the depth, quality and fidelity of real strings just isn't the same. Again, the number one issue is cost.

OK, so the vote was we were going to do the string date. Cros conceded to the vote and was OK with it, but he was late coming to the studio the day we recorded the strings. We were at A&M Studios in LA to overdub the strings on the track we had already recorded at Neil's ranch, because A&M had a huge room. I was early that day, because I love string dates. There's nothing like it, especially when they're going on a piece of music that I co-wrote. Nash and I worked directly with the conductor to get the part together and he wrote a beautiful chart for us.

We were getting ready to do the strings and the orchestra was set up in the studio. Now when I was with Joe Walsh, we carried around nose glasses and took Polaroid pictures of people with them on, and for some reason this had caught on with the CSNY camp. So, we bought about sixty pairs of nose glasses and put them on the orchestra. It was so funny to see those dignified older ladies and gentlemen in such a formal setting as a string symphony orchestra… and they all were wearing nose glasses.

I'm sure no one had ever asked them to wear nose glasses before, and they were really enjoying it. One guy already had a big nose, mustache and glasses, and when he put the nose glasses on, it didn't look any different. The orchestra loved it and they actually played the track wearing them. They really had a great time. It was absolutely hilarious and I took several pictures of them. It looked insane.

I got to go out with the sixty piece orchestra and play the tympani part that was written out for that song. It was absolutely thrilling and brought back old memories of playing with the symphony in Canton and my high school orchestra, but this was a whole other level. These musicians were incredibly skilled at what they did. It was such an exciting experience for me. It was about a three or four hour process  tuning up, getting the chart worked out, getting the balance, sixty pairs of headphones, setting up sixty music stands, lights on the music stands, about forty microphones…it was a huge deal just getting set up. It took all day. That's why it's really expensive, but the outcome is worth it if you have the money. Then the orchestra warmed up and a couple of takes into it, they nailed it beautifully.

Crosby still hadn't come. It wasn't that he was so against it, it just wasn't his thing. Graham had gone back and forth with Crosby about the strings and Graham had won, but he wasn't done with the argument and he wanted to have a little fun with Crosby. He came to me and asked what I thought we could do. So, we conspired to play this brilliant trick on him.

Back in the '80's we had a piece of gear called a Harmonizer. What they basically did was take a vocal or guitar or any sound and it could "detune" it. What that would do is put it slightly out of tune, which if you only go a few cents out of tune, it actually widens the sound and it doesn't sound out of tune, it makes it sound larger. Our engineer was Niko Bolas, who's a fabulous engineer/producer, and had been with us at Neil's ranch when we recorded the tracks. I had made many records with Niko, who also worked with Fogelberg and Neil Young. He's also a nut. He had just engineered a huge beautiful session and it must have made him feel really proud to pull that off and do a great job.

Here's what Graham thought, and I totally give Graham all the credit, because he's the culprit. He asked Niko if he could put all the strings into the harmonizer and put them out of tune for playback. If you put them slightly out of tune, they just sound bigger and wide and cool, but we went a few steps past that. We probably put them nine or ten per cent out of tune, so at first they sounded OK, but then you'd eventually realize they didn't sound right. Crosby would have no way of knowing that we'd inserted the harmonizer into the string tracks.

Crosby finally showed up at the studio about an hour later, and we acted all excited like, "David's here, let's play him the track." We'd told Graham we'd play it completely straight, as if the strings sounded so good that they'd convince Crosby that we'd done the right thing. We sat him in the engineer's seat, which was directly in the center of the board, cranked it up and played the song. The song was now completely finished and we were all sitting around with these proud looks on our faces, like, "Isn't this unbelievable?"

Crosby has the gift of perfect pitch and it's amazing. In over thirty years, I've never heard him sing out of tune. Ever. He listened to the song, and we all gave a big sigh, like we were euphoric and nearly drawn to tears with it's beauty. Cros was dead silent. Then he turned to Nash and he said, "Uh…can I have a word with you out in the hall?" and they walked out the door. We had this agreement with Nash that we'd play it straight-faced like we all thought it was beautiful. That was hard to pull off. Fortunately, studios are soundproofed, so when they went out into the hall, we roared. Neil said we were evil.

According to Graham, Crosby said something like, "Graham, we can't use the strings." Graham said, "What? We just spent $40,000 for strings and you're telling me we can't use them?" Cros said, "We can't use them. They're out of tune!" Somebody cracked the door open because we couldn't stand it and we had to hear what was going on, and they were going at it. Graham kept insisting that the strings were beautiful and Cros was in complete panic. The whole time out in the hall Graham never caved or let on while Cros was freaking out. Then he said, "Well, I guess we better go tell Stephen and Neil."

They walked back into the control room, and we're the ones who blew it. There were about nine of us in there, and everyone was dying laughing. Crosby lost it. He knew we got him. Graham probably knows Crosby as well as anyone in the world, and he knew exactly how to get him. Crosby has a history and a reputation as a prankster. He loves to play pranks on people and he's a good sport, because he can dish it out and take it, too. But this time, I think we finally nailed him. It was the mother of all pranks. I have to hand it to Graham, it was brilliant. It was probably the funniest moment of all thirty years of CSN. Of course, after all this, we did unplug the harmonizer, sat him down, and played the song for him with the beautiful strings. He was moved.

Even today, the prank lives on. If we're in the studio working on a keyboard part and we start having some trouble with it, someone will say, "Hey, let's put a little harmonizer on it." Then David will look up and, with a twinkle in his eye, give him the finger.

1988, Crosby, Stills & Nash Summer Tour

The band for the 1988 CSN Summer Tour was David Crosby, Stephen Stills, Graham Nash, Mike Finnigan on keyboards, Bob Glaub on bass, Joe Lala on percussion and me on drums. The last show of the tour was in San Diego, and the techs decided to pull out all the stops. The movie "Spinal Tap" had come out in 1984 and one of the biggest jokes in that movie was the eighteen inch Stonehenge prop for the stage. Graham had a song he played at the grand piano during the show called "Cathedral," which had a line about Stonehenge. We thought that Graham needed a Stonehenge prop, too. The crew constructed a replica of the piece out of styrofoam and slowly lowered it from a lighting truss while Graham was playing. It was a very amateur lowering, which made it even better. It landed right on the piano. They had also put a smoke bomb inside the piano, which started smoking during the song. Graham could hardly keep his composure.

Later that same show, Graham invited his daughter, Nile, to come out and sit at the piano with him for the song "Our House." Nile was just a little girl at the time, probably about six or seven. It was so cute. She sat there beside her daddy smiling adoringly at him, while he played the piano and sang the song to her. It was so wholesome…all they needed was a couple of glasses of milk and some cookies sitting on the piano and it would have looked like something out of the 50's.

The crew didn't know that Graham was going to have Nile sit at the piano with him, so during the line in that song, "...two cats in the yard..." they lowered two stuffed toy kitties, but while lowering them, the two cats bumped against each other and it looked…at least it to us… like they were humping! We almost stopped playing we were laughing so hard. It was a great way to end the tour!

CHAPTER TWENTY

<u>1989, Joe Walsh, Tampa gig</u>

In the fall of 1989 my tour with CSN was finished for the year and I was off. Joe Walsh called me and asked if I'd be available for a "one off." We call shows that are just one show in the middle of a month "one offs." I don't know why, I just think of it as you do one show and then you're off for a while. Joe didn't have a band together at the time, but he knew he could call Rick Rosas and me and we could do a show on the spot with just a good sound check. I was supposed to fly down from Ohio to play a gig with Joe near Tampa, Florida.

At the time, Joe and Rick Rosas were in Chicago doing radio shows with Steve Dahl. I did the show with Joe once and I remember Steve had a snare drum and a cymbal in the control room to do rim shots after jokes. Joe and Rick were really great together on the radio so they were doing a lot of shows. Rick is one really funny son of a gun. Joe and I had a musical partnership and a friendship, and believe me, we did our share of stupid crazy things, but Joe and Rick had a different kind of partnership. They were more like Jerry Lewis and Dean Martin.

Rick would always do anything, and would wholeheartedly throw himself into whatever they were doing. People used to call in to the show and ask them ridiculous questions and Rick and Joe would talk to them. They told stories and jokes or called up friends and talked to them while they were on the air. Joe used to call me sometimes when he was doing a radio show and I'd tell the trombone story or something. Sometimes he'd talk about what he wanted me to say before we went on the air, but sometimes he just called me out of the blue and I was immediately on the radio.

The band was coming from all parts of the country and connecting through Atlanta so we'd all arrive in Tampa at the same time. Smokey, Rick and Joe were flying down from Chicago, some members of the band were coming in from L.A., I was flying down from Ohio, and then we were going to meet and fly the last leg of our flight together. My plane got in first, an hour before the other flights, so I got something to eat and then went to the gate to meet Smokey, Rick and Joe. Their plane finally arrived and I was kinda staring ahead, waiting for them to get off the plane. They were flying in first class, so they were some of the first passengers to get off the plane. And there they were. I couldn't believe what I was seeing. My mouth dropped open as I looked at them in astonishment...and then I laughed.

Joe and Rick had kept themselves busy during the two-hour flight from Chicago to Atlanta by making themselves outfits made entirely of newspapers they'd brought on the plane. They used scissors to cut out the pieces for the newspaper clothes and then Scotch-taped them together, making an entire ensemble for each of them. It must have looked like some kind of weird home economics class on the plane.

They walked off the plane trying to look as though nothing was unusual, wearing their newspaper and Scotch tape suits, rustling loudly with each step. They were each wearing a complete paper outfit over their clothes, including a coat, shirt, pants, hat and even shoes. The paper shoes were taped over their regular shoes, so they had great big giant shoe feet. When they saw me laughing and the look on my face, they tried, but they just couldn't keep from cracking up. They actually had tears in their eyes from laughing so hard. They were really enjoying this whole outrageous scene they were making... a sort of "cut out man" in 3-D.

The people who were waiting at the gate and the people getting off the plane didn't know exactly what to think, but they were all laughing, too. I can just picture the stewardess saying, "Bu-bye!" I'm sure it took a crew to clean up the paper scraps and mess on the plane... and it's not like we were at a small rural airport. No, we were at one of the biggest and busiest airports in the world. Since we were taking a connecting flight together, I started walking toward our next gate like I didn't know them, but we were all laughing so hard it was obvious we were together.

We had to walk quite a distance to our gate, with them still wearing their paper suits, rustling and looking like walking billboards or something. Imagine this in the airport today. They'd be wrestled to the ground and taken into custody. In fact, they would have never made it on the plane with the scissors. Still wearing their ensembles, Rick and Joe boarded the plane to Tampa and wore the paper clothes the entire flight. After we landed, the tape and paper were starting to be affected by the humidity and the clothes started coming apart, making them look even worse. Joe and Rick kept the clothes on, though, and even wore them in the limo to the hotel and checked in that way, with the paper clothes kinda half on and half off. It was fantastic and absolutely hilarious.

I have to tell you, back in those days Joe was out of his mind, and mixing in Rick and me was like adding gasoline to fire. I never knew what Joe was gonna do next, but I really enjoyed the elaborate ridiculous things he was capable of doing. Like me, he was always thinking of creative things to do for entertainment. How did his brain work? He thought, "Let's see, we have newspapers, we have tape, we have scissors and two hours to kill...hey, let's make outfits!"...well sure, that makes sense. Knowing Joe so well, I can just picture him smiling and kinda laughing to himself as the light went on and the idea first dawned in his brain, and how he must have been laughing as he told Rick, who, as I said, was always up for anything. When Joe talks to you about doing something like that, he kinda puts his face close to yours, squints his eyes, puts his arm around you and talks really softly while he's laughing and kinda nodding, so it's like you're conspiring to do something.

I wish I'd been there on the flight for the construction of the outfits, but being surprised with them coming off the plane wearing the clothes in finished form was just spectacularly funny. I gotta laugh just thinking about it. What a couple of nuts! I only wish I would have taken some pictures, but the image of them in their horrible paper clothes is burned in my memory forever.

1990, Crosby, Stills and Nash, "Live It Up"

The album "Live It Up" had five producers....CSN, Stanley Johnson, and me. Back then, that was a lot of producers. At the time, a lot of the classic bands were trying to go with the flow and "update" their sound, because it was getting to be hard to get radio airplay with their classic sounds. At the time, radio stations were playing old classic rock but not new classic rock, an unfortunate trend that I still see today.

When we cut the "Live It Up" album, the idea was to update the CSN sound. In hindsight, that's never a good idea when a band has had spectacular success with a classic sound. We knew what fans wanted to buy, but we also wanted radio stations to play the songs, so probably half the album has songs that depart from the classic CSN sound. We didn't use as many vocals and we just didn't have the kind of songs that CSN fans had come to expect. We were

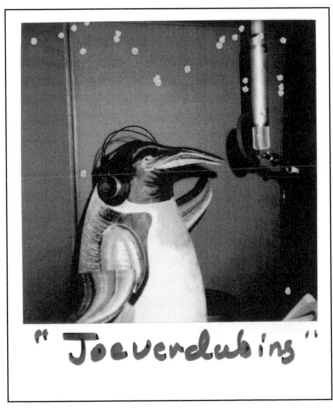

"Joeverdubing"

9 thought you said 1½ cents —

Gerry Tolman

all trying to break out from being treated like we were an oldies act. Joe Walsh was also having the same problem getting on the radio and tried the same thing…a lot of the classic rock groups did. Musically, it just didn't work. With that being said, there are still some really great songs on that album.

I had been in the studio recording the album for a couple of months and I was getting a little crisp, so I needed a break and came home. Back then we didn't have MP3's or email, so they Fed Ex'd me a DAT, or digital audio tape, of the mixes every day. Along with the daily DAT's I received… and this was Graham Nash's doing… they included Polaroid photos of a huge inflatable penguin doing different things in the studio. They'd pose the penguin at the board with his arms on it like he was mixing, or with headphones on like he was singing. All fifty-nine pictures had captions and were hilarious. I saved every one of them.

I'd listen to the DAT's and then call the guys at the studio and we'd talk about the mixes. It was very respectful of them to include me in the loop, and I really appreciated it. Don't ask me about the picture on the front of the "Live It Up" album. I didn't have anything to do with it and I don't think it has any meaning, but the record company did make little plastic hot dogs to promote the album.

SLICE SAYS, "HI, JOE"

John Vanderslice

1990, Crosby, Stills & Nash, Live it up Tour

The band for The Live It Up Tour was David Crosby, Stephen Stills, Graham Nash, Mike Finnigan on keyboards, Jorge Calderone on bass, Kim Bullard on keyboards, Michito Sanchez on percussion, and me on drums. To go along with the new updated sound, CSN decided to make the stage show a huge production and spent something like a million dollars for props, which was a lot more money then than it is now. There were big picture frames that, I think, were supposed to be windows, that swung down into view during one part of the show. There were a couple of great moments, like when a ship seemed to sail across the back of the stage during "Wooden Ships." In the middle of "Suite: Judy Blue Eyes," there was a light over Stephen that was like...well, did you ever see those flood lights for the opening of a shopping center? It would shine straight down on him and was so bright it looked like a scene from Star Trek...like they were going to beam him up.

The band and crew made fun of the slide show of kids during "Teach Your Children," and there was a big stained glass window that appeared behind us when we played "Cathedral." There was so much stuff on the stage that after the first show we had to send about half of it back because, time-wise, it was impossible to get it all set up. They'd hired a guy from New York who was a set director from Broadway, and he just didn't get the concept of a traveling show. The thing I remember the most was how hot the stage was with all the extra lights. Unfortunately, the Live It Up album and tour were named after my song, which was on the album. The whole time was a struggle for classic rock musicians, and what we tried just didn't work out. No one person was responsible, but I have to give us an A+ for trying.

At this particular time, my son, Joe Jr., who was now in the fifth grade, wanted to be an astronaut, and wrote a song for them during math class called "SRB Separation." We thought it might be fun to record the song and send it to NASA and see if they'd play it for the astronauts, so I recorded it with him. David Crosby had a friend who could get us to the right people to talk to about the song, and he introduced us to Jeanie Cunningham. Although the astronaut office declined using Joe Jr.'s song, our effort started a relationship that lasted for many years with several of the astronauts, pilots and members of the astronaut office. The group included Jim Wetherbee, Bonnie Dunbar, Charlie Armstrong, and Pierre Thuot..

Jeanie Cunningham

For the next few years whenever CSN played in Houston, I invited them all to the show. We found out that there was an astronaut band called "Max Q," which is a technical term, and asked the band members to sit in with us. But although many of them came to the shows, they were too humble and shy to play with us. That was one of those things that was hard for me to understand...they would fearlessly face being launched in a space shuttle, but wouldn't sit in, even at soundcheck, with CSN.

Jim Wetherbee, Joey & Me

Several of the astronauts invited us to their shuttle launches, and although I was always working and couldn't go, Susie and Joe Jr. did fly down to try to see two of them. They were given VIP passes in the section where the friends and family sit. Both times Susie and Joe Jr. flew down, the shuttle didn't launch. The liftoff was cancelled just a few hours before the launch time, but it was really an exciting experience for them to be invited down.

The astronauts were some of the finest men and women I have ever met. You could tell what superb character they all had, and that they were chosen for certain personality qualities, as well as for their courage, knowledge and skills. They loved the space program the way I love music. I related. Jim Wetherbee, who was also the drummer in their band, took us all around and gave us a private tour of the NASA Houston facility. He eventually became a Commander and one of his many shuttle flights was the one which took John Glenn back into space. Eventually I invited the astronauts to a Joe Walsh show when I played with him in Houston. It was fantastic getting to meet those heroes.

That was the tour that I started asking Joe Jr. to come out on stage and play tambourine during "Teach Your Children," and the seeds for a musical career, instead of one in space, were planted. All the CSN guys, band and crew, were always really wonderful to Susie and Joe Jr., and they went to a lot of gigs that summer. I remember walking into the dining room at one of the shows, and David was sitting there

having a serious conversation with Joe Jr., who was sitting across from David, soaking in everything he said. David was telling him that he'd rather go back to jail for the rest of his life than ever do drugs again, and how drugs had stolen his musical creativity for so long. Can you ask for a

Me, Joe Jr., & Christopher Stills

better drug program than that for your kid? I can't tell you what that meant to me.

Joe Jr. had taken quite a liking to David, Stephen and Graham, partly because they'd always joke around with him, but especially because they let him come out on stage during the show. They made him feel so at home, that he'd started thinking he was part of the band, and even got a towel after "Teach" and would put it around his neck like the rest of the band guys. After the show, he'd say, "Great show, guys," to David, Graham and Stephen as we walked back to the dressing room. He'd been to a lot of gigs by now, and had gotten familiar with the songs.

I got a cassette of the show we'd just done and was listening to it in the car as we traveled to the next city after the show. It was late and dark and Joe Jr. was in the back seat...I thought he was sleeping. I said to Susie, "Fast forward the tape to 'Cut My Hair,' I want to check on something." From out of the darkness of the back seat, Joe Jr.'s head suddenly appeared between us, and he leaned forward, turning his head toward me. With his voice full of disgust for my lack of knowledge about David's song, he corrected me. "It's "Cut My HEAD,' Dad," he said, like I was a complete idiot. Susie and I lost it. "Cut my HEAD?" I asked Joe. "What do you think he was doing...shaving?" We couldn't stop laughing. Hey, hasn't everyone heard the lyrics to a song a little differently than what's actually being said? I still refer to that song as, "Cut My Head."

During the tour that year I got to visit the Meyers Lake Carousel, which is now in Bushnell Park in downtown Hartford, Connecticut. It's now known as The Bushnell Park Carousel. We stopped by on our way to the gig and I rode one of the horses...I was glad the guys weren't there to see me.

David was still totally thrilled about life, and he wanted to do everything. At that particular time in his life, he was like a kid at Christmas...every new day was like a gift for him. Like a little kid with a toy truck, apparently David thought it would be a fun experience to drive the tour bus, so he just HAD to do it. Susie, Joe Jr. and I were driving in our car to the gig in Pittsburg, when Joe Jr. turned around and looked out the back window because David's tour bus had just pulled up right behind us on the Interstate. "Hey, Dad," Joe Jr. said excitedly, "David's driving the bus!" David's driving the bus. Perfect. The funniest part was, he looked the part. He was so pleased with himself, smiling from ear to ear, while he watched our reaction in the car. Joe Jr. grabbed the video camera and took pictures of him. It was hysterically funny.

We arrived at the huge show at Three Rivers Stadium in Pittsburg, Pennsylvania, where we were opening for The Grateful Dead. Trying to blend, we'd all worn tie dye. I followed the buses past security and into a world that looked like a time warp to the late 1960's. When we went inside, we got instructions like "Don't drink anything that you didn't open, and don't put your drink down." It was like being at Woodstock. There were thousands of people with backpacks, bare feet and VW vans with flowers painted on them...where do you get one of those? I have a photo looking out from my drum set at 80,000 fans, all dressed like hippies from the 1960's. Jerry Garcia sat in with us for "Wooden Ships" and he played pedal steel guitar on "Teach Your Children." It was a fascinating concert to play and watch the fans...they went crazy when we played "Woodstock"...because they were probably all there. Hey, David, Stephen and Graham were!

1991, Joe Walsh, "Ordinary Average Guy"

Joe was going to record another album and had signed with Epic Records. I met him in New York City to talk with Michael Caplan, who, at the time, was the head of the Artist Relations Department. I wondered why I was going along for this meeting. While I was at the meeting, Joe surprised Michael and me by announcing that I was his co-producer for

Me & Smokey

his "Ordinary Average Guy" album. I had to sign papers to make it official, and then a couple of weeks later, in October, we headed down to Chattanooga, Tennessee, to record.

The band was Joe, Rick Rosas, Chad Cromwell and me, with Dave "Snake" Reynolds engineering. We did a couple of double drummer things and got some great tracks. I wrote the song "School Days" for that album. We decided that we wanted to move to another studio and since Gary Belz was a good friend of Joe's, we went to his studio. We finished the record in Memphis and mixed it there as well.

The photo of Joe on the front was taken with Joe actually jumping on a trampoline. I loved the action and the Joe-ness of it...I think it's the best album cover of all his records. He had a hit single "Ordinary Average Guy" off it, and it turned out to be a great album. We had a hard time getting started, because in January of 1991 we had invaded Iraq in The Gulf War. It was the first time we'd ever gotten to see live footage from the front lines. We were riveted and weren't getting anything done, so we had to move the TV out of the control room. Once the record was finished, we went out on tour to promote the album.

1991, Joe Walsh, Ordinary Average Tour / Doobies

It was around this time that Joe Walsh, Rick Rosas and I brought "cut out man" to a whole new level. We always had our supplies with us...tape, scissors and magazines...so we were always ready to create our masterpieces at a moment's notice. We were flying first class on a very long flight, and we had a lot of time on our hands. Joe Walsh and I were sitting beside each other, and Rick was sitting across the aisle one row ahead of us. Rick noticed that there was a Japanese businessman in the row in front of Joe and me who had put one of those light-blocking sleep masks on, and was already sound asleep. We all thought that it looked hysterical.

A few minutes later, Joe leaned over to me, looked me in the eyes and said quietly, "I dare you." He had cut out two huge staring eyes from a photograph in one of the magazines, and had applied double-sided sticky tape to the back of each eye. Dare me? He handed me the eyes. I stood up and leaned over the seat, and then very carefully put the eyes on the sleep mask. The man in the seat next to the businessman was losing it laughing. The businessman never even stirred, and slept for most of the flight. The stewardess never said anything to him because she hadn't seen me apply the eyes and she didn't know if he had put them on the mask himself. Finally, he woke up and took the mask off...he couldn't help but see the eyes...and got really mad. Hey, don't look at us...do we look like the kind of guys who'd do such a thing? It was some of our best "cut out man" work. We were totally out of our minds at the time, and the Ordinary Average Tour provided even more opportunities to express ourselves.

The Ordinary Average Tour was one of the craziest and most fun tours I've ever done. It was complete insanity every night. The band was Joe Walsh, Rick Rosas on bass and vocals, Al Kooper on keyboards, Chad Cromwell on drums, and me on drums, percussion, flute, keyboards and vocals. This was the tour that I did "stick toss" with Chad. Like I said, I was really uncomfortable since he wore glasses and I was afraid I was going to hit him in the eye with a stick. The "you'll poke your eye out" thing was big with my Mom when I was growing up. But stick toss was just a fraction of the onstage insanity.

For starters, Joe told jokes between the songs. He had this one really great story about a pirate with an eye patch and a hook. The pirate said he lost his hand when it was eaten by a shark or something, and that was how he got the hook. Then Joe supposedly asked him something like, "But what about the eye patch? How'd you lose your eye?" The pirate said that a sea gull was flying over and pooped in his eye. Then Joe asked the pirate, "Well, how did that cause you to lose your eye?" and the pirate said, "First day with the hook." Then I'd do a rim-shot. He told that joke every night, and it always was really funny to me. He had flawless delivery, and told it every time like it was the first time.

Joe had planned the stage set up, and it clearly was designed by someone absolutely out of his mind. He wanted it to have an "ordinary average guy" kind of feel, so we had all kinds of props on the stage. There were things that made absolutely no sense, but I could tell they made Joe laugh, so they were up there. We had a huge inflatable dinosaur, a large banana, an inflatable doll for "I.L.B.T.'s," an old rusty barrel, and a real washer and dryer. One of the techs, Doug Sturgis, put on an apron and maid's hat and came out on stage while we were playing and pretended to do laundry. Instead of sitting on a rack, the keyboards were sitting on an ironing board. There was a guy made of stuffed clothing dressed up and laying in a lawn chair on one side of the stage. We called him "Big Bob." Joe had a battery operated cave man that kind of wandered around on the stage beside him while we played, and I had a battery operated white rabbit on an equipment case beside me that kinda hopped around. We actually carried a helium tank on the road with us, and every show Doug would fill balloons and tie them to the equipment and mic stands. Joe learned to play trombone, really badly, I might add, and did a trombone solo in "Rocky Mountain Way' each night.

During the song "Ordinary Average Guy," there was a sound byte of a bowling ball flying down the alley and hitting a strike. I did the sample on the record and we used it live. For that song Doug set up play bowling pins on one end of the stage, and Joe would actually bowl across the stage. After a while he had his timing perfect, so that when the sound effect came up of the ball hitting the pins, his ball was hitting the pins on stage. We enjoyed that every night. OK, you had to get in a good mood just looking at the stage set up. I couldn't help but remember my circus gig when I was in high school.

Add to that Joe's clothing choices throughout the tour. Sometimes he'd wear totally mismatched rhinestone embellished shirts and pants and weird shoes or boots. Sometimes he looked like a clown, his clothes were so crazy and bizarre, but it was his joke...he was doing the laughing. He was really amused by it. Sometimes he would put on layers and layers of coats, sweaters, vests, shirts

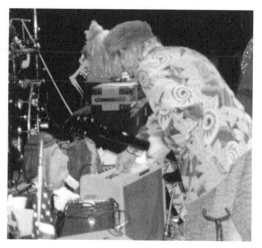

and scarves and stand there taking them off when he first went out on stage. And the hats...he had insane hats.

One of the most creative and interesting things he did was "Aluminum Foil Man." He'd come out on stage with part of his outfit made of aluminum foil. He made the foil part himself and it looked it, which made it even better. He really enjoyed making the foil clothes and hats and would kinda chuckle while he was making them. It had this Viking, "B" movie, science fiction, George Jetson kind of insane feel. The hats were especially weird and creative. We never knew what Joe was going to do. He was just unbelievably fun that tour. It was really entertaining for me, so I imagine it was for the crowd...and I know Joe was really amused by his creative endeavors, too. He was like that...he laughed to himself and enjoyed the joke of what he was doing while he was doing it.

We were opening shows for the Doobie Brothers that summer. If we do a whole tour with another band, we can't help but become very close friends. On this tour there was a lot of musician camaraderie because of mutual respect for each other's talents and material. It was a really great match. Both bands had similar fans from the same era, and we were drawing great crowds. We didn't know the guys from the Doobies before the tour, so the first night we all stood on the side of the stage and watched each other's show.

Joe & Pat Simmons

We set up our equipment with all the props we had on the stage in front of the Doobies equipment. They also had two drummers, so there were four drum sets on the stage every night. I loved that! Night after night, we watched each other's shows, until one night, we noticed that they would play about half of their hour and forty-five minute set, and then take an onstage break and introduce the band and talk to the crowd for a couple of minutes. The guys that worked for them would bring them water and a fresh towel or something. Then they'd finish their set.

One night, Joe came to me and said, "Hey, let's talk to their guys. Why don't we dress up like waiters holding trays with drinks and serve them during their break?" So, that night Joe, Rick and I put towels over our arms and served them their drinks on a tray. At first it really threw them and they were kinda in shock and then they thought it was hilarious. The crowd recognized us and they really got into it.

The Doobies immediately had to retaliate, and the following night had security guys bring us drinks during our set. The course was set, and, during that tour band pranks were brought to a whole new level, particularly due to Joe's influence. The next night, Joe went out to serve them wearing a big tuxedo coat with tails and Rick and I were wearing funny hats or something. We didn't notice it at first, but Joe wasn't wearing any pants with his coat. None. He went totally commando. When he walked out on stage, the audience didn't notice, but when he turned his back to the audience to give a drink to one of the Doobies, Joe's coat opened and Pat almost dropped his guitar and died. The audience didn't have any idea what was going on, but by then, we did. I couldn't believe Joe had the nerve to do something like that. I thought we had totally topped anything they could do, but I was wrong…it just escalated.

The Doobies were not to be outdone, so when we played in Columbus, Ohio, we were playing "Life in the Fast Lane," and all of the sudden three tanned muscular professional male dancers came running out from backstage. Normally, if anyone came running out from backstage, security would immediately grab them and escort them out of the venue, so the Doobies had to have had them in on it. The dancers spread out across the front of the stage and started stripping off their denim jeans and bumping and grinding in their little Speedo outfits with their butts shaking in our faces. It was still daylight, so you could really see them. I looked out and did a double take. I couldn't believe what I was seeing. It was horribly hilarious and the crowd really went wild. I don't think they cared if it was part of the show or not.

Joe amazingly kept his composure and kept playing, although he was laughing really hard at what was going on around him. It was during the part of the song where Joe had a lot of solo guitar work, but he never missed a note. He even went up and played guitar leaning into the one guy, jamming like the dancer was in the band. We were all really cracking up. The Doobies were all standing along the side of the stage enjoying their prank, laughing their heads off. It was a masterpiece. Hey, the Beach Boys had cheerleaders at the time. I'm sure the Doobies were just trying to raise the bar for our show. The dancers stayed onstage for the rest of the song. The Doobies really got Joe good with that one. So, was it over? Are you kidding?

The next night in Cincinnati, the pranks continued. We had a barrier behind the drum sets to kind of hide the Doobies equipment during our show. The barrier was big enough that people could get behind it and not be seen by the crowd. During our show we always did "stick toss" every night, so while we were tossing the sticks back and forth, all of the sudden we saw rubber chickens being thrown back and forth from behind the barrier, but it looked like it was part of our act. Then the Doobies stood up and doused us with silly string. I don't know

how many cans they used, but it totally covered us like a giant web. My son, Joe, was between the drum sets picking up the sticks we missed that fell on the floor, and was handing them back to us. He was already ducking flying drum sticks, but now he was completely covered with silly string.

We had our own prank planned. That same night, while the Doobies were playing "Jesus Is Just Alright with Me," Joe decided to pull a Biblical-themed prank. He came out dressed as Noah with a sheet wrapped around him, including his head. He was walking all bent over like he was old, and led some exotic animals, including an ostrich, across the

Joe as Noah

Stephen & Kristen Stills Wedding

Toledo 1995

Little Richard & Me

Smokey Wendell, Drew Carey, Me, Joe Walsh & Bernie Kosar

Gerald Johnson, Graham Nash, Stephen Stills, Joe Vitale Jr.,
David Crosby & Mike Finnigan - New Jersey 1996

Crosby, Stills & Nash - Rock N' Roll Hall of Fame Induction Ceremony 1997
Performing "Wooden Ships" Photo by: Joe Vitale Jr.

Joe Jr.'s first gig

Stephen Stills Blues Band
Back: Doug Hamlin & Gerald Johnson
Front: Mike Finnigan, Me, Joe Jr. & Stephen

Joe Walsh, Craig Doerge, Rick Rosas, Russ
Kunkel, Me & Mike Finnigan in Chicago

Feed the People

Conway Studios Los Angeles - CSNY Recording "Looking Forward" 1999

Photo by: Claudette Sooter

Above: Stephen & Andy Mixing "Man Alive"

Photo by: Beth Jordan-Kroll

John Langenstein & Me at Fenway Park (Red Sox vs. Yankees)

Tom Bukovac, Joe Jr. & Will Owsley

Joe Jr. & Me with the completed "Man Alive" album 2005.

David's birthday

Stephen's 60th birthday

Me & David Santos at The Louvre

Joe Jr. in Edinburgh, Scotland

David, Mike & James impersonate
street sign in Sweden.

Peter Frampton & Me   Mike, Jeff, Me, David & James

Above photos by: Jeff Pevar

Photos by: Buzz Person

David Santos, Me, David Crosby, Paul Rogers & Stephen Stills - London

Photo by: Buzz Person

Alan Rogan, Joe Jr. & Graham Nash

Andy Newmark & Me

Phil Collins & Me   Photo by: Jeff Pevar

Paul Rogers & Me

Tina the Fish...

The unnamed West Coast Hotel

*Pat Simmons, Me in Versausage
& Hutch Hutchinson*

My good friend Mark Lane, Australia 07

Sydney Harbour Bridge

Zoo photos by Buzz Person
Above: Mason Wilkinson

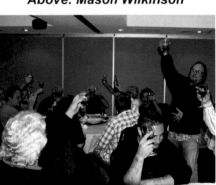

We DO have the same hair!!

Left: Mike "Coach" Sexton

Right: Donald "Buddah" Miller

Squatty Barrera, Thom Lowry & Me

Crosby, Stills & Nash performance photos by: Buzz Person

Stephen Stills, Me, Graham Nash, Kevin McCormick & David Crosby 2008

Photo by: Buzz Person

Back: John Tompkins, Jimmy Hatten, Aaron Swetland, Ron Covington, Jeff Chergosky, Ian Ayler, Todd Caldwell, Stephen Stills, Mike Klvana, Graham Nash, Gregory Hancock, David Crosby, Bill Long, Em Lehman, Kevin McCormick, Mason Wilkinson, James Raymond, John Gonzalez

Front: Michael Murphy, Stan Sooter, Jage Jackson, Rance Caldwell, Mouse DeLaLuz, Joe Vitale, Mike Warbington, Wayne Ballard, Crook Stewart, Will Nash

Howie Albert, Zakk
Wylde, Ronnie Albert

Leah Felder, Don Felder,
Stephen Stills, Alice
Cooper, Jack Blades, &
Tommy Shaw

Doug Hamlin, Kevin
McCormick, Jack
Black, Wyatt Issacs,
Stephen Stills

Bonnie Raitt

Alice Cooper

Phil Keaggy

Jackson Browne

Wavy Gravy

Garrison, John
Good

Keek Mitseff

Cheech Marin

Jim Manzo, Joey
Molland, Hutch, Raz

Eddie
Kramer

Jay Leno

Alan Rogan

Brian Wilson

Jeff Foskett

My touring backstage pass collection 1971-2002

Joe Vitale
"Plantation Harbor"
Shirt used on cover

Joe Vitale
"Rollercoaster Weekend"
Shirt used on cover

My NEW album!! "Speaking In Drums" 2008
To order go to: www.joevitaleondrums.com

My son's killer debut album!! "Dancing With Shadows" 2008
To order go to: www.joevitalejr.com

front of the stage. Joe had paid someone something like $1200 to $1500 to rent them from the Cincinnati Zoo. The animals were pretty freaked out from the loud noise the band was making, but they only walked across the stage one time.

The Doobies were into the success of their dance-themed prank, so the next show, they hired some strippers to come out on the stage and dance while we were playing. Not just strippers, but nasty strippers. They didn't serve us, but came out and did some kind of bump and grind dance. The Doobies nailed us again. We had no idea they were capable of something like that. They just didn't seem like that kind of guys.

The idea was not just to pull off a prank, but to momentarily mess with your head while you were playing the show. In Pittsburg, Big Bob the stage prop which was the figure made of stuffed clothing, was actually a person that night. He sat there and didn't move once the entire show until Joe mentioned him…then he got up out of the chair, waved at the crowd and walked off stage. It really threw Joe, who was used to it being a dummy. You could see a little fear mixed with confusion pass over his face and then he got it…another Doobie prank.

In St. Louis, both bands decided to prank Joe, and switch off band members with the Doobies on "Rocky Mountain Way." The talk box solo part was pretty long, and Joe had to keep facing forward because he had the tube in his mouth. It was the perfect time to switch. One by one, we traded off our instruments with the Doobies while the song kept playing. Then we went out front and sat in seats they had saved for us in the front row. So, there was Joe playing, and all of the sudden he looked down at the front row, and his band was sitting there. It really took Joe by surprise. He looked at all of us sitting down there, but the music was still playing behind him. It just didn't compute. Joe was so stunned he stopped playing, turned around and saw the Doobies playing, and just lost it.

It was like chess, and night after night on the tour, each band tried to win with the best prank. We finally pulled the prank that ended the contest. We were playing a minor league baseball stadium gig in Portland, Maine. We decided that since the Doobies seemed to like dancers so much, we'd hire some to serve them their drinks and dance for them. Since they had already done that to us, we had to raise the bar. Joe had someone go out and find some professional women impersonators and hire them for the show that night. These guys totally looked like women.

They came out on the stage and started dancing. There was one dancing in front of each guy. Then the dancers turned and faced the Doobies with their backs to the audience, opened their outfits and flashed the guys. So the "girls" that had been dancing for them suddenly showed them their packages. This prank had everything. Dancers, surprise and horror! Whoa! How do you top that? After that show, they said, "You win, we quit," and the pranks stopped for the rest of the tour. There was no way we could take the bar higher. I'd never say either band won. I think it was a draw.

This was seventeen years ago, and people still come up to me and say they saw the band that tour and talk about "stick toss" and the dancers. It was a great time and memory. We actually have video footage of some of the pranks. After thirty or forty years of touring, most shows are just a blur, but that tour and those gigs are something I'll never forget.

1991, Father Guido Sarducci, "Santa's Lament"

As the tour was winding up, Joe had moved on to another joke. He had decided to run for Vice President of the United States and took his joke to the max.   In San Francisco, Don Novello, as "Father Guido Sarducci," the character he played on Saturday Night Live, introduced Joe and announced his candidacy at a press conference on CNN. This opened up the craziness for the following year's "Vote for Me" tour, and an entire patriotic-themed wardrobe for Joe to indulge himself. It also brought Joe and "Father Guido" together for a collaboration on a song called "Santa's Lament."

The two of them had started to write the song and they needed a band, so they hired me. Father Guido came to my home for several days to record it. We recorded the track and I ended up writing part of the song as well as producing it with Don. Although he didn't really speak in broken English and wasn't a priest, I really loved how totally Italian Don was. When my parents heard Father Guido Sarducci was coming to my house for a few days, they wanted to come over and meet him. Italian AND a priest? Who could ask for more, unless he'd been a doctor, too? They'd never watched Saturday Night Live and thought he was a real priest or something, so when they met him they kept calling him "Father." I could tell Don was really enjoying that, and I have to admit, I was, too.

The song is about a bunch of little kids asking for high tech toys, and Santa's lamenting about all the expensive things they want instead of a football or a doll. One asks for real estate, another wants a yacht. He also complains about Rudolf's attitude, mentions the liability of Rudolf's nose during hunting season, and the kind of snacks people leave for him. We needed some children to sing part of the song and do some speaking parts, so we asked Joe Jr. and some of Susie's nieces and cousins' children to come over.

Susie's cousins, aunt and Mom came over to watch the recording, and it was really fun. The eight "kids," who sang really sincerely, are now out of college and most of them are married. There's nothing like the sweetness of children's voices, even if they're on a comedy song. The kids who sang were Jamie Gaston, Adam and Jared Singer, Amy and Ashley Swihart, Jami and Natalie Tondra, and my son, Joe Jr. We named them "The Becktones." After we had done all we could with the song, we shipped the master tape out to Joe and he put a great guitar part on it. "Santa's Lament" was released for Christmas that year, and I still always hear it on the radio around Christmas time. I only have one cassette of it, but I understand it's on the CD called "A Classic Rock Christmas."

L to R: Natalie, Jamie, Joe Jr., Adam, Jared, Ashley, Jami & Amy

CHAPTER TWENTY-ONE

<u>1992, Joe Walsh, "Songs For A Dying Planet"</u>

Joe called me and was going to record another album "Songs for a Dying Planet." The best part was that he was using Bill Szymczyk again as the producer. It was like old times! Fantastic! When I looked through the window in the control room and saw Bill, I always was calm and confident that if he said whatever I did was cool, it WAS cool. If he didn't like it, I accepted that because of all his knowledge and years of experience. It was also really great to see Bill and Joe working together again.

Bill was living in North Carolina at the time, so we recorded in Charlotte at a beautiful studio called "Reflections," which has since closed. We were there in January…great timing if you live in Ohio. One of the cuts on the album was "Theme from Baroque Weirdos," another "weirdos" song. I wrote it at home and Joe and Bill acknowledged that they couldn't beat the track and the demo became the master. I thought about calling it "Theme from Broke Weirdos," but we decided to change it back to "Baroque."

Joe was a ham radio operator and knew Morse code, so the secret message on that album was "Register and vote for me" in Morse code. The message was apparently too secret, and didn't get out the vote for Joe. The album cover was a crazy looking futuristic machine, which was a piece of artwork I had first seen back in 1972. Bill and Joe loved that thing and tried to use it for every album Joe recorded, but it never seemed to work. Finally, they had a title that made sense with the art and were able to use it.

1992, Joe Walsh, Vote For Me Tour

When Joe called me to go out for the Vote for Me Tour, I knew his campaign was going to be really fun. I was in. The band that tour was Joe Walsh, Rick Rosas on bass and vocals, Zak Starkey on drums, and me playing drums, keyboards, flute and vocals. It was really fun for me to get to play a tour with Zak, who's a really great guy and a fantastic drummer. He eventually went on to play with "The Who." He didn't get the gig with Joe because he was Ringo's son, he got the gig because he's a superb drummer in his own right. He really wasn't into doing stick toss, so we didn't do it very often that tour.

Since he was running for Vice President, which was much funnier than running for President, Joe adopted an Uncle Sam-themed wardrobe for most of the tour. I have no idea where he shopped, but he had flag capes, a huge top hat, flag vests, a flag top coat, and flag shirts and tee shirts. For whatever reason, he also sometimes wore a coonskin cap or a cowboy hat with really brightly colored Indian headdress feathers stuck in the band. I guess he wanted to look All American.

A group from Australia called The Brothers, who really were brothers, opened the show for us every night. They played bagpipes. At the beginning of our set, they'd start at the back of the theater and walk down the center aisle to the front, playing the bagpipes. Then we'd start the first song in the key of the drone of the bagpipes. It was really powerful and the crowd always loved it.

One of the brothers looked just like Tom Cruise. We used to tell the audience that we had a special guest in the audience that night... Tom Cruise...and the girls would just go crazy. Then we'd bring him out and they'd really go nuts, because when you first saw him, you'd think that's who he was, but once you got a good look at him, it wasn't Tom Cruise. It was always interesting to see realization set in.

Rick, Joe and I were always trying to amuse each other. It wasn't like there was a competition between us, we just really liked to make each other laugh. It seemed like the more outrageous we got, the funnier it was to us. One night Rick invited us over to his room to watch TV. He'd noticed that usually the image on the

Joe on the campaign trail.

screen didn't change for a long time during the news. So, knowing how much we loved nose glasses, he had drawn them on the TV screen over the CNN news anchors with magic marker.

I think Rick just wanted to show us that he was artistic, creative, and intellectually informed in a primitive, yet sensitive, way. Once Rick had showed us his TV, we realized we could decorate the news people with all kinds of accessories. We could add glasses, hats, sunglasses, hair, mustaches, beards, sideburns, freckles, necklaces, bow ties...all kinds of things. It was especially fun when we all did one together. It was hilarious to us and this got to be another "thing" we did that tour. Somehow Rick discovered that the marker came off the glass with toothpaste, so it didn't even cause any permanent damage. Don't try this at home. Remember, we're professionals.

1993, Walsh / Frey Tour

In 1993, Joe Walsh and Glenn Frey, who hadn't worked together since 1980 with The Eagles, decided to tour together, so we did the Walsh/Frey Tour. The band had two drummers because I played a lot of keyboards because of all the Joe Walsh and Eagles material. The band was Joe Walsh, Glenn Frey, Marty Fera on drums, Michito Sanchez on percussion, Bryan Garofalo on bass, Duane Sciacqua and Danny Grenier on guitars, Barry Sarna and Tom Canning on keyboards, and the four piece horn section, Al Garth on saxophone and violin, Chris Mostert on saxophone, Greg Smith on baritone saxophone, Darrell Leonard on trumpet, and backup singers Laura Creamer-Dunville and Shaun Murphy. It was one really great band.

I had known Marty Fera for a while since I used to go to see his band at Josephina's in L.A.. I even sat in once in a while. Then Marty got the job with Glenn Frey, so we were on the road together. When Joe toured with Glenn, he wanted me there for the same reason I played with the Eagles...so I could play other instruments, like keyboards, flute and also double drum. We had a ball, because with both Marty and Machito, we had quite a rhythm section going on back there.

It was a great tour and we ended up doing Joe Walsh, Glenn Frey, and Eagles songs...what a lineup! It was fun to play so many hits and it made an interesting combination of songs for the set list. In hindsight, I guess they were testing the waters for a possible Eagles reunion. Although they had claimed they'd work together "when hell freezes over," the following year in 1994, The Eagles were back together.

Anytime you get Joe on the road, he gets ornery. That tour we had a lot of people on the road and we had a lot of fun on the stage. There really wasn't room up there for Joe's elaborate props, because there were four guitar players. Four. And a bass player. There were a lot of amps in front of the drums. Joe had come to rehearsal with an amp that really sounded great, so Glenn said he had to have one, too. They were both playing through identical amps for the tour.

Glenn & Joe

Midway into the tour, we were playing "Life in the Fast Lane," and Joe's amp started breaking up on him during the main riff. Joe was really frustrated, so Joe, being Joe, went back and started kicking and beating up the amp in the middle of the song. Then he took his guitar off and put it through the grill cloth on the front of the amp. The crowd loves it when you do things like that and they thought it was part of the show, so they really cheered and clapped. But Joe wasn't doing it for the crowd…he was just really mad at the amp. Fortunately, there were two guitar players and the rest of the band who were still playing, because suddenly, both Joe and Glenn's guitars just stopped.

The reason both the guitars were no longer audible was because Joe, by mistake, had taken out Glenn's amp. Meanwhile, Glenn immediately noticed that his amp had stopped working, and turned around just in time to see Joe finish it off by shoving his guitar through the front. He stood there with his back to the audience and his mouth hanging open in disbelief, looking at Joe like, "What the hell are you doin' to my amp?" The rest of the band couldn't help but see what was going on, and we all started laughing. It was so unbelievably hilarious. Luckily, Glenn didn't get mad at Joe. So, for the rest of the tour, Glenn played through Joe's repaired amp, and Joe had to play through something else, because Glenn's amp was totaled.

When we played in Cleveland, I had some of the guys from the band come to my home for dinner on our day off. We were leaving for Indianapolis later that night, so the band came in the tour bus, which they parked on the street in front of my home. I was looking forward to having everyone over for a fantastic Italian meal. Susie made lasagna and we all were having a wonderful time. There were really a lot of us and we kind of split up a little. A bunch of us went downstairs to listen to some music, and some of the rest of the guys were upstairs watching TV or talking. It was a really nice evening, but then it was time for all of us to leave.

I remember that it was night time, and Marty walked out on our front porch and saw fireflies, what we call "lightning bugs," for the first time. I couldn't believe that he'd never seen them before, but Marty couldn't get over them. To him it was a complete wonder…all those bugs lighting up and flying around in my front yard. It was really neat to look at them through the eyes of someone who had never seen such a thing.

Susie and Joe Jr. walked out to the bus with us, and I wheeled my luggage around to the side and loaded it into the bay. It's always so nice for me when I get to stop through home in the middle of a tour. We all said our goodbyes and Susie and my son watched as the bus pulled away and then walked back into the house. Susie had started cleaning up when my son ran into the kitchen. He was completely white. "Mom!" he shouted, with horror in his voice while he pointed to the family room, "They left Joe Walsh sleeping on our couch!"

"No, they didn't!" Susie shouted back, equally horrified. They both ran into the family room, and my son pointed to Joe Walsh, who was all snuggled up in the pillows and afghan and was still sleeping like a baby, on the couch. They stood there for a minute, looking at each other, then Joe, and then back at each other, trying to figure out what to do next. "Don't wake him up!" Susie whispered desperately.

How could that happen? Well, you know how a big Italian meal affects you…you get sleepy. Joe had curled up at the one end of the couch and buried himself in the pillows with an afghan over him. We eventually had all ended up in the dining room for coffee and dessert and were sitting around talking. I asked, "Hey, where's Joe?" and Smokey said, "He must have gone out to the bus to sleep." There were a lot of us there, and the view from the dining room table was the back of the couch. We couldn't see him. When we left, Smokey assumed Joe was in his stateroom sleeping on the bus, because the door was closed.

I used to tell Susie stories about all the outrageous and crazy things Joe and I did all the time on the road. All these thoughts were going through her mind. She knew Joe and I stayed up all night a lot of the time…what was she going to do with him when he woke up in a few hours? She pictured Joe drawing on our water color paintings with magic markers. Was she gonna have to stay up all night with him or what? She REALLY didn't want to leave Joe alone and wide awake with nothing to do.

Susie grabbed the phone and started calling everyone who she could think of who was connected with the band. Unfortunately, this was still before we had cell phones on the bus. She knew once we went to bed on the bus, we wouldn't get up until we got to Indianapolis.

Meantime, after we had gotten out to the interstate and were rolling down I-77 for a while, "Smokey intuition" kicked in. He thought he just better make sure Joe was back in the stateroom sleeping. It was like Smokey was a mother hen…better check on the kids. He looked into the stateroom and there was no Joe. He quickly looked around for Joe…and it's not that big inside the bus…and then yelled to the driver, "We left Joe! STOP THE BUS!"

Well, you can't really just stop a bus or do a U turn on the Interstate. We had to get off at the next exit and then get back on and come back to the house. Minutes seemed like hours back at my home. My son Joe heard the bus pulling up and got Susie, who "greeted" me at the door. She wasn't smiling. With a voice bordering on hysteria, she pointed upstairs and nearly shouted, "You left Joe Walsh on the couch!" We had to wake Joe, who was buried in the pillows and still sleeping. He really enjoyed hearing what had happened and kept laughing about it. He put his arm around Susie and got his face up really close to hers and, laughing, said, "I bet you were *so freaked out.*" Susie looked back at him and laughed. "Ya think?" she asked. Then he laughed some more. He chuckled all the way out to the bus. I knew how Joe was. I could tell he was going to enjoy this for a long time.

1993, Joe Walsh / Hot August Nights

Joe Walsh called and asked if I could do a string of three gigs that August at the Ohio State Fair and two Navy bases. I didn't need to bring any gear, because it was going to be supplied at the gigs. The first one was in Columbus, Ohio, so Susie, Joe Jr. and I drove down. We arrived in Columbus and went over to the gig for a sound check. Rick Rosas was playing bass, and Joe had gotten Phil Jones for the extra drummer. When I showed up there were two drum sets and keyboards set up. I don't know who was supposed to play or what happened, but the keyboard player never showed up.

Joe Walsh, Rick Rosas, Phil Jones and I were there. Joe Jr. was sixteen. Joe Walsh looked at me, then he looked at Joey, then he looked at me, and then looked at Joey again. He said, "Can he do this? Can he play my music?" and I said, "Yeah!" so Joe Jr. was the drummer, and I was the keyboard player. I only played drums on "Funk #49" because there was no keyboard part, and "The Bomber," because I didn't think Joe Jr. knew that song. He played "Rocky Mountain Way," all the James Gang material, and all the Walsh tunes, including "Life in the Fast Lane." Although Joe Jr. was only sixteen, he knew all the songs and played great, with a lot of confidence and authority, and without any rehearsal. It was a heck of a challenge and he rose to the occasion magnificently, just like a pro. After that first show, Joe said, "Are you coming to the other two gigs? Joe Jr. said, "Yeah," and Joe Walsh said, "You're hired," so Joe Jr. did all three gigs. I was so proud of him.

CHAPTER TWENTY-TWO

1993 & 1994, Dan Fogelberg, River of Souls Tour

Dan Fogelberg called me in the late summer of 1993, and I went out and played drums on two tours in a row with him. Robert McEntee played guitar, and for the first leg, the bass player was Timothy B. Schmit. That was really cool since I had just finished working with Joe Walsh and Glenn Frey. The second leg of the tour was in 1994, and we lost Schmit because that was when The Eagles got back together. We replaced him with Mark Andes on bass, from the groups Firefall and Heart.

Rehearsing at Dan Fogelberg's ranch that fall was like no other rehearsal I'd ever experienced. It was like going on vacation to an exotic mountain resort. Like Dan, the ranch was totally unique. It was in the mountains and everywhere I looked there

Dan, Timothy, Me & Robert

was a breathtaking view. The night sky was pitch black and filled with thousands of bright stars every night. The air was clean and clear and the spectacular mountain views were constantly changing. The Victorian home was artistically designed and furnished by Dan, the complete Renaissance man, who was also a fantastic cook.

His master bedroom had a little round turret room above it, accessed by a spiral staircase. The round room was about a twelve foot circle, and up in that room, with 270 degrees of windows, Dan had a baby grand piano where he could play and write music. The view was beyond description and it changed not only with the seasons, but hourly with the time of day and the weather. No wonder he wrote the kinds of songs he wrote. I couldn't figure out how he got the piano up there and I had to know, so I asked Dan. He told me that before the builders put the roof on, they used a crane to lift the baby grand piano three stories up to the room. Dan's ranch was around nine hundred acres, which he partially leased to some of the ranchers up there. The land butted up against a national forest, so all the thousands of acres next to the ranch would remain untouched.

It was paradise up there. We didn't turn on the TV for two weeks, and it was wonderful not knowing what was going on in the world. Dan did occasionally watch TV, though. A few years before, he turned me on to a TV show he taped called "Mystery Science Theater 3000." Dan loved that show, especially when they made fun of him and his music in some of the episodes. There was one episode where they poked fun at Stephen Stills, too. Dan thought the show was hysterical and was a big fan. When I came back to Ohio, Susie, Joe Jr. and I started watching it and became devoted fans of the show, too. We taped and watched every episode until it went off the air in 1999. It's one of our favorite programs and we still watch our tapes of it. It was fun to share that with Dan…the sense of humor of that TV show.

We'd practice all day up at the ranch, and then about 6:00 PM, he'd go down to his wine cellar and break out some incredible bottle of wine for us. We'd have a glass of wine together while we listened to the classical music he'd put on, and then he'd make us dinner. He was like a world class cook and everything he made for us was absolutely delicious. What a class act.

One afternoon on a day off, a couple of us took the top off his Jeep and drove around the ranch taking pictures of the scenery. It was fall in Colorado, the air was crisp and the Aspen leaves were colored a bright golden yellow. The tree bark was shining white in the Colorado sun, the pine trees were a rich dark green and the sky was a clear bright blue. The grey stone in the mountains already had some touches of glistening white snow. I even caught a rainbow in the one photograph. See how sensitive I got from hanging out with Dan? Even so, I just can't adequately describe what we were seeing, and what Dan saw every day up there on his ranch. I took some photographs with my point-and-shoot camera even though I knew no photograph could ever do the scenery justice.

There were thousands of amazing shots we could take everywhere we looked. I just took a few pictures, but they came out spectacularly beautiful. So beautiful, in fact, that Susie had them specially enlarged and printed and I sent Dan a set that he had framed. Susie entered another set in The Quail Hollow Camera Club's photo contest for me. I won several ribbons and was embarrassed at the club's show when the other photographers asked me questions about what lens and shutter speed I'd used and I had to tell them I'd used a fixed-focus point-and-shoot camera. It was the beauty of that place that made the photographs so stunning. Hey, but at least I was being artistic like Dan!

In contrast to his artistic side, Dan was also a rugged outdoorsman. As you already know, I was raised in the city and the only horses I rode growing up were on the merry go round at Meyers Lake Park. During rehearsal at Dan Fogelberg's ranch, he asked if anyone wanted to go riding. He had a lot of horses. My wife, Susie, owned a horse when she was growing up, and had convinced me to go riding a couple of times in a very controlled trail riding situation. I had minimal experience, but I was game. After all, Dan, who was a very experienced rider, was our trail boss.

Dan took me down to the barn to pick out a horse for me to ride. To Dan's tremendous amusement, I referred to some of the newborn horses in the pasture as "ponies," …much better, I thought, than calling them "horsies" like I usually did. He laughed out loud and kindly corrected me, "Those are foals, Joe Bob." On our walk down to the stables, I described my horseback riding experience. He said, "Oh, OK, I have the horse for you. She's a twenty year old mare named, 'Honey' and she's very mellow." I said, "Sounds perfect."

He taught me how to saddle her up and before hitting the trail, he suggested that I ride her inside the riding barn, so we could get used to each other. She was a great horse, a sweetheart. Everything went well, so, off we went to hit the trail…me riding Honey, while Dan rode his personal horse, a large gray stallion.

As a kid in the 50's we had our share of cowboys on TV, and it felt just like being part of an old western, riding horses through the mountains. As I said, it was autumn in Colorado, the sky was deep blue with white puffy clouds, and the warm mountain sun was shining down on us. The air was clear and fresh, and it was totally quiet except for the sounds of the horses' hoofs on the trail, the birds and the breeze rustling the leaves on the aspen trees. The view was spectacular. I could tell that Dan loved sharing his world with me. I had never experienced anything like it, and I loved being there. There is probably a place in heaven just like it.

On our journey, Honey quickly realized she had a greenhorn on her back and stopped to eat the grass. Dan was slowly riding away from me, and I didn't like him getting too far in front. He was so at home on horseback. He wore his boots, hat, and gloves and looked like a real cowboy. I said, "Let's go, Honey," trying to reason with her, and I started bouncing the reins on her neck. "Giddyup!" She didn't respond. Apparently my voice held no authority. I yelled up to Dan that Honey wouldn't move. Dan yelled back to lightly kick her in the sides. I did. No response. I yelled up to Dan again, and told him that she wouldn't budge. He said, "Aw, man!" Being an experienced rider, he came galloping down the hill riding full speed towards me. "Whoa!" he commanded.   He came to a screeching halt, pulled out a switch, smacked Honey on the rear and yelled, "Git, Honey!" Honey took off in a full gallop.

I've never been on a horse that went that fast. On a horse, this was apparently third gear. The only time I ever got reckless with a horse was when I'd ride the horses that went up and down instead of the stationary ones on the Meyers Lake Carousel. I was scared to death, but I must admit, it was an incredible feeling, going that fast on the back on a horse. Between hysterical laughing, Dan yelled, "Pull on the reins, Hop A Long!"

When Honey finally stopped, I bent down and quietly told her it wasn't me who hit her. By now, the horses were getting thirsty, so we rode over to a small pond. Dan, being the kind gentleman and friend that he was, reminded me that horses liked to play in the water and that after Honey had her drink, to immediately get her out of there. He knew that she'd have thrown me into the pond and Dan felt I'd had enough excitement for one day. For the rest of the time at the ranch, he called me "Hop A Long Joe Bob."

We rode for about another hour through his spectacular wilderness ranch and brought the horses back to the stable, took their saddles off, and brushed and fed them. I have thousands of great memories of touring with Dan, but this was a day I'll never forget. Dan was so good and patient with me. He was like a Boy Scout leader taking a Cub Scout camping.

Once we started the tour, Dan and the band flew in a small plane, a King Air, which is a twin engine prop plane. It wasn't just small, it was very small. As I've explained with my many stories about flying, over the years I've had a lot of bad experiences, so I was especially wary of flying in small private planes, which I considered more dangerous.

We played in Erie, Pennsylvania, and the next gig was in Chicago. Dan and the band took the plane, and I went with the crew on the bus. Dan knew about all my bad flying experiences and said he wanted me to be comfortable when I was traveling. He said if I ever decided to fly with them I was welcome, but taking the bus with the crew was fine with him, too.

It was at least a nine hour drive to Chicago. When we finally got to the hotel, we asked for the room number lists for Dan and the band. The hotel said that Dan and the band hadn't arrived yet. There were no cell phones at the time, so there was a lack of communication. We got on the phone and nobody could find them or knew where they were. We figured that they should have been there an hour after taking off in the plane, and we started getting really worried.

We eventually found out that Dan and the band had taken off in the plane that night from Erie, Pennsylvania, and were headed for Chicago over Lake Erie, when the cabin of the plane completely filled with smoke. An overloaded electrical circuit sparked and heated up enough that it caused a fire inside the walls of the plane behind the electrical panel, so they couldn't even get to it to put out the fire. They took the fire extinguisher and doused the panel, which took out the electrical circuits. They were flying at night over Lake Erie with no electricity.

The pilot had to make an emergency landing in Cleveland, with the emergency vehicles on the runway and everything. The pilot was excellent and landed the plane without any incident. Dan and the band got out of the plane as fast as they could. Then they got a hotel, went to bed and didn't try to call, since by then it was the middle of the night. The road manager was able to book another plane, which brought them to Chicago the next day. It was just one of those nightmarish things you think would never happen, and it really scared everyone, even Dan. Thank God, I didn't get on that plane and have to go through another horrible flying incident with an emergency landing. Whenever something like that happened, I always thought of all the other rock & roll bands and stars that have been killed in small plane crashes. I didn't want to be one of them, so I stayed on the bus with the crew. I still got to spend a lot of time with Dan and the band, though.

Sometimes we had some spare time and Dan would want to play a game to pass the time. One of his favorite games was dominos, which he played all the time with the band guys. I'd never realized that it was an actual game. To this day, I don't know how to play it even though sometimes I watched the other guys playing it with Dan. He showed me how to play it one time, I tried it, got bored, and never played it again. I thought dominos were just used to set up an intricate design in a gymnasium, and then someone knocked them over so they'd fall one at a time.

All the gigs on Dan's tours were great, but if you worked with Dan Fogelberg, the gig you'd want to do was at Red Rocks Amphitheater in Colorado. Red Rocks is a beautiful natural amphitheater carved into the mountains and we always sold out when Dan played there. I remember that one time when we played there, the guys from Firefall, which had been Mark Andes' band, came and sat in with us.

Once in a while when I was touring with Dan, we'd play for a weekend celebrity auction at a fantastic resort. For example, we did one in Hawaii, one in Puerto Rico, and one at the Resort at Squaw Creek in California. People would donate really cool expensive things that were autographed, which were auctioned off to raise millions of dollars for charity. There were always a lot of celebrities there. Pierce Brosnan, Robin Williams, Alex Baldwin and Richard Dean Anderson were some of the celebrities at Squaw Creek.

During the day the celebrities skied in races. They were paired up based on their abilities, celebrity verses celebrity, and they had to ski down a pretty good-sized mountain. I've always been really careful with my arms and legs  because I'm a drummer, so I never got into skiing. My two favorite mountain sports were downhill afghan and cross country sofa. Dan Fogelberg, however, had spent the better part of his life in Colorado, and like everything he did, he was an excellent skier.

Dan was matched to race against Richard Dean Anderson, who played MacGyver on TV, who's also a tremendous athlete and world-class skier. Dan didn't win the race, but he gave him a good run for his money. I watched Dan race and I took a lot of pictures, including one of Dan crossing the finish line of his race. We played the concert that night and it was really cool to look out into the audience and see so many recognizable faces that appreciated Dan's music. He was the perfect class act for that event.

1994, "Top the Rock" Concert at the Rock & Roll Hall of Fame

It seems to me that The Rock & Roll Hall of Fame has always been in Cleveland, and yet it seems like only yesterday that my son, Joe, and I played for the "Top the Rock" concert. This event at The Rock & Roll Hall of Fame was held out in front of the building when the last I beam was put on the top. There were a lot of artists who autographed it, including my son, Joe Jr., and me.

The concert was fantastic and included Jerry Lee Lewis, The Outsiders, The Michael Stanley Band, Gary Lewis and The Playboys, some of The Raspberries, and several local Cleveland artists. It was a great moment for me when I got to play "Great Balls of Fire" with Jerry Lee Lewis. He totally rocked!

Me & Gary Lewis

The huge inflatable woman from The Rolling Stones tour was there, making an interesting visual. I was really honored to be part of a concert involving the completion of the construction of the building.

1994, Crosby, Stills & Nash, 25th Anniversary Tour

Meanwhile in 1994, it was the 25th Anniversary of Woodstock and Crosby, Stills and Nash had just released an album called "After the Storm." They had used different musicians than they usually had playing on their albums, to try to do something different. They were out on the road doing gigs with those musicians and I remember going up to Blossom Music Center and sitting in with them. It really felt weird because of all the years I'd played with them.

They were going to play at the 25th Anniversary of Woodstock that summer, and did a really great job, but David wasn't feeling well and was starting to get noticeably sick. By that fall, he was in the hospital and the doctors told him he had to get a liver transplant. I was scared to death for the guy, because at one point in the hospital he was in critical condition and the doctors had given him just a few more weeks to live unless a matching organ was donated. Fortunately, David was given a new liver and a new lease on life.

Facing death and then having the surgery be so successful, David came out of the hospital with a heightened appreciation for life. I could tell it was quite an awakening for him. Also, because of all the press, a son who David didn't even know existed came to see him. Out of the difficult ordeal David had faced came an unexpected blessing, a son named James Raymond. David discovered that James was not only his son, but also an extremely talented musician, and the two bonded in a very deep way. They started a band called "CPR," standing for Crosby, Pevar and Raymond, and toured during CSN's off time. Eventually James Raymond and Jeff Pevar would join the band and tour with Crosby, Stills and Nash.

Life is sometimes like that, surprising and unexpected. The dark places in life sometimes lead you to a new and wonderful place you couldn't have imagined and never would have gone to otherwise. I've been there in some very dark stretches of my life, and there have always been good things on the other side of that darkness. If you're going through a tough time and you're reading this book, don't lose hope.

1994, Tom Bukovac

Sometimes in life, you're doing one thing and it leads to something else which is quite remarkable. This was the case when I met Tom Bukovac. I first met Tom in 1994 when I was producing a project in Cleveland. We needed a guitar player, so I asked Dale Peters from The James Gang, who was playing bass on the project, if he knew of a local guitar player. He said to ask the keyboard player, who said he knew a guy...Tom Bukovac. He said Tom had moved to Nashville, but he happened to be in Cleveland visiting his Mom. I said to call him and see if he could come the next day and work with us for about a week. Tom said, "Absolutely," and showed up the next day. He plugged in his guitar and started warming up...I was stunned at how great he was...my jaw hit the floor. He was one of the finest guitar players I'd ever heard.

About a year later, the great Willie Weeks, who was Wynonna Judd's bass player at the time, called and asked me if I knew of a guitar player for Wynonna. I said, "I not only have the guy, but he lives right there in Nashville. Here's his name and number...and save yourself some time...just call him and hire him. He's fantastic." Although Willie Weeks has always respected my musical sense, he said, "We have to go through the proper channels here in Nashville and audition him. " My response was, "Nah, Willie, just hire him." Willie laughed and we said goodbye. Three days later, Willie called me and said Wynonna had auditioned Tom and hired him on the spot. I said, "Duh!"

Due to his own talents, efforts and personality, Tom has become the top guitar session guy in Nashville...quite a feat with all the great guitar players down there! He's an absolute pleasure to work with. Over the years, Tom played on several songs I was writing and recording which eventually ended up on my third solo album, Speaking in Drums, which was released in 2008.

1994, Jackson High School Band Trip To The Fiesta Bowl in Arizona

Toward the end of elementary school, when Joe Jr. had expressed a desire to learn to play drums, there was only one person who I trusted to teach him. I had him take lessons from Phil Zampino, who I'd taught to play drums many years before. I knew Phil was an excellent teacher and would teach him to play drums correctly. He took lessons from Phil for years and had natural talent and a love for playing. No one ever had to tell him to practice…he just did it. He'd already started writing and recording songs, so music and band became his main interests during his high school years…well, that and girls.

Joe Jr. was in the Jackson High School Band, which was called "The Purple Army," under the direction of Tim DeStefano. The Purple Army was enormous, with about 310 members, but it wasn't just quantity, it was quality. It was a show band, not a corps band, so by the end of every performance, the audience was on their feet clapping and cheering…clapping and cheering…what every musician craves. The band was everything you'd ever dream a high school band experience could be. It was exceptionally well run, had extremely organized and hysterically funny parent band boosters, and the students were highly motivated to work hard and achieve excellence. I couldn't have been happier that my son was in that band.

One time, before he could drive, I picked him up from a basketball game where he was playing in the pep band, which used to pretend to read the newspaper while the other team was being introduced. "Who'd your team play tonight?" I asked. "I don't know," he said thoughtfully, "…blue," referring to the color of their uniforms. Well, that narrowed it down. "Did you win?" He looked over at me. "I'm not sure," he answered, nodding and smiling, "but we sounded great!"

It was around that time that he also started taking guitar lessons because he'd noticed that the guitar player was always out front. Much later on, he started taking vocal lessons from Lois Whytsell, a fantastic singer I sometimes use on demos. I knew he needed a strong foundation for a lifelong career in music, and he worked hard to get better and better and build that foundation.

I went to the football games to watch him play in the band at halftime every chance I could. It was an added bonus that the football team usually won. Joe Jr.'s sophomore year the band was taking a trip to Arizona to march and play in The Fiesta Bowl Parade and game, so Susie and I volunteered to go as chaperones. Chaperone? Me? What were they thinking? The amount of people going on the trip was enormous. Someone actually told the kids, with a straight face, that the band was going on three separate flights, so that if one of the planes crashed there'd still be enough band members left to march in The Fiesta Bowl Parade. Like they'd really do that. We really enjoyed that joke.

We left for the trip right after Christmas and spent a week in Arizona. We didn't get much sleep because we had to get up before the kids and stay up after they went to bed. I think my biggest contribution was killing a spider in one of the kid's bath tubs. That's something no one's ever asked me do during all the years I've been on the road. We went to a lot of activities arranged to entertain the kids during the week we were there and finally went to the parade and proudly watched our band march by. Then we went back to the chaperone bus. "Is everybody here?" someone asked. No one was quite sure, so we sat there waiting. It was hot in the bus and we wanted to get going. Finally, one of the men took charge. We get things done. "Everybody who's not here, say, 'Aye.'" Obviously, no one said anything, so we left. We were in town and had probably only gone about a mile, when we heard shouting and screaming. We looked out the back window of the bus to see several of the chaperones… red-faced, waving their arms, and running after us. Oops.

On New Year's Eve we went to a barn out in the desert and had a barbequed dinner. Then we waited for midnight while the kids danced. I was a "watchdog" so the kids who went outside to try to sneak away from the group to "make out" didn't get too far out in the desert because of the rattlesnakes and scorpions. I must have done a good job, because after we got back, the other band boosters presented me with a "Watchdog Award." I've played on stage with some of the loudest bands in rock & roll, but I can't begin to tell you

how much racket 300 kids can make when it's finally midnight on New Year's Eve…especially when they noticed, two hours early, that it was already midnight in Ohio.

The next day we dragged our fried selves to the Fiesta Bowl game and the band held a flag as big as the whole field. I remember that the guy who owned the flag looked like Santa Claus. Then some of the band kids got underneath the flag and made it appear to wave. I have to tell you, it was spectacular. Mission accomplished, the next morning we packed up and flew back to Cleveland and the snow. I wouldn't have missed it…but I was also glad to get back home.

It was really important to me that Joe learned as much as possible in high school band, because I remembered how important the fundamentals had been for me in my career. By this time, Joe Jr. had firmly changed his career ambitions from being an astronaut to being a professional musician. I never doubted that he'd be successful. He was showing a talent and drive that was well beyond his years. Tim DeStefano had the band perform a song Joe Jr. wrote and scored his junior year, called "Southern Getaway." The Jackson High School Band Director his senior year, Thomas Holiday, had the band perform a symphony Joe Jr. wrote and scored, titled "Encounter." I was confident he was in excellent hands.

CHAPTER TWENTY-THREE

<u>1995, The Stephen Stills Blues Band, The Cool Party Tour</u>

The following summer in 1995, I went out with The Stephen Stills Blues Band for The Cool Party Tour. This turned out to be one of the most fun tours I've ever played on during my career. Because of his surgery, rehab and the birth of his son, Django, David was out of commission for a while, so Stephen put together a great blues band. At the start of the tour, Stephen had Mike Finnigan on organ, keyboards and vocals, Gerald Johnson on bass, and Mark Williams on drums, since I was still finishing up the tour with Dan Fogelberg.

Stephen's tour manager at the time was Denny Jones. One day I got a call from Denny, and he said, "Hey, this is Denny Jones. I'm out here on the road with Stephen  Stills, and he'd like to talk to you." I said, "Put him on!" Stephen said that Mark Williams had made a commitment to do another tour, so he asked if I'd come out and play the rest of the shows with him. Having finished the tour with Dan, I said, "Absolutely!" Working with The Stephen Stills Blues Band was always a fantastic experience.

We shipped my gear and I took a plane to Portland, Maine. I already knew Mike because we had worked together for years with CSN and I had met Gerald Johnson a few years back at an L.A. musicians club, called Josephina's. Gerald, who was from Steve Miller's band, was playing in a band with Mike that night. When I found out Gerald was in the band, I was really excited because he's a fantastic bass player and a really fun person.

Me & Gerald

I immediately liked him and really enjoyed playing with him. I also met Thom Lowry, who was Stephen's guitar tech, for the first time. Besides being an excellent guitar tech, Thom ended up being a very close friend of mine.

I really didn't need to rehearse with Stephen since I already knew all his material, so we just had a really lengthy sound check. It was a really cool band with such a great vibe. What a great tour! There were a lot of CSN crew guys so it was like being with family again. Denny Jones turned out to be a real character, to say the least…the cream of the crop of tour managers. He was a brilliant sports history expert and knew everything about sports. We couldn't stump him. We could ask him any question and he'd know the answer. People really like Stephen, so in practically every city he was offered the chance to do some really fun things when we weren't performing. Sometimes Stephen came, and sometimes he didn't, but Denny accepted a lot of the offers and set up things to do that included the band and crew. It seemed like we were always doing something together during our time off, and it was like being on the road with a group of friends.

That summer Stephen had hired a nanny named Kristen to care for his daughter, Eleanor, who was about seven. Kristen, who was from Portland, Maine, took care of little Eleanor on the road. Denny Jones just loved little Eleanor and used to give her jobs to do, like bringing the towels out to guys on the stage or giving us our drinks of ice water when we came off the stage. Denny would give her a couple of dollars each night as her pay. He was so good with her. You should have seen the two of them walking around together backstage...they looked like Yogi Bear and Boo Boo. We all loved Denny and I'd do any tour Denny was road managing. He had the perfect temperament and ideas for the road. He also went the extra mile for Stephen every time he asked. Sometimes it's the little things that mean a lot.

One time Stephen lost his putter, and he gave Denny the job of finding it. It took about three days of searching and investigating, but Denny eventually found it at a hotel where we'd stayed. Stephen had apparently put the putter down on the bed and it had gotten covered up with the blankets. An honest housekeeper had turned it in and the hotel had it. That's the kind of thing Denny would do...it wasn't all music business, it was personal things, too

We went to a lot of baseball games that summer. A lot. Denny loved baseball, so if there was a game in any city, we'd head for the stadium when we had a night off. We went on a picnic and sailing in Toledo and saw eagles...the birds, not the group...nesting in trees on Lake Erie. But the most hilarious day was when we went to King's Island in Cincinnati, Ohio, for a gig. It was a

Captain Stills & crew

beautiful Ohio summer day, so the entire band and crew were out in the park. It was hot, so we decided to go on the log ride that ends up going into the water. I remembered accidentally going on a similar ride at Disneyland several years before, and knew that the first part of the ride was a roller coaster. I really hate roller coasters. I said I wanted to take some pictures, so Susie and Joe Jr. went on the ride with Stephen. They were having a great time with him and were calling him "Captain Stills," so, of course, they had him sit in the front seat. They all came screaming and laughing into sight at the end of the ride and really got drenched when the log hit the water.

Since they were all pretty wet, we decided to go on the White Water Canyon ride, which was like going white water rafting down a river in a large inner tube. They all dried off waiting in line for the ride and I took a picture of us "before" and "after." We went on the ride and all got soaked...really drenched...I don't think we could have gotten wetter if we'd jumped into the water. Here's another example of Stephen's creative mind solving a problem. We were all walking around the park dripping wet, when Stephen said he wanted to go into the gift shop. We waited outside. Pretty soon, Stephen came out wearing all new dry clothes...even shoes. He'd left his wet clothes in the dressing room. He just kinda laughed about it when we asked him where his other clothes were. What a character!

One of the nights off, Stephen wanted us to all go see the movie "Congo." Stephen reads a lot, and he thought it was going to be a really serious thought-provoking movie. Susie has never gone to a violent or scary movie since I finished her off early in our marriage with a double feature of "Jaws" and "Earthquake." Susie was really concerned about going to a possibly gory movie we thought was about war in the Congo.

We all went to the theater. Stephen and Denny Jones sat in front of us with a huge tub of buttered pop corn. The movie started. A couple of scenes into the movie, all of the sudden there was the Earth from outer space, and Susie said, "What is this, Star Trek?" and she started laughing. Then we saw the gorilla named "Amy." It was so obviously someone in a suit. We all started laughing. Stephen and Denny still thought it was going to be a serious movie and were annoyed that we were laughing at everything, so they moved. It wasn't too long until seeing the gorilla started cracking them up, and we heard them laughing really hard a few rows over. It became a big band joke that tour and as soon as Congo came out on video, we bought it so we could watch it on the bus and laugh at it even more.

We were playing a lot of outdoor places and it was an especially hot summer, so Stephen had gotten a floor fan to keep cool during the show. I always crack up when I see the old fans with the blades exposed in antique stores…they just have litigation written all over them. The fan Stephen was using had a metal screen on the front so the fan blades were protected, but it was vibrating and making a lot of noise during the show. Stephen had the crew take the screen off…you can see where this is going. The crew guys said, "OK, but you're going to expose the fan blades," and Stephen said, "I know that, just do it. Take the screen off." That night during the show, Stephen had to make an adjustment on his amp, so he walked back and as he turned, his guitar cable got swept up by the fan blades.

The fan was slowed down, but the blades kept turning and started to reel him in like a big fish. It was like the fan had caught a marlin. OK,

we were in the middle of a show. For a moment, it seemed like Stephen, who was still playing, was trying to decide, "What should I do? Put the guitar down?" He was playing such a great guitar and didn't want to see it chopped up in a fan. What if the blades cut into the cord? Each revolution was pulling him closer to the fan. So, Stephen planted his feet and stood his ground, and the fan started wobbling and flopping… kind of hopping towards him, like it was a creature from The Twilight Zone or something. In a sci-fi movie, the crew would have "reversed the polarity" to save

Stephen and the guitar, but this was real life, so Thom, who saw what was happening, just unplugged the fan. The next day, Thom put the screen back on the fan and taped it up so it wouldn't vibrate and make so much noise. For the time being, Stephen and the guitar were safe.

But the fan wasn't finished with Stephen, and there was a second fan incident that tour. We were playing outside and this same fan, which was about the same size as a Fender Twin Amp, was running. By then, the crew had put a black grill cloth over the front of the fan so it didn't look ugly on the stage mixed in with Stephen's beautiful amp array, but air would still blow through it. It looked so much like an amp, that when we were playing "Love The One You're With," Stephen walked back to turn up his amp with his eyes still looking forward at the audience…and reached down…and instead of turning up the amp, he turned up the fan. We all saw what Stephen did and started laughing. Then he noticed that his guitar wasn't any louder but there was a lot more air blowing, and he started laughing, too. It was one of those great moments that happen on stage where the band shared a laugh together but the audience never caught on as to what just happened.

We traveled through a lot of beautiful countryside that summer, and I had my point-and-shoot camera on the road with me. One day, we were traveling on the bus between shows in the Vermont area, and we started seeing some spectacular scenery. Stephen was lying on the couch up front reading a book. He had a new really high-end camera, a 2

Denny & Mike clean the bus windows.

¼ inch negative Hasselblad. Stephen loves photography and he probably has taken 100,000 photographs. We started traveling through an area with absolutely stunningly beautiful countryside.

Stephen's camera was lying on the floor beside the couch. To look out the window, he'd have to do something like a sit up. We were all really getting off on the scenery, and doing "ooo's" and "ahh's" and saying things like, "Oh, wow, look at that!"

Stephen was engrossed with what he was reading, and yet couldn't help but hear all of us. He didn't want to miss the scenery but he didn't want to stop reading. In one of the best examples of multitasking I've ever witnessed, without ever looking up, Stephen reached down and picked up the camera. Then he held it up over his head, pointed it facing out the window in the direction we were looking, and snapped a picture. About five miles later, someone would say, "Hey, look at that lake, it's like glass!" and, still not looking, up would come the camera, he'd point it out the window and snap another picture. Stephen never stopped reading. What I'd give to see the pictures he took that day.

1995, Stephen Stills, The National Anthem

This was the tour that the Cleveland Indians were really on fire and the fans…including me…had hopes that the Indians would go all the way and win the World Series. Unless you were an Indians fan back then, you can't imagine the excitement of having that dream. It had been a LONG time since we'd been to The World Series. There was even a comedy movie made about the Cleveland Indians. Hey, our team wasn't a joke! We wanted to win! There had been a baseball strike and in other cities the fans seemed to be holding a grudge against their teams. Not in Cleveland. The stadium had been sold out every game since it opened, and tickets were next to impossible to get. Tribe Fever had swept the fans. Everyone knew all the players by name, and the fans loved them all, including Mike Hargrove, the team Manager.

What a lineup! The team was Sandy Alomar, Carlos Baerga, Albert Belle, Orel Hershiser, Wayne Kirby, Kenny Lofton, Dennis Martinez, Eddie Murray, Charles Nagy, Tony Pena, Manny Ramirez, Paul Sorrento, Julian Tavarez, Jim Thome, and Omar Vizquel, just to name a few. It looked like we were finally going to make it to the World Series, so it was especially exciting for me when Stephen was asked to sing "The Star Spangled Banner" to open one of the Indian's games at Jacobs Field in Cleveland. Stephen takes all things patriotic to heart and really wanted to do an excellent job. He stayed at The Sheraton in Cuyahoga Falls and really rested his voice. Singing "The Star Spangled Banner" a capella in front of a stadium full of fans has to be one of the most frightening and challenging performances any vocalist can face.

We drove to the game in the tour bus and pulled into the stadium basement to park. Who knew there was basement parking at Jacob's Field? Stephen had brought along the entire band and crew. We had tickets for seats, as well as access to a box upstairs. When it was nearing game time, we all went down to the field. Stephen only had a pitch pipe to get him started. I remember him saying how important it was for him to start on the right note, because otherwise the song would climb out of range. I really admired him for caring so much about singing it well. I knew he'd nail it.

We all got to go right down to home plate with him and stand there while he sang. Someone blew the note in the pitch pipe, and Stephen took a deep breath and started singing. I remember seeing his name in the stadium lights, and seeing the lyrics on the screen. Susie took photos of him as he sang, growing more confident with each note. He sang it beautifully and the crowd roared when he finished. You could see the look of triumph and satisfaction all over his face. It was a great moment.

Stephen & Slice

I was a big fan of all the Indians, but I particularly wanted to meet Jim Thome. He was standing nearby, but I didn't want to bother him right before a game, so I didn't go over. Heck, I wanted to meet them all. I had a lot of fun playing baseball as a kid, and had really special memories playing catch with Thurman Munson in my neighborhood.

Some of the Cleveland Indians were in a band together and I remembered seeing Omar Visquel on TV one night saying, "I want to play Led Zepplin rock & roll!" I wanted to send him some drum sticks, but I didn't think he'd know who I was, and I wasn't sure how to send them so he'd get them, so I didn't do that, either. Being there with Stephen was such a fantastic experience, because we finally did make it to the World Series that year.

The Stephen Stills Blues Band continued to travel across the country that summer, and later, toward the end of the tour, we played at a winery in California. David Crosby came to see us perform. It had been about nine months since his surgery and he was feeling great. He sat in and sang "Long Time Gone." His voice was as powerful as ever. Stephen and David talked afterwards and they decided that since David looked and felt so well, they could gear up and tour the following year as CSN.

The tour had been fantastic and I'd really enjoyed myself. The band, crew and Stephen had all been a lot of fun and the music had been excellent. For me, that tour even ended on a very special note. We'd ended up in the northeastern part of the country by the time we finished the tour. Our last show was in a small town with no major airport nearby. I was going to have to make a lot of connections and it was going to take me all day to fly home. The truck driver was going down to Nashville, and he said he was taking the Interstate right past where I lived. He said if I wanted, he'd be glad to drop me off. I thought that was a great idea and decided to do it because I'd be home at least twelve hours earlier than flying.

During the night on the trip home, out in the country where it was pitch black, he pointed and said, "Hey look, it's the aurora borealis." I'd never in my life seen it. He stopped the truck and we got out to get a better look. It was awesome...these huge colored bouncing sheets of light in the sky, shimmering and waving. It was like nothing I'd ever seen before...like special effects in a sci-fi movie. What a fascinating way to end the summer tour.

1995, Joe Walsh, The National Anthem

It continued to be a huge year for the Indians, and we did finally make it to The World Series, where we were playing The Atlanta Braves. Joe Walsh was asked to sing the National Anthem at Jacob's Field in Cleveland, and he invited me to come along. I went up to the game with Joe and during rehearsal, he said he wanted to sing, "...and the home of the...Indians," instead of "and the home of the brave," since we were playing the Braves in the series. I don't know if Joe was just kidding, or if he really would have sung it that way. The production people saw absolutely no humor in this. They were immediately ready to pull the plug on his whole performance if there was any chance he might sing it that way. I know Joe pretty well, and I wasn't sure what he was going to sing until after he was finished. To everyone's relief, he sang it the way it's supposed to go.

Although I loved baseball, I'd never been to a World Series game. I would have gone and happily sat in the worst seats in the house, but I was with Joe Walsh, who was singing the National Anthem, and we were given the red carpet treatment. We had great seats but it was really cold for baseball, about 45 degrees, with the wind blowing off the lake. It was worth it, though...I got to see and hear Joe sing and the Indians won that night. Tribe Fever continued!

CHAPTER TWENTY-FOUR

<u>1996, Crosby, Stills & Nash / Chicago Tour</u>

In 1996 CSN co-headlined our summer tour with the group Chicago. One night we'd headline and they'd open the show, the next night they'd headline and we'd open the show. The two bands actually flipped a coin to see who would start first. Chicago won, so we started the tour with them headlining the first show. We agreed to make a couple of exceptions. When we played in the city of Chicago, they headlined, and when we played in L.A., we headlined. It was a fantastic pairing and an excellent show. Both bands were drawing about the same amount of fans, and both bands attracted the same age group.

The band for that tour was David Crosby, Stephen Stills, Graham Nash, Mike Finnigan on keyboards, Gerald Johnson on bass and me on drums. Opening night of the tour was in New Jersey. We thought we'd start the tour off with a really great practical joke on David Crosby. The guitar techs have a whole rack of each guy's guitars backstage to keep tuned and ready to bring out onstage. Some of them are truly priceless. We wondered what would happen if one of the guitars had an "accident" on the way to the stage.

I had a hacksaw on the road with me and sawed through the back of the neck just past the metal "truss rod" on a cheap guitar that looked just like one of David's priceless Martin Guitars. A truss rod is a metal rod that goes through the guitar neck, which is used to keep the neck straight when the strings are tightened and tuned. With the truss rod sawn through, the neck would be easy to snap. We were all set. Everyone in the band and crew were in on it and gathered at the sides of the stage. This was going to be great. As we all waited to see him freak out when his priceless guitar was broken right in front of his eyes, I was hoping David didn't have any heart problems.

His guitar tech, John "Gonzo" Gonzales, went backstage and started to bring David his acoustic guitar, which we had replaced with our doctored duplicate. Then Gonzo faked tripping when he handed the guitar to Cros. What an actor! He stepped right on the body of the guitar and the neck snapped. Gonzo pretended to look appalled and shocked. The audience gasped. It was perfect!

Cros was only stunned and horrified for about a second…and it was a really great second, I gotta tell you…but then he realized that it wasn't his Martin Guitar. We were really disappointed that we hadn't been able to get him after all the work and expectations we'd had. We all did enjoy his appreciation of what a horrible moment that would have been if it had been for real, and all the trouble we'd gone through just for him. We could see it in his eyes and how he was grinning…Cros can really dish it out, but it's hard to get him…anyone else would have totally lost it.

It was really a great tour. We took a break in West Palm Beach and Stephen married Kristen Hathoway on May 27, 1996, at The Ritz Carlton. Kristen looked absolutely beautiful and I think Stephen was the happiest that I'd ever seen him. Mike Finnigan was the best man, and sang a beautiful ballad for the ceremony. Both bands, CSN and Chicago, were there, and after the small but beautiful ceremony, we all smoked cigars and drank champagne. Unlike most marriages and receptions, we were on tour, so Stephen and Kristen couldn't just leave and go somewhere…so we all went up to their suite. Wasn't that thoughtful of us? I'm sure they didn't want to be alone on their wedding night! There was a grand piano in the room, so I started playing oldies. Kristen's Mom was there and a bunch of us sat around the piano and sang together until about one or two in the morning. It was a really great and memorable night.

David, Stephen, Graham and I all had a lot of past connections with Chicago, and the band members all got along really well. I already knew the drummer, Tris Imboden, and we became really good friends that tour. Tris played a fantastic drum solo every night and I enjoyed watching him. I already had a relationship with Chicago's manager,

Jim Guercio, who owned and operated Caribou Recording Studios in Colorado. I also already knew the guys in Chicago. Jimmy Pankow and the Chicago guys played the horn parts on my album, Plantation Harbor, in the song "Sailor Man." I also had spent time with Jimmy when I recorded Don Felder's album.

Chicago was a really great band to have on tour. They're all excellent musicians and their band was incredibly tight. I loved hearing them play. They have a totally devoted fan base, and I noticed their fans that were my age were bringing their kids, who had also become fans. We sold out nearly every show.

The most memorable night of the tour was when we played in St. Louis. It was an outdoor gig in an amphitheater, and a tornado had struck nearby about an hour before our show. The people were already coming in and getting in their seats. A main grid went down and it knocked the power out for a huge area. It was about 7:00 PM and the show was going to start in about an hour, so the crowd waited for the power to come back on. Pretty soon it was show time, and we still had no power, but it was still light out, so it was no big deal. We had no power or PA system, so we not only couldn't play, but we couldn't make any announcements. The crowd could see that there was no power, so they knew why the concert wasn't starting. At least the storm had gone past us and it wasn't raining on them.

That night Chicago was opening and we were headlining. The crowd waited. Nine o'clock passed, then ten o'clock. The crowd was still waiting out in the pitch blackness, except for the reflection of lights that were miles away in the city. The dressing rooms were also dark, so we got back on the bus so we could have some power and lights. The promoter brought in a generator so we could do the show and started wiring it up. Around eleven thirty, the generator was ready to go. The crew fired it up and Chicago went out to start the show. They put the PA and the amps on it and that was OK, but when they added the lights, the generator blew out. Back to square one.

By midnight the promoter finally got another generator there and hooked it up. As soon as we could use the PA, we explained to the crowd that we could only use half the PA, the amps, and a portion of the lights. God bless that crowd. They sat there all night and were still waiting for us to play. I think it had become a "thing" with them, and they were determined to see it through. Chicago started at midnight, and we didn't go on until 2:30 in the morning. We were so tired by then, but the crowd had all stayed and waited…I think only about ten people had gone…so, we wanted to give them a good show. Although we were beat, it was actually kinda fun.

The problem was that we were going to play near Milwaukee the next night. It was a long way. Chicago played, got on their buses and left. Normally we would have already played and our trucks with all the equipment would have been on the road by about one thirty in the morning. Since we had started so late, we didn't finish until about five in the morning, and our trucks didn't leave until about six. The they had to drive all the way from St. Louis to Milwaukee with our lights, equipment and PA and set up again when we got there. The truck drivers could hardly make it.

We were able to sleep on the bus and got in about four or five in the afternoon and had to do a show that night. Since we had headlined the night before, we had to open the next night, which gave us even less time. The crew had to set up without any sleep. I think we started about twenty minutes late...that's how close it was. We just made it. The drivers and crew really came through for us.

That summer my son, Joe Jr., was playing great and I wanted him to sit in on the song "Woodstock" during our show at Blossom Music Center in Ohio. If anyone hasn't seen CSN do their version of "Woodstock," let me tell you, it's not the folksy tune from the 60's that it used to be. It rocks! I've always thought CSN should put it on one of their albums.

Joe Jr. loved playing to that song. He'd practiced it and the entire CSN set over and over. He was playing at a fantastic level, so I had no qualms whatsoever about his drumming abilities. Joe Jr. had invited several of his friends to the gig, so I really wanted him to have a chance to play. I had been asking Stephen if he could play for the show, but the CSN guys had seen Joe growing up since he was a baby, and they still thought of him as a kid, as "Little Joe," as they called him. Stephen didn't give me a definite answer and we started the show. Now I didn't have time to get a final answer out of him.

Me, Tris & Joe Jr.

It was a packed, sold out show. Joe Jr. came out onto the side of the stage and was standing with Susie, watching us play. The band played the entire show and had come to the last song, which was "Woodstock." Joe Jr. had never played or rehearsed with the band, but he knew the song and I knew the enormous crowd didn't faze him. I thought, "What the heck," because I knew he'd play great. I motioned for him to come over and I moved aside so he could take my place behind the drums. The three guys usually look back before we start, but for some reason that night they didn't, so they didn't see that Joe Jr. was going to play drums instead of me. I counted off and he started playing. We weren't playing double drums…he was the only drummer, and he was kicking ass. I was so proud!

I was standing nearby playing cowbell and Joe Jr. was playing so well that the three guys thought it was me. Stephen finally turned around and saw him playing drums with me on cowbell and looked at me with confusion for a second. I think he thought that I must be sick or something since I wasn't playing. I smiled and signaled back that I was fine. Then Graham and David turned around and saw him. He was playing so well that Graham shook his head, laughed and flipped him off. Then we all laughed. By this time all three guys were watching Joe Jr. and were nodding and beaming like it was their own son playing. The crew had gathered on the side of the stage, and they were clapping and smiling like he was their son, too. As I said, up to that time, the band and crew still thought of him as "Little Joe," just the kid they had watched growing up since he was a baby. None of them had realized what a talented musician this kid was by now. That night, with Joe playing near our hometown, was the highlight of the tour for me.

1997, Stephen Stills, "Man Alive"

I started out the year working on Stephen's solo album, which we ended up working on for the next eight years. Only one of those original songs went on "Man Alive," which was finally released in 2005. All the rest went on the CSNY album "Looking Forward," which came out in 2000.

1997, The Drew Carey Show

While I was in L.A. working with Stephen, I got a call to see if I was available in about three days to do the Drew Carey Show with Joe Walsh. I guess it was a last minute idea for the show to include music along with cameo appearances of people from Cleveland. Even though the show is taped in L.A., the setting for the series is Cleveland, Ohio, so Drew and the writers had the brilliant idea to include former and current Clevelanders and use them as extras in the party scenes. Besides the local news people who were on the show, special Cleveland guests were Mayor Michael R. White, Little Richard, Cleveland Browns star quarterback Bernie Kosar, and Joe Walsh. Since Little Richard was going to be able to come and play keyboards, they figured we could do "Rocky Mountain Way." Rick Rosas lives in L.A. and I was in town working with Stephen, so we had our band together and were invited to be on the show.

The plot of the show was that Drew's beer company, Buzz Beer, was going out of business so they decided to have a party for all their friends with free beer. Mimi and Drew had a fight in the office, as usual, and she decided to get even with Drew by putting the flier for his party in the newspaper. Drew's home was swamped with people, including Joe Walsh and Little Richard, who were supposed to be visiting the Rock & Roll Hall of Fame.

First of all, it was really a thrill to hear that we were going to do the Drew Carey Show, but when I heard that Little Richard was going to be there and play with us, I was blown away. I mean, he's a legend. The show was supposed to take place in Drew Carey's real home town of Cleveland, so I felt right at home on the set with the Chief Wahoo sticker on the refrigerator. I looked around and I remembered how people from northeastern Ohio enjoyed picking up the subtle inside things, like the Ghoulardi tee shirt and poster.

The people doing Drew's show were some of the nicest people I've ever worked with on TV and they were very accommodating and patient with us. Mimi was especially helpful and kinda coached us on what we should do during the shots we were in when we weren't playing music. She said we should be completely casual and act like we were at a real party, and really introduce ourselves and talk to the other people who were in the scene.

In the regular set for the outdoor scenes, Drew has a pool table in the backyard. When I saw it on TV, the backyard looked a lot bigger, but when I was actually there, it was really a small area. We had a drum set, our band equipment, and a lot of people from the party crowded into the little area. The stagehands actually had Joe stand on a box to raise him up a little, and they put my drum set on the pool table.

Then the director wanted us to play "Rocky Mountain Way" with Little Richard on keyboards. "Rocky Mountain Way" is in the key of E and Little Richard's favorite keys are C and G. He had learned the song for the show in the key of C. It's hard to  transpose on the spot. I remember Little Richard came over to me before rehearsal while Joe was warming up, and he said, "Hey, Joe, I thought this was in the key of C." I said, "No, we're gonna be doing it in the key of E, like the original recording." He told me he'd learned it in the key of C, and asked if I could talk Joe into playing the song in that key. Well, I knew that wasn't going to happen, but I said I'd see what I could do.

Little Richard was from the old school of the 50's. He always played a real grand piano and never played an electronic one, and he's known for playing on an eighty-eight key grand piano. Grand pianos are so expensive, heavy, and hard to keep in tune, that most people take a grand piano shell and stick a synthesizer into it, so it looks just like a real grand piano. Fortunately, that was the case with the piano Little Richard was going to play. With a synthesizer, I could transpose the key, so he could play a song in the key of C, but it came out playing in the key of E. I don't think Little Richard had any experience with electronic keyboards at that time, so he didn't know the key could be transposed electronically. So, that's what I did. When he wasn't paying attention, I just transposed it from E down four steps to a C, and told him Joe said it was fine to play the song in the key of C, rather than try to explain it. Little Richard was so happy.

But, during the rehearsal in the afternoon, someone must have tripped on the power cord, because the power went off for a second and the synthesizer in Little Richard's grand piano reset back to the original key. All of the sudden, Little Richard said there was something wrong with his keyboard, so I went over and hit a bunch of buttons real quick and changed it back. One of the most fun things was when we fired up the gear, and Little Richard started playing and singing…and we all joined in. He's so awesome, the real deal. He's such a natural and his voice was still great. He had to be in his 60's then, but he sure didn't look it, even up close. I saw him this past year, and he still sounds and looks great. What a thrill it was to have Little Richard right there playing "Rocky Mountain Way," a song I co-wrote. I can't tell you how great that experience was for me.

I also became friends with Cleveland Browns quarterback, Bernie Kosar, while we were doing the show. We exchanged information and a few years later when I was playing with CSN down in Florida, I invited him to our show. The whole experience taping Drew's show was really wonderful and fun and Drew couldn't have been nicer to us. Mimi was fantastically helpful to us, and the whole cast and crew made it a really good memory for all of us. Since I was positioned on the set right behind Joe, I got a lot of camera time. Rick Rosas did a great job, and you can see Smokey standing in the background in a lot of the shots.

Joe and Drew really hit it off and he made several more appearances as a reoccurring character playing himself. It's always fun to see people who are really from Ohio on that show, and I'm glad I was included in the Cleveland cameo special, which seems to run a lot more often than any of the other episodes….at least here in Ohio.

1997, Rock & Roll Hall of Fame Induction Ceremony

It was May of 1997, the only year the ceremony was ever held in Cleveland, and Crosby, Stills and Nash were being inducted into the Rock & Roll Hall of Fame. For me, that was fantastic! Stephen made Rock & Roll Hall of Fame history by being inducted twice the same night…once for The Buffalo Springfield and a second time for Crosby, Stills and Nash. Since the ceremony was held in Cleveland, we played a warm up gig at The Agora the night before. The band was David Crosby, Stephen Stills, Graham Nash, Mike Finnigan, Gerald Johnson, and me. Our performance was going to be taped and televised multiple times and would live forever in Rock & Roll Hall of Fame history. We wanted to sound great and a gig the night before really helped us get ready.

That year the inductees included the Jackson Five, our old friends the Bee Gees, Crosby, Stills and Nash, Joni Mitchell, Parliament-Funkadelic, The Buffalo Springfield and The Young Rascals, one of my all-time favorite bands. What an unbelievably great roster!

Since we were attending and playing for the induction ceremony and dinner for the event, everyone in the band had tickets, which were about $1500 each. I was taking Susie and my son, Joe, and Graham surprised me by generously picking up the

Me, Susie & Joe Jr.

cost of their tickets. He didn't make any big deal about it, he just did it. Graham's like that. He's a very generous, giving person. We all really appreciated it.

There was a host of celebrities there that night who were attending the event, introducing inductees or giving the induction speech for the honorees at the ceremony. Michael Jackson was there being inducted with the Jackson Five. He came down to the stage area during sound check wearing that small white mask he sometimes wears, but didn't talk to anyone or stay long. I didn't see him anywhere in the audience during dinner. James Taylor was there to induct Crosby, Stills and Nash and Michael Douglas was there with Stephen. My son, Joe, got autographs from several of my heroes, including The Young Rascals and legendary Beach Boy, Brian Wilson.

I noticed that Diana Ross was sitting at the next table with Barry Gordy. She was there for The Jackson Five's induction, and was sitting with her chair back against mine during the dinner. I held her in such awe, admiration and esteem...the voice on all those wonderful Supremes singles from the 60's...one of my favorite girl groups. I leaned over and whispered to my son and Susie, "Look who's behind me." "Get her autograph, Dad," Joe Jr. urged, but I was too shy and said I couldn't do that. The next thing I knew, Joe Jr. had gotten up and walked around the table to ask her for it. She was really gracious and signed his booklet.

The Bee Gees were sitting a couple of tables away and it was so cool to see them inducted, remembering when CSN had recorded at Criteria when The Bee Gees were recording Saturday Night Fever. They were really having a great time over there...it was a fabulous night of celebration. CSN had been on a roll since 1969 when their first album had won a Grammy. It's been a great opportunity to work with so many Rock & Roll Hall of Fame musicians during my career, including The Eagles, CSN, and Neil Young.

1997, Crosby, Stills & Nash Summer Tour

We continued the CSN tour and headed south. We were going to perform at the Jackie Gleason Theater in Miami, Florida, and arrived at the gig in one of the band tour buses. We pulled up to security and one of the guards started giving us a hard time. He wasn't going to let us into the gig. He wouldn't move the blockade and the bus driver wouldn't drive through it, even though we were yelling for him to do it. OK, who would get a tour bus to try to sneak into a gig? It would cost way more than tickets. The argument continued to escalate and things were getting pretty hot. We couldn't believe it. Finally, Graham had had it, and went out the door at the front of the bus to talk to the guard, face to face. In honor of where we were trying to go, we encouraged Graham by saying, "To the moon, Alice!"

Again, who wouldn't recognize Graham Nash? Did they think we'd hired a look-alike? Thom Lowry, who's a good friend of mine and the guitar tech that tour, went right off the bus after Graham. Thom is a black belt. Graham started to move the blockade. The guard shouted and took a step toward Graham, and in seconds…and I mean SECONDS…Thom Lowry took him down and that guard was on the ground. Thom was talking to him in a very calm and controlled manner and explained that he shouldn't move or he'd get hurt in that particular hold. That immediately calmed the guard down. Thom let him up and the guard let us drive inside and do our sound check for the gig. We all had a new and greater respect for Thom, and I had to compliment myself for my excellent choice in friends!

1997, Rock Walk / Stephen Stills Induction Ceremony

Besides doing the CSN tour that year, I was also doing a lot of work with Stephen on his solo album and with The Stephen Stills Blues Band when CSN wasn't on tour. The Stephen Stills Blues Band played several shows along with The Bruce Willis Blues Band for the grand openings of Planet Hollywood restaurants, where Bruce Willis was a partner. Bruce seemed more like a rock & roller than an actor and was completely at home on the stage. He's a fantastic blues singer and harp player and had an excellent band with him. The shows were really cool, because they'd close the street down out in front of the restaurants. The walls of Planet Hollywood restaurants were filled with tons of Hollywood memorabilia from movies.

Meantime that year, Stephen was filling his own walls with Stills memorabilia. It was a year of awards for Stephen. He had already been inducted into the Rock & Roll Hall of Fame for both CSN and The Buffalo Springfield. Then, during our CSN tour that September, Stephen was inducted into "The Rock Walk" in L.A. The Guitar Center on Sunset Boulevard has a "Rock Walk" out in front and leading up to the door, which is kinda like the stars on Hollywood Boulevard. You can probably find almost every notable rock & roll guitar player in the world making up that walk. The Rock Walk is made up of beautiful squares that look like they're made of black granite, with the artist's hand prints, name, and date of induction on it.

The hand print impressions are made at the induction ceremony, followed by the artist writing his or her name below the prints in the wet cement. The impressions are later cast into a permanent square and then placed in the walk. There are always photos taken of the artist holding up their hands covered in the cement. Crosby, Stills and Nash were playing a seven day stretch at The Fillmore in San Francisco, so The Stephen Stills Blues Band guys who were also in CSN...Stephen, Mike Finnigan, Gerald Johnson and I...got up that morning and flew down to LA to perform with Stephen after the ceremony.

Bruce Willis came and introduced Stephen as not only a fantastic musician and singer, but also as his friend. It's a really cool ceremony and a tremendous honor which gets national attention in the press. Stephen looked fantastic in one of his trademark Hawaiian shirts and graciously thanked everyone for the honor. After the induction, we went into the store for a while and there was equipment all set up, so we played about three or four tunes. Bruce Willis knew me from the gigs we had done earlier that year, so as we brushed shoulders when I was walking to the stage, he said, "Hey, Joe," and I said, "Hey, Bruce," As he was walking away from me, he said, "It's early." It had already been a long day for me. "I hear ya," I answered. It was a really long, but a really great day. If you ever go to The Guitar Center on Sunset Boulevard in L.A., Stephen's square is right before you walk into the main entrance of the store.

After we played, we hopped back on a plane, flew to San Francisco and played again at The Fillmore that night. We'd heard rumors that Neil might come, and about the fifth night, he showed up. He sat in and did "For What It's Worth" and "Ohio." David, Stephen and Graham had been talking to Neil about playing together again, and I think that they were just kind of testing the waters. The crowd loved it. It was really cool to see the four of them up there singing and playing together. It was even better to hear them again. What a fantastic vocal blend!

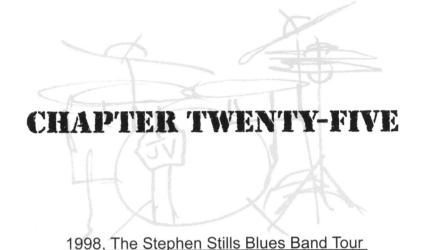

CHAPTER TWENTY-FIVE

1998, The Stephen Stills Blues Band Tour

In 1998, The Stephen Stills Blues Band toured with Mike Finnigan on keyboards and vocals, Gerald Johnson on bass, my son, Joe Jr. on percussion, and me on drums. The band was used to playing together and the show was going along really well when Stephen walked out in front of his "monitor" to play a guitar solo for the crowd. Monitors are speakers that are about fifteen inches tall and point toward us so we can hear ourselves playing. They make a small barrier between the band and the crowd and Stephen really loves to get right out in front of them and close to the fans during his guitar solos. He stands at the edge of the stage, bends over his guitar and plays while the crowd reaches their arms out toward him. It's a really exciting moment of showmanship and the crowd really gets into it and connects with him. It always generates a lot of applause and cheers. When Stephen was nearing the end of his solo that night, keeping his eyes forward on the crowd, he backed right into the monitor…and fell backwards over it.

He wasn't hurt, but he landed flat on his back. I don't know how it didn't knock the wind right out of him. He was laying there on his back with his knees bent over the monitor, and, unbelievably, was still playing his guitar solo…he never even paused. It looked like when you lay on your back and put a bed pillow under your knees, except Stephen was on the stage in front of a huge crowd and never missed a note. I don't now how he did it. He totally held onto his concentration and just kept playing. It was a good solo, too.

Thom Lowry, Stephen's guitar tech, and someone else from the crew ran out and lifted him back onto his feet, and the crowd cheered… they thought it was part of the show. Through all that, even while he was being lifted back on his feet, Stephen never stopped playing. I gotta tell you, I was really impressed. First, that he didn't get hurt falling backwards like that, and then that he had the composure to keep playing without ever missing a note. I couldn't believe it. He made what could have been really embarrassing into a fantastic show moment.

1998, Joe Walsh, "Rocky Mountain Elway"

ABC wanted to use classic rock songs re-recorded with new words for Monday Night Football that year. The Denver Broncos, with star quarterback John Elway, were going to be playing and they needed a song for them. Since Joe Walsh and our band had lived in Colorado when we wrote "Rocky Mountain Way," it seemed natural to use that song for the Broncos, especially since "Way" rhymes with "Elway." The Monday Night Football people had written new lyrics, but of course, Joe altered them.

OK, I'm from Ohio, and I can't tell you how many times John Elway and the Denver Broncos crushed our dreams of the Cleveland Browns going all the way to the Superbowl. We just could never get past them. But I really respected John Elway as a fantastic football player, and it was really cool that we were going to cut a reworded version of "Rocky Mountain Way." Joe came to Ohio for two days and we rewrote, shortened and re-recorded it. Then Joe taped a music video which they showed on Monday Night Football. It was a really fun project and I got to go to the Superbowl with The Stephen Stills Blues Band and see John Elway and the Broncos play and win the following year.

Hollies / Byrds / Buffalo Springfield / CSN / CSNY
Reunion Tour Plan

Back in 1987, The Buffalo Springfield had nearly reunited to do a reunion tour. It was now eleven years later, and, once again, there was talk of a reunion tour. But this time, it was a fantastic plan, a fan's dream concert, and my son and I were going to be included. The Hollies, The Byrds, The Buffalo Springfield, CSN and CSNY were talking about reuniting to do a huge reunion tour the following year with all five acts on the bill...The Mother of All Tours! Graham Nash, who was always coming up with brilliant ideas, had the idea in the back of his mind for years, and it looked like it was finally going to happen. Stephen called me and told me the plan, which was still in it's early stages. He was really excited and all for it. I started to think it was really going to happen.

It was obviously going to be a mega tour and Joe Jr. and I were both going to be playing assorted instruments with the different groups. We'd either play drums, percussion or keyboards, along with back up vocals. Apparently someone had talked to all the major players and everyone was tentatively willing to do it. It would have been the most talked about and must-have ticket for fans that year. Can you imagine the song lineup each night? We expected to play huge venues and I was really excited about it, too. What an opportunity! What a tour to play...rock & roll history! I got excited just thinking about it. Once again, things fell through and the tour never happened. Graham's amazing idea for a tour is still possible, but there will be a day when it can never happen.

1999, Superbowl XXXIII, The Stephen Stills Blues Band

Stephen has a LOT of friends, one of which is Jim Irsay, who owns the Indianapolis Colts. Sometimes Jim sends his private jet to pick Stephen up to go to games, just because he likes him so much. I think Stephen is one of Jim's favorite artists and friends. Every Superbowl, all the owners of the teams each hold a huge party the week leading up to the game. The Colts weren't in the Superbowl in 1999, but Jim Irsay threw an elaborate Superbowl party in Miami that year. He called Stephen and asked him to play for his party, so

Stephen called our Blues Band guys and set it up. What a great gig. We not only got to do a show at a fantastic private party on a yacht, but we also were given tickets to the Superbowl.

On Friday, Susie, Joe Jr. and I flew to Florida. We were all glad to get out of Ohio in January. The next day was Saturday, which was the day of the party. We all got in the van with Stephen and the band and headed to the gig. We didn't know much about it or what it was going to be like, except that it was going to be on a yacht. We pulled up to the pier at the marina, and boarded a beautiful, three story yacht which was docked and waiting for us. All of our gear was already loaded on the yacht, which was lavishly decorated with exotic tropical flowers.

Each deck had a band, a bar, and fantastic food. The top floor had a reggae band, and we could go outside on the deck and look out over the water. Our floor, the rock & roll deck, had mountains of shrimp, an elaborate bar, an outstanding dinner, and fruits and desserts everywhere. The coolest thing for Joe, Susie and me was that Bob Newhart, doing stand up comedy, opened the show for The Stephen Stills Blues Band. All of Bob Newhart's TV series were favorites of ours and it was such a treat to get to see him do a show, especially since we got to sit about eight feet from him. His humor is so unique, with all his pauses and stammers and perfect timing…he's absolutely the best. After the show, Joe Jr. was walking around outside at the back of the yacht and ran into him. He said Bob Newhart was really nice to him and they talked for a while. I think that was the best thing about the whole trip for him…or maybe it was the cheerleaders.

The Miami Dolphins' cheerleaders were there in their uniforms and posed for pictures with some of the guests. Joe particularly enjoyed that. Yeah, maybe that was his favorite part. He still has the photograph on his wall. Eventually we went up to the top deck to enjoy the view. It was dark by this time, and the moon and stars were shining on the Intercoastal Waterway as the yacht cruised by all the sparkling lights along the way. The warm ocean breezes smelled like salt water. What a night! It was spectacular!

The next day, we went to a nearby hotel and met a bus Jim Irsay had rented to transport all his guests to the game. I'd never been to a

Superbowl game before. The Denver Broncos played the Atlanta Falcons in Miami for Superbowl XXXIII. The stadium was obviously sold out and there were people and performers everywhere. Each seat had a souvenir cushion and the entertainment was unbelievable. The pre-game entertainment was Kiss with a fantastic pyro show. Then Cher sang "The Star Spangled Banner." The halftime show starred Big Bad Voodoo Daddy, Stevie Wonder, Gloria Estefan, and tap dancer Savion Glover. It seemed like there were as many performers on the field as fans in the stands. They really put on a show.

The commentators for the game were in a covered booth right in front of us. It was really exciting to see Pat Summerall, John Madden, James Brown, Terry Bradshaw, Howie Long and Cris Collinsworth covering the game. We got to see John Elway win his second consecutive Superbowl and be named Superbowl MVP. What a fantastic career! We knew we'd be seeing John again in five years when he would be inducted into The Professional Football Hall of Fame in my home town, Canton, Ohio.

1999, Crosby, Stills and Nash Winter Tour

Crosby, Stills and Nash did a short run of gigs in February of 1999. The band was David Crosby, Stephen Stills, Graham Nash, Mike Finnigan on keyboards and vocals, James "Hutch" Hutchison on bass, Joe Jr. on percussion and drums, and me on drums. We referred to it as "The Valentine's Day Caesar's Run," since we did the same shows every year for three years running. We played two nights in Atlantic City, two nights in Las Vegas, and two nights in Tahoe. For someone from Ohio, the four feet of snow that fell in Tahoe while we were there was spectacular, but to them it was just a "dusting." After the gig in Tahoe, Robin Williams, Kevin Nealand, and Mike Myers came backstage… you can imagine three comedians together. They were absolutely hilarious.

This was the last tour that CSN used a percussionist in the band. Even though it was a short one, I'm so glad that Joe Jr. was able to do the tour as a band member with me. He'd come a long way from being "Little Joe" with the tambourine on "Teach Your Children."

1999, Crosby, Stills, Nash & Young, "Looking Forward"

Stephen and I were in the studio in L.A. working on his solo album. I could tell Stephen was really excited because the songs were coming out great. I stayed in L.A. and continued to work on the material, while Stephen went up to Neil's ranch and played him the songs. Stephen could tell Neil really liked them, so he asked him if he'd like to come down and put some guitar on his record. Neil said absolutely yes.

About a week went by and then Neil called Stephen to set it all up. He said something like, "Since I'm coming to L.A., how about if I bring a couple of my tunes down and get you to play on 'em?...and I'll check with David and Graham…maybe I could get the three of you to sing on 'em." It was obvious that something was brewing. Before he came to L.A., Neil must have spoken to David and Graham, because I got a phone call from Stephen who said that I should come to the studio. It sounded to me like a go…a CSNY album. This was going to be great and the timing was perfect. I knew Stephen's material and I'd gotten a glimpse of David's and Graham's new tunes when I was just hangin' with them. Neil always brings killer tunes to any project, so this was looking sweet. It seemed like every few years the four guys had tunes that uniquely worked together to make an album, so Neil came to L.A. to put the guitar parts on the songs. We met at Conway Studio and were standing together outside when Neil drove up, making quite an entrance driving one of his vintage cars. He parked the car and got out wearing torn jeans and some kind of weird hat with his wild hair and sunglasses. He looked over at us and said, "Let's rock!" I loved it. This was rock & roll!

It was the first day at the studio with all four of the guys there. As with any album, the first day was really fun and really important…it was show and tell day…it was "what you got?" Each of the guys played their songs and after listening to everyone's material, the excitement level was really high. We mapped out our plan over a great dinner. The next day we started to work on the album, the vibe was great, and we continued throughout the winter and spring of 1999. We worked really hard on it and I had the pleasure of working with Donald "Duck" Dunn for the first time. We took the months of June and July off while Neil toured, and resumed working in August at Neil's ranch. He still had all the animals and turkeys, and invited us to stay at The White House again. Everyone kept their cars away from the goats…much to my disappointment.

We worked on a few more tunes and they mixed the rest of the songs. We were there for about three or four days finishing it up. It sounded great and I thought I'd completed the project, but Neil asked me to stay and lend an extra ear for the mixes. He said he valued my opinion, so I stayed another two or three days. I checked the mixes listening in the control room, while Neil checked the mixes driving around the ranch in his truck. Hey, whatever works. The album was released later in the year.

CHAPTER TWENTY-SIX

2000, Sonic Foundry / Sony loop libraries

A friend of mine contacted me and asked if I'd be interested in putting together a "loop library" for his company, Sonic Foundry. Hey, I'm not exactly a computer guy, so I wanted to know what the heck a loop library was. He explained that it was software that had digital sounds on it which could be used to write songs or make records on a computer. Some of the sounds were single beats or notes, and some were longer patterns. They could be repeated over and over, making it possible to construct an entire song using layers of the loop libraries...for drums, guitar, bass, keyboards, etc. He asked if Joe Jr. and I would be interested in doing a Latin Percussion library. We thought it was a great idea and decided to do it.

It was a LOT of work, and I never could have done it without Joe Jr.'s computer knowledge. The first library sold pretty well, so next we thought we'd be creative and do a library of rhythms and sounds from items that weren't musical instruments. We made the rhythms and beats with pots and pans, crow bars, bumpers, trash cans...etc. That library ended up being called "Junkyard Rhythms." It's hard to believe that all those sounds and rhythms are made from objects instead of instruments. We hear them used all the time in TV shows, movies and commercials.

Sonic Foundry was purchased by Sony, who asked us to do a third library. I went through all the libraries that Sony had, and I realized that they didn't have one of the Hammond B3 organ. I was used to using an organ in songs, and with my music background, I knew that particular sound has been a staple in classic rock and blues. Joe Jr. and I created "Organ Donor," followed by a second B3 library, "Organ Recipient." I've heard from lots of musicians who appreciated having it. I played on both organ libraries myself, but my son, the computer genius, produced, engineered and edited it. Finally, we put together "The Vitale Collection," which includes drums and percussion. I love the creative aspect of the libraries...that songs can be constructed using software and a computer. It opens up musical composition in a whole new and creative way. It's like having a band at your fingertips.

2001, Stephen Stills solo album, "Man Alive" continues

Stephen had asked me to produce his solo record with him back in 1997, but as I said, most of the songs we recorded for the "Man Alive" album had been used on the CSNY album "Looking Forward." We were basically starting from scratch. I figured we'd do the vocals at Stephen's, but when I asked him where we were going to record the tracks, Stephen said, "Right here." Stephen had everything we needed to record...except for one thing... someplace to isolate the drums from the guitars when we recorded tracks.

No problem! Stephen pointed at the back porch off the studio and said, "There's our drum room. Build it." I called my Bunion Brothers partner, guitar player and tech, Doug Breidenbach, and we proceeded to enclose the porch for Stephen's studio. It wasn't exactly one of the jobs I'd expect as a co-producer of an album, but, hey, it's rock & roll...anything for the artist! It took us about two weeks to finish the extension to the studio and we even made it look like part of the original house. Yeah, the Bunion Brothers were proud of our finished project. All those years ago when I was building my soap box derby car, I never imagined that someday I'd be using what I learned to build a studio drum room for Stephen Stills.

After the construction was finished, my next priority was, " Let's talk about songs." Stephen had tons of material that were outtakes or unfinished pieces of material scattered throughout two inch masters, quarter inch mixes, DATS and even cassettes. One of the jobs that Stephen gave me as co-producer…thanks, a lot…was to go through all that material and make notes, document tapes and see what was there. I found lots of great material...probably enough for about ten albums.

One of the songs we found was a two-inch 24 track master of the song "Feed the People," recorded in 1979. We decided that we loved the song but probably needed to re-cut it, although the chorus vocals were incredible. We re-cut the track with Stephen on guitars and bass, Joe Jr. played percussion, and I played drums and keyboards. We digitally extracted the original chorus vocals and gave our new music track and the old chorus vocals to Joe Jr. to blend together. Easier said than done. Because of all the years and transfers, the vocals weren't a true A-440 pitch. Joe Jr. tuned them up to A-440 and discovered that the tempos were a little different. He worked several days and brilliantly placed them in the track with the correct pitch and tempo...an amazing piece of digital surgery.

Studio Photos by: Joe Vitale Jr.

Someone sent the resurrected song to UNICEF at The United Nations and in 2004 Stephen was honored with the UNICEF Children's

Champion Award. Joe Jr. told Stephen he should write a cook book called "Feed the People" and publish it when he released his solo album "Man Alive." Most people don't know this, but Stephen is a fantastic gourmet cook, and everything he makes is out of this world. It would

have been THE cookbook to own...I've eaten at his home so many times over the years, and everything he's ever made has been unbelievably delicious.

One day while I was working at Stephen's, he said he wanted to do a new song and to set up to record two acoustic guitars and two vocals. I said, "Who's the other guy?" and he said it was going to be Neil Young. I

thought, "Man, this is going to be cool." Neil showed up around noon and in three takes, they nailed it. It's amazing to watch those two guys work together. The song was called "Different Man." I wish all songs were that easy to record. What a couple of pros.

After all the records that I'd made with Stephen over the years, this

one was very special to me because it was basically just the two of us and we shared the mission. He showed me a great deal of respect, as I did him, and we had a lot of fun making decisions together, whether easy or tough. We worked on the album over a period of eight years and it was finally released in 2005... mission accomplished!

2002, Dan Fogelberg Tour

In 2002, I rehearsed and then went out for what was to be my last tour with Dan Fogelberg. Dan's life seemed to be at such a wonderful point. He looked healthy and was full of energy and life. He had just married Jean and was the happiest I'd ever seen him. He was excited for all of us to meet her and talked about her all the time when she wasn't there with him. Dan referred to her as the love of his life, his soul mate…he was one happy man. They were planning to build their dream home in Maine and talked of sailing on the ocean, which Dan loved. He also spoke of retiring in a few more years, but I never was sure he was serious.

The band that summer was Dan, Mike Hanna on piano, Mark Andes on bass, Robert McEntee on guitar and me on drums. We had all played together with Dan so many times that now it was very comfortable, like a group of old friends. Dan planned an acoustic set in the middle of the show, so he could play his entire range of songs, from acoustic to rock & roll, each evening. He also had us each do a  song from other bands we'd worked with, so Robert did a blues tune, Mark Andes did a Firefall song with a flute solo I got to play, and I got to sing "Rocky Mountain Way."

We rehearsed at Dan's ranch and again we were given the royal treatment. After rehearsal each day, Dan got a bottle of excellent wine, turned up the classical music and cooked dinner for us. After dinner, we'd sit out on his back deck with either another glass of wine or espresso, and look at the thousands of stars in the Colorado night sky. Because of the altitude and the clearness of the air, they were always the brightest I'd ever seen. Then Dan would pass out Cuban cigars, and even though we weren't regular cigar smokers, we smoked them together. A guy thing. Up on the hill back of Dan's home, we could see and hear the elk running at night.

Because of the influence of Dan and my experiences on his ranch, I had come to a place of tremendous respect for this Colorado life Dan lived. I understood the peaceful contentment of the hardworking lives of the cowboys, ranch hands, and the people who chose to live there.

I guess I'll always be a city slicker, though, and I never knew what to expect…I had some pretty interesting experiences for someone who was raised in the city. One day we were leaving Dan's ranch to pick up some supplies, and we had to stop the Jeep until a porcupine got off the road and out of our way. I'd never seen one and I didn't realize how big they were. They were probably as common to the people who lived up in Pagosa Springs as ground hogs were in Ohio, but for me, it was an exciting experience.

The tour was about six weeks long and we played theaters, casinos and amphitheaters. They were the perfect sized venues for Dan's music, and that summer he seemed to have a special connection with the audiences. He sang and played guitar with the perfection his fans had come to expect throughout all the years of his career and he was really enjoying performing.

Dan was always very quick-witted and ready to joke around. In Cleveland, we were on the stage during soundcheck and someone tried to get into the tour bus… and set off the alarm. It was making a rhythmic beeping and Dan immediately started in playing and singing "Day Tripper" to it. I especially enjoyed the tour, because Dan usually had a plane, but that year we had too many guys and Dan had Jean with him, so we took a bus and we all rode together. Great Band. Great times.

When I said goodbye to Dan at the end of the tour, I had no idea I'd never see him alive again. In the early summer of 2004 I tried to contact Dan to see if he was going to tour and got no response. I left messages at his ranch, in Maine and with his management. It wasn't like Dan not to respond, and I started wondering what was going on. I made a few more calls, but no one had heard from him or knew what he was doing.

Eventually I got a group email from Dan and Jean with the horrible news that he had advanced prostate cancer. They said they were going to fight it with the most advanced cancer specialists and treatments in the world. The email was kind and gentle and expressed their love for everyone. They knew how devastated everyone was going to be when they received the news. Here they were facing Dan's cancer, and yet thinking of others. They said they were upbeat and hopeful, and asked for some space. Then, they broke off contact with nearly everyone. I can understand that…they would have been getting calls and discussing the cancer every day…it would have completely taken over their life. They wanted to fight it and, as much as possible, enjoy the time Dan had left together. I tried to find out how Dan was doing over the next few years, but I heard everything from "the cancer is in complete remission" to that he was at death's door.

I knew Dan had sold the ranch and I didn't have his current email, phone number or the address in Maine, so I couldn't send a card to let him know I was thinking of him, although I'm sure he knew. Then I heard that his guitars were for sale in Nashville, which I took as a very bad sign. Finally, I got a phone call from Kenny that Dan had passed away, fortunately before his death was reported on the news. His wife, Jean, has sent beautiful and eloquent group emails to his friends since he passed away. His passing still seems unbelievable and impossible, and it was a very sobering and sad time for us all. Dan left me so many wonderful memories that it seems like he's just away enjoying life on the ranch or sailing in Maine with Jean and that I'll see him again. I hope that someday we'll play music together again in a much better place.

CHAPTER TWENTY-SEVEN

2003, Crosby, Stills & Nash Tour

Stephen called and said we needed a bass player for the CSN tour that year, so I told them I had the guy and suggested that he call David Santos. I first met David Santos in 2001 when I went to Nashville to record Bobby Gatewood's album "Finally Home." My friend, phenomenal guitar player Tom Bukovac, was playing guitar and producing the album and David Santos was playing bass. He was a fantastic bass player and we really hit it off, so I knew he'd be great for

Photo by: Buzz Person

the tour. Stephen trusted my judgment and had David fly to L.A. to audition. In an hour, Stephen hired him. The band for the 2003 CSN Tour was David Crosby, Stephen Stills, Graham Nash, Mike Finnigan, David Santos and me.

Of the band and crew members who have worked with CSN, I've been there the longest, closely followed by Rance and Mike Finnigan. Besides being an unbelievable musician, B3 player and vocalist, Mike

Finnigan has been a good friend since the day we met. He's one of those people always described as having "star quality." He's the story and joke teller…Mike should definitely have his own TV show. When Mike sits down with you and has that twinkle in his eye, you know you're in for a great time. The best stories Mike tells are those  he re-enacts as the story unfolds…he can have the entire bus in stitches. Sometimes we'll settle back in the bus and say, "Tell us a story, Uncle Mike-ie."

CSN has a huge fan base in the United States, and we did a lengthy tour that year with four separate legs to it. They also have a big fan base in Italy, and several great Italian guys came all the way from Italy to see us. Since they came all that way and they run a huge fan club for CSN, the band invited them come to our soundcheck. They came over to see me and say hello during the soundcheck because they're Italian and they liked it that I'm Italian, too. They spoke very broken English. I'm not criticizing…you should hear my Italian! One guy came up to me and said, "Hey, are you-a gonna play "Long-a Time Gone?" So, I said, "Why, yes," and I laughed. I got up on the stage, went to the piano and started playing a polka, like, "oompa oompa oompa, da da da, oompa oompa oompa, da da da." Then I started singing, "Long-a Time Gone, what's a matta you? Long-a time gone, what's a matta you?"

Normally, I don't ever make fun of other people's songs, especially songs my boss wrote, but David Crosby has a really great sense of humor, and David can dish it out, OK? So, by now, I was singing into the mic and the rest of the band guys had started playing, and Stephen, Graham and David were all laughing. Then they all came up on the stage and started singing, and David picked up his guitar and started playing. All the stage hands and the people stopped what they were doing and stared at us. They couldn't believe it. The

Italian guys loved it. That's become one of the inside family jokes with CSN. We wanted Crosby to do it that night at the show, but he wouldn't go that far with it. Geez, he's put out a record since then, you'd think he'd do a "remix" version of "Long-a Time Gone."

2005 Crosby, Stills & Nash European / USA Tour

We rehearsed in LA for two weeks before we started the 2005 CSN European and United States Tour. The band was David Crosby, Stephen Stills, Graham Nash, Mike Finnigan on keyboards, David Santos on bass, James Raymond on keyboards, Jeff Pevar on guitar and me. I went home to Ohio for a week after rehearsal and then flew from Detroit to Amsterdam, where I met the rest of the band. It was about an eight or nine hour flight, with two meals and two movies. Some of the band guys who'd gotten there first were waiting for me at the airport. After being on the road for over forty years, it's not that thrilling to go to a city I've been to twenty or thirty times before… sometimes I even know the street names. This tour, however, was going to be new and exciting.

It was June, and driving from the airport to the hotel, I looked around and saw windmills, spring flowers and beautiful canals all through the city. We had a couple of days off to adjust to the time change, so David Santos and I would leave the hotel in the morning, walk for hours and still be in Amsterdam. We stayed at The American Hotel and performed our first show at a big festival at Pepsi Stage. I didn't realize how big CSN was worldwide until I got that far away and we had such a huge fan response. The people were really nice to us and I couldn't help but notice that nearly everyone was in good shape. They all seemed to either walk or ride bicycles, so there wasn't a lot of traffic. And where did we eat, since we were in Europe with really fit people around us? McDonald's. We called McDonald's "The American Embassy," and even though there were warnings about mad cow disease, we figured McDonald's would be safe. In fact, we made a point of it to eat at McDonald's in every country we visited.

After the show in Amsterdam, we drove to Paris. We got in late at night and checked into our hotel. To me, it looked just like any other city, but when I woke up the next morning and opened my drapes, there was the Eiffel Tower! I reflected back on my artwork in Santa Fe and my brief career as a sidewalk artist. I immediately became the artist "Van Joe." We had a day off in Paris, so Mike Finnigan, David Santos, James Raymond and I took a train over to The Louvre. The guys seemed to instinctively know where I'd fit in. When I arrived at The Louvre, I realized that I had a once-in-a-lifetime opportunity. It hit me like a lightening bolt and I was filled with inspiration. Thoughts crossed my mind of going back to the hotel, sharpening my pencil and whipping out some masterpieces…and setting up my art stand right outside on the sidewalk. I was sure my work visa would cover it. I spotted a place that would be perfect, but the guys weren't very supportive. Musicians. Graham has a great eye for art, and if he'd been with us, I knew he would have realized my genius and backed my venture. Imagine, I was at the entrance of one of the most famous art museums in the world…empty-handed. We went inside to admire the works of my fellow artists.

I was especially excited to see some paintings by Vincent Van Gogh, my favorite artist, who interestingly enough has a name similar to mine. While David Santos was pointing out something in the brush work, his hand must have gotten into the infrared beams in front of the art work and he set off the alarm. We all started scattering and some guards came over…we walked away from David like we didn't know him. Since they didn't arrest David, we continued touring the museum together. I saw there was a huge line to see the Mona Lisa, but we waited to see it. I don't
know exactly what I was expecting, but I was surprised to see how small it was. I found myself looking at the painting and thinking of "cut out man," since we'd made one using her body and had added my face. We finally left The Louvre and headed outside to see the sights of Paris.

We could see The Eiffel Tower in the distance, so we had no trouble finding it. It was bigger than I'd imagined...way bigger than it looks in pictures. We stood under it but didn't go up because the line was too long. It was our only day off in Paris, so we walked the two or three miles to the hotel and since it was such a beautiful day, we ate beside the Seine River.

After the gig in Paris we drove to Brussels, Belgium, which reminded me of a gig in the Midwest. We went back to Amsterdam, stayed at the same hotel and played another festival. Then we flew to Helsinki, Finland. What sticks out in my mind was that at 3:00 in morning it was still light out, like in Alaska...daylight all summer. We saw beautiful scenery on our ferry boat ride to Stockholm, Sweden, where I got a fantastic hot dog. I loved the beautiful stone roads. And what a treat to go to Oslo, Norway! We were asleep and the bus driver stopped and woke us all up so we could look at the scenery. It was stunningly beautiful, with waterfalls, mountains, rainbows, and lakes.

Then we flew to London where I met Susie and Joe Jr. They had flown all night, but I was anxious to show them all the tourist sights, so we walked over to see Big Ben, Parliament, and Buckingham Palace, which was across a beautiful park. We were in England about ten days and hubbed out of London to our various gigs. The band traveled through the streets of London in our tour bus on the way to Edinburgh, Scotland, and we all were enjoying seeing so much of the city. Susie, Joe Jr. and I went up to the second story of the tour bus and found Pevar and his girlfriend, Inger Jorgensen, playing the guitar and singing Beatles songs. We got to see a lot of the countryside, with  the beautiful stone fences lining the pastures. We arrived in Scotland and toured the castle in Edinburgh on a foggy, cold, rainy day, which gave it a lot of atmosphere. The castle was fantastic, and I couldn't help but think of the fun Joe Walsh, Rick Rosas and I could have shooting items out of the cannons.

After Scotland, we went back to Manchester, England, where Graham Nash was born and raised and then played in his original band, The Hollies. Then we traveled back to London, where we played at the Apollo Hammersmith Theater. We had a lot of people come to the gig…David Gilmore from Pink Floyd, Paul Rogers from Bad Company and Free, Brian May from Queen, and my dear friends, Alan Rogan and Andy Newmark. It was just fantastic to be in London and see the red telephone booths, the black taxi cabs, and all of the beautiful architecture. On our last day in London we rode on one of the double-decker buses and then the subway, called The Tube,

Mike, Pevar, James, David & Me

to see the crown jewels and the Tower of London…just one week before the terrorist attacks. Then Susie and Joe Jr. flew back home, and I continued the tour with CSN.

In Bonn, Germany, we went to Beethoven's house and saw his priceless piano…all roped off with signs that said "Do Not Touch." Graham was looking at the piano. I knew what he was thinking. Like the devil on his shoulder, I thought, "Touch it…touch it!" just willing him to ignore the sign. Graham reached out…and didn't just touch it, he PLAYED it. I couldn't believe it. Inside my head, I heard angelic choirs singing. I loved Graham for doing that! The piano was really out of tune, by the way, probably since no one was ever going to play it again anyway.

After Bonn, we played in Frankfort, Germany, which was a more cosmopolitan town. Then we got on the bus and drove to Montreaux, Switzerland, for the Montreaux Jazz Festival. We arrived late at night, about 2:00 or 3:00 in the morning, and as we were approaching the city… I just couldn't help myself…I opened the bus window and yelled…"RIC-CO-LA!" The guys shook their heads in disgust and said, "We can't take you anywhere!" I laughed and did it again. It didn't echo like in the TV ad, by the way…maybe I needed more altitude.

The next day I got up and walked along Lake Geneva. There was music everywhere, street vendors, art, and food, with the Alps in the background. It was spectacularly beautiful. We were there for about two days, and with our laminate passes we could get into any show. Backstage at one of the shows, I met BB King, who was also playing at the festival. Phil Collins came to our show and brought his beautiful son, Nicholas, who  was about four or five. His son was starting to play drums and the two of them sat right behind me on the stairs where I walked up to my set. It was really fantastic to see Phil again, and to meet his son.

The best part of the tour for me, personally, was when we drove over the Alps and into my homeland, Italy. I got to see the vineyards and forests, the mountains, and the shoreline of the Mediterranean Sea…it was as beautiful as I'd imagined. When we got to the hotel in Milan, we had a day off and met in the lobby before we all went out to dinner. I was really looking forward to eating in Italy and was excited to be able to compare their cooking with my family's…after all, both were "authentic" Italian cooking. Italians love to cook for friends, family…hey, anyone…it's part of who we are…we like to feed you to show our love. I knew there would be restaurants everywhere. One of the guys went up to the concierge and asked where the nearest Italian restaurant was located. I looked up and thought, "He's kidding, right?" The concierge looked up, started laughing and speaking in Italian. Then he switched to broken English and said, "We no have-a "Italian" restaurant...we have-a "restaurant." We all laughed.

I'd asked my Aunt Katy what to eat in the different cities, so I knew what delicious Italian foods were the specialties of each area. After Milan we went to Luca, which had spectacular ancient Roman structures. Just west of Luca is Pisa, with the Leaning Tower of Pisa. We had a day off and went over to the Tower. I can't fully explain how I felt seeing it in person after I'd seen it all my life in pictures, but it was fantastic. It's an ancient structure which was a bell tower, and it was built like a silo, with a spiral stairway on the inside of the wall. It seemed like a million steps while we were climbing it, and

the higher we got the more we could tell it was leaning. Now, I'm kinda claustrophobic and I definitely don't like heights, but I was determined to go to the top, no matter what.

We got to the first level, which has four bells and a twelve-foot round dome-shaped plexi-glass center, so we could see all the way down to the bottom on the inside of the building. That was terrifying. We kept climbing. To get to the very top, we went above the bell level on another spiral staircase. The steps are

about one foot wide and we were hugging the inner wall of the walkway...and then we came out on the top of the Tower...it was REALLY frightening...but we made it! The Tower really leans and the guardrail was only about 3 feet tall...I heard many people have fallen off it. We went down to the ground

level and all did the tourist thing… got a photograph taken so it looks like we're holding up the building. We followed my Aunt Katy's advice and had a great Italian dinner that night.

After visiting a couple more Italian cities, we went to Barcelona, Spain. It's absolutely beautiful, with lots of amazing architecture, scenery and stores. The weather was gorgeous, so we walked everywhere on our day off there. We played the show and Stephen played "The Spanish Suite." Stephen speaks Spanish during the song and the people loved it. That was our last show and then we flew home after five fascinating weeks in Europe. We took a couple weeks off and then resumed our tour in the United States. It was a fantastic summer!

The year ended on an unexpectedly horrible note. Tragically, Gerry Tolman, Stephen and Graham's manager, was killed in a one car crash December 31, 2005. I got the terrible news that New Year's Eve as I was sitting down to dinner. Gerry was driving near his home that morning when his car hit some water and hydroplaned into a telephone pole. He'd died instantly. The accident had happened that fast, in just a few seconds, and he was gone. It was unbelievable and I was really shaken up, as I sat there and the news sank in. One week from that night, it would have been thirty years since Gerry and I first met and became friends. The people all around us celebrating New Year's Eve sharply contrasted with my feelings. I was reminded again of how short and unexpected life and death can be.

CHAPTER TWENTY-EIGHT

<u>2007 release, Stephen Stills, "Just Roll Tape"</u>

On April 26, 1968, Stephen Stills was at a Judy Collins session in New York City. After she was finished, Stephen offered the engineer some cash if he could stick around for a few hours and record some demos of the songs he'd been writing. The engineer agreed. So, Stephen, with just his acoustic guitar and vocal mic, sat down and in a couple of hours recorded what were to become some of rock & roll's most classic hits, including "Suite: Judy Blue Eyes," "Helplessly Hoping," "Wooden Ships," "Change Partners," "So Begins the Task," and "Black Queen." Can you believe the list of songs? Once the songs were recorded in 1968, I imagine the engineer cut an "acetate" copy of the tapes for Stephen to take with him. An acetate was a record made out of a material that only had the capability for a limited amount of plays. The quarter inch tape remained at the studio, which was a common practice at the time.

In 1969, the tape that Stephen had made and left at the studio was only one year old. That particular studio would sometimes rent rooms to bands for rehearsals if they weren't booked for recording sessions. A New York musician, named Joe Colasurdo, had a band which occasionally rehearsed at the studio. On his way there one day, he walked past a dumpster in the alley behind it. Joe saw that, for whatever reason, the studio had thrown a bunch of boxes containing tapes in it. He was curious and looked through the discarded boxes. One of them had Stephen Stills' name on it. By 1969, everybody knew who Stephen Stills was…except, maybe, the person who threw out the tape…so Joe rescued the tape from the dumpster and saved it for over thirty years.

Graham and I have a good friend, Dan Curland, who we call "Mystic Dan." He owns "Mystic Disks," a record store in the city of Mystic, Connecticut. If Dan doesn't have whatever album you're looking for, from any era, he'll find it. He's found several vinyl albums I was looking for, when I couldn't find them anywhere else. In the summer of 2003, Joe Colasurdo was in Mystic, Connecticuit, and saw Dan's cool record store, so he went in. Since Dan is such good friends with the entire CSN family, he has a lot of CSN memorabilia and posters displayed on the walls of the store. Joe asked Dan if he was a big fan of CSN, and Dan said that Graham Nash was a personal friend of his.

Joe asked if Dan was able to get in touch with Graham and Dan said, "Yes." Joe gave Dan his contact information and asked if Dan would tell Graham that he had a tape from 1968 with Stephen Stills' name on it. Dan, being a collector himself, knew the value of the tape and called Graham immediately. Graham called Joe, who brought the tape to him when we played in New York.

What an amazing treasure! I remember Graham calling me over to his bus, which was parked outside of our hotel. He said, "Joe, come on my bus, I want to show you something." I walked into the bus and Graham said, "Look at this." There, lying on the booth table, was the old tape box from the studio containing the tape which Stephen recorded back in 1968. I picked it up. It was, in fact, the master tape. I started reading the song titles…I was stunned. There was something like seventeen songs. Here was a treasure which was almost lost forever. We all owe Joe, Dan and Graham. I think it's such a cool story of how the tape found it's way back to Stephen.

Graham, who was already a brilliant archivist, knew exactly what to do. He told me he was gonna have the tape "baked," which meant the tape was actually baked in an oven at a controlled temperature and time, a temporary means of restoring old tapes. Then he immediately had the tape transferred to digital. After the tape was transferred to digital, Stephen hired Joe Jr. to digitally prepare the master for print. What a suitable title Stephen chose for the album he made out of the demos…"Just Roll Tape." That's what Stephen always says when he's working out an idea for a song in the studio and wants to get all his ideas down on tape.

As a writer, I find it's often really interesting to go back to the original demo I recorded for a song. Sometimes, it's surprisingly good, sometimes not. In Stephen's case, the songs and performance were fresh, complete and brilliant. The beauty of the songs and the clarity of the guitar and vocal performances were reflective of the quintessential Stills. The graphics on the CD are an actual scan of the songs listed on the outside of the tape box. Those songs were released on the album "Just Roll Tape" in 2007 on Rhino Records. They're something to hear.

<u>2007, The Stephen Stills Blues Band Tour</u>

We were all set to go to Australia and New Zealand the first of the year in 2007, but then David got the flu. It was a particularly nasty strain, accompanied by a horrible cough and pneumonia, that was "going around" that year. David has a tremendously powerful voice, so I imagine his coughing was powerful as well. Someone told me that David coughed so hard he threw his shoulder out and then he ended up in the hospital with pneumonia. His doctor didn't want him to leave the country when he was recovering from being so ill, so the tour was postponed until fall. It took David a long time to regain his health, so Stephen went out with The Stephen Stills Blues Band and toured most of the year.

The band was Stephen Stills, Kevin McCormick on bass, Todd Caldwell on keyboards and vocals, and me on drums and vocals. Mike Finnigan was touring with Joe Cocker, so Stephen had to get an organist and found Todd, a great keyboard player from Texas. We did the first leg of the tour with Kevin, who normally plays bass with Jackson Browne, but he had prior commitments, and couldn't do the second leg of the tour. I suggested Kenny Passarelli, who had worked with both Stephen and CSN in the past. Knowing Kenny's and my history with Joe Walsh, Stephen cautiously hired Kenny, but warned us we had to behave ourselves on the tour. Of course, we assured him that we'd behave…well, pretty much.

I love playing with The Stephen Stills Blues Band, and it was a particular treat to be touring with Kenny Passarelli again. We played smaller venues and got a great response from the crowds. We mostly played at clubs and theaters, but, once in a while, let's just say we played at a club that looked better on paper than it looked in person. When we arrived at one club, which I won't name, I had a funny moment with myself and my Dad in heaven. I remembered many years ago when I was going to play with The Echoes and quit my Dad's band, and he'd shouted that I was going to end up playing in dives when I was sixty if I went into rock & roll. Here I was, nearing sixty, and I was definitely playing in a dive that night. Thank God, it was just for that one night!

One of the hotels on the west coast we stayed in, which shall remain unnamed, was completely bizarre, from the lobby to the rooms. From the outside, it looked just like any other hotel. The inside, however, was a whole different story. Kenny and I walked in, took one look and immediately started laughing. The lobby looked like Dr. Seuss had furnished it, and the front desk looked like it had been attacked by flower children, with brightly colored flowers painted everywhere. Kenny and I looked at each other and said, "What is this, Disneyland?"

Besides the oversized furniture in the lobby, that Kenny and I HAD to get our picture taken with, there were even more surprises upstairs. On the way upstairs, even the interior of the elevator was covered in a bizarre fabric print. We got to our rooms, which had red walls, and were amazed at the furnishings. The TV stand looked like it was wearing a hat and the light fixture on the ceiling, which was made of three colored glass globes on movable metal arms, looked like it was from the sci-fi movie "The War of the Worlds." Sometimes hotels have robes in the

room, right? Well, check it out…this hotel had robes that were animal prints…ours were zebra, which matched the covering on the bed's headboard…which was wavy, like the back of a Victorian couch. Kenny and I put our robes on over our clothes and asked a friend of ours to take a picture of us. We posed like fashion models. Our friend was laughing so hard the pictures were totally jiggled…this one is the best of the three he took. Everywhere we looked there was something that made us laugh. It got even better.

I was unpacking when Kenny phoned me and said, "Did your friend Tina come to your room?" "What friend Tina?" I asked. "I don't

have a friend named Tina." Kenny laughed. "You will. Come over to my room." I went over to see what was going on. There had been a knock at his door and Kenny had answered it. There was a person from the hotel standing there with a goldfish in a bowl, which came with a note from the fish. It said something like, "Hello. My name is Tina and I'm here to keep you company during your stay with us. I hope it's an enjoyable one…" The note went on about feeding it and changing the water. Tina's note closed by asking Kenny to talk to her once in

a while. Yeah, the hotel even had "pets" delivered to our door. I have a picture I took of Mason, standing outside the hotel talking on his cell phone, which I think is really funny. He's telling management to never book us there again.

2007, Versausage

We played throughout the spring, summer, and into fall, and there were always those days off with time on our hands. Kenny and I had to find things to do. As I've said, you can't buy rock & roll clothes now, so, you have to make them. I'm always looking for ideas for stage clothes, even though I generally end up wearing a black tee shirt and blue jeans. Once I spilled bleach on a black tee shirt, and it made an orange-ish red stain. It was a pretty interesting and cool looking stain. I started thinking I might be able to make some tee shirts, so while I was at the drug store with Kenny one afternoon, I picked up some bleach. "What'd you do, get spaghetti stains on yourself?" he asked.

We went back to the hotel and about two hours later, I called Kenny and asked him to come down to my room. I held up the shirt and he said something like, "Wow! What a cool shirt!" and I proudly said I'd just made it with the bleach I'd just bought. Kenny paused, looked at me, back at the shirt, then back at me and said, "You're out of your mind." He said that I should wear the shirt to the gig, and then said, "I want one."

I gave Kenny the second one I made, and after Todd, the organist, saw them on us, he wanted one, too, so I made him one. Soon, we were all wearing them to the gigs.

So, I started my line of tee shirts, which I called "Versausage." The trademark logo is four sausage links connected in a V. Stephen's always ready to be part of the craziness on the road, so one night we all walked in wearing my Versausage creations and he said, "And who are you wearing?" like we were on the red carpet. "Versausage," I answered. That night at the gig, he launched my tee shirt line by announcing that the band was all wearing "original Versausage."

One of the highlights of the tour was our show at the Los Angeles House of Blues. A month before the gig, I'd asked Rick Rosas and Joe Walsh if they wanted to come to the show. Joe, Kenny and I hadn't been in the same room for years. We had quite a reunion get together…and of course, we asked Joe to sit in and play "Rocky Mountain Way" with us. It was the three of us with both Stephen and Todd, and we did an unbelievably great live version of it. It was amazing…we hadn't played together in so many years and it sounded just like Barnstorm again. It was a great night. As we reminisced, Kenny and I were very thankful that there was nothing like U Tube in the old days when we were on tour with Joe Walsh…a feeling shared by most rock & roll musicians.

We finished the tour playing on four of the Hawaiian Islands. When it comes to touring, that's where you want to end your tour. I came home after having had such a great tour, and had about two months before starting rehearsal for the CSN Australia / New Zealand tour. I spent the time working on this book and the albums Joe Jr. and I were each recording.

2007, Crosby, Stills & Nash Australian & New Zealand Tour

The band was David, Stephen, Graham, Todd Caldwell on keyboards and vocals, Kevin McCormick on bass, James Raymond on keyboards and vocals, and me on drums and vocals. Although I was looking forward to going to beautiful Australia and New Zealand again, I was dreading the long flight, especially since I was flying from Cleveland, Ohio, since I'd returned home after rehearsal. Long story short, my bag was lost for two days, but the airline finally found it and got it to me. I

James & Me by the Opera House.

loved New Zealand. I couldn't get over the fact that there are both penguins and tropical birds. Of course, I had to feed them. The scenery was breathtaking. I bought a DVD so I could show Susie and Joe Jr.

We moved on to Australia. After four visits to Australia and New Zealand over the years, I finally saw the Southern Cross for the first time. I had played on the original cut of Stephen Still's song "Southern Cross" on the Daylight Again album and had played it at gigs for decades since, but I'd never seen it in person. It was absolutely amazing, and I understood why Stephen had been inspired to write a song about it.

We were able to get a private tour of The Opera House in Sydney. It's such an architecturally fascinating landmark and the building's exterior even looks like the sound of concerts inside would be superb. It was really interesting to see how it's acoustically designed. You can see the Sydney Harbour Bridge from there, and I was fascinated that people actually pay $150 to walk across the top of it. I must have taken 15 pictures of tourists on the top of the bridge, just because I don't like heights and, to me, it would have been horrifying. We took

a VIP tour of Taronga Zoo, and I got to pet a kangaroo, a giraffe, a baby koala bear, and a few things I wasn't sure what they were, but they were interesting. I saw a Tasmanian Devil and other Australian animals. When I was petting the koala bear, which was the highlight of the entire day for  me, the girl zookeeper holding it said, "Hey, you both have the same hair," referring to the grey I now have. Everybody in the band looked at the koala and then my hair and laughed. Hey, thanks!

The flight home was really long, as it always is, especially since I was going back to Ohio. This time, my bag arrived with me. It was well worth the trip...it's a beautiful part of the world and I can't wait to go there again.

CHAPTER TWENTY-NINE

2008, Crosby, Stills & Nash Tour

The band for the 2008 CSN Tour was David Crosby, Stephen Stills, Graham Nash, Todd Caldwell on organ, Kevin McCormick on bass, James Raymond on keyboards, and me on drums. The band sounded great, as usual, and we were having a fantastic time. We started the tour on the west coast, and immediately, I began to express myself. My hotel room in Seattle had a huge piece of artwork on the wall. It was of a life-sized man, but he had no face...it was like a silhouette. I needed to make it more interesting. I grabbed a magazine and cut out eyes, a mouth, a smile, and a tie and taped them to the picture. The maids were freaking out, because they thought I'd done something permanent to the artwork. The CSN guys heard about it, and 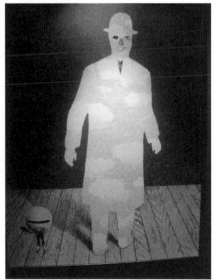 one by one, stopped by my room to see it, like it was an art exhibit. Everyone thought "cut out man" was hysterical...hey, it's what I do... so we all started doing "cut out man" at every hotel.

We're creative people…we need things to do…and how some of those things have changed over the years. With rock & roll musicians, it used to be about who had the best guitar, mic or drum set.   Not any more. Now, since the dawn of the computer age, it's all about who has the best high tech toys. This past summer we were near Detroit the day the new iPhone came out and was available for sale. It was the coolest toy on the block…the thing everyone had to have. We had the day off and Todd Caldwell, our organ player, took a cab over to the nearest mall and bought one. It came loaded with every "whistle and bell" known to man. He ran into someone from the band in the hotel lobby when he got back from the mall. He proudly whipped out his new Star Trek-like communicator iPhone and said, "Check it out."

Whoever he was talking to, answered, "Aw-w-w-w, Dude, the new iPhone." He was totally drooling. Word got around fast…it was Breaking News. Crosby was the first to hear, then Nash, then James Raymond. Crosby said, "He WHAT? How dare he go to the mall and not tell me he was going?" Nash agreed. "This is treason."

The next day we met in the lobby at 3:00 PM to go to soundcheck, The room was thick with iPhone Envy. While we were waiting for the buses to pull up, somebody called Todd Caldwell's cell phone. I think it was Cros, because he said really loudly, "Hey, somebody's cell phone's ringing. It sounds like a new iPhone to me." And so the razzing began. Finally, in his defense, Todd answered, "Hey, if you'd gone with me, you wouldn't have been able to get one anyway. I had to stand in line for a half hour, and I got the last one in the store." It seemed like the razzing was over.

That night at the show, in front of thousands, Graham introduced the band as he did at every show. When he got to Todd, he said, "Give a warm welcome to Todd Caldwell, our B3 player, and his new iPhone. Show 'em your new iPhone, Todd." Everybody laughed. I wasn't one who was suffering from iPhone Envy. All I need in life is to be able to be in the middle of nowhere on the bus, and have someone be able to call me. If I'd wanted one of the new phones, though, I'd have been the first to jump on his case. I thought, "Ok, let's put this razzing to rest."

The next day, Graham, David, and James all found a store that wasn't sold out and bought new iPhones. So, everybody was happy, right? That night, Graham walked into the dressing room at soundcheck and wistfully said, "I almost had it." We wondered what it was that Graham had wanted so much. He got an enormous ornery smile on his face. "When I was at the phone store, there was a huge, six foot tall cardboard iPhone. I offered a lot of money to buy it, but they wouldn't sell it to me. My plan was to have Mason put it on the stage right next to Todd and the organ for the show tonight." I pictured it in my mind for a few seconds, nodding my head….Todd… the enormous cardboard iPhone sitting next to him the entire show…the lights on it…yeah….great idea, Graham. We all started laughing. It would have been awesome. What I learned from the iPhone saga is, either bring enough iPhones for the whole class, or keep your mouth shut.

You'd think that after all these years we'd be a bunch of old, settled musicians, in our hotel rooms quietly watching the news on TV at night. Well…no. Not yet. In May, Graham had appeared on American Idol, singing a duet with Brooke White, who was one of the contestants. They sang "Teach your Children," and it really worked well for both of them. In fact, it worked so well that Graham said that maybe they'd do another song together sometime.

I brought a song idea to him and he liked it, so we decided to write the song together. After several nights in my hotel room studio, complete with my ironing board keyboard stand, we got the music done and we were starting on the vocals. We had the night off in Tuscon, Arizona, so Graham came over to my room and we started doing the vocals. We were having a great time…

we were rockin'…and it started getting louder and louder. It was about midnight when we heard a knock at the door. It was a very loud knock, for us to be able to hear it over the music. We were annoyed. Since he thought it was one of the other band guys, Graham yelled, "WHAT? Can't you hear that we're working in here?" I yelled, "Stop knocking! We're recording!" The knocking got even louder.

Graham had had it, so he opened the door and yelled, "WHAT?" Standing in the doorway was a 6'5" security cop, who was in his twenties. He hadn't come to do backup vocals. He calmly said, "You guys gotta keep it down." I looked at him and started laughing. What a reverse…usually, the old guys are telling the young guys, "It's too loud. Turn the music down." I paused for a moment and enjoyed my memories of past hotel carnage.

A few days later, I was again taken back to memories of being on the road with CSN. We were leaving for soundcheck and I looked up into Crosby's bus… and saw David in the driver's seat, ready to drive to the gig. He looked totally at home behind the wheel and, I swear, if he'd been a cat, he'd have been purring. He was leaning forward on the steering wheel and gave me this big 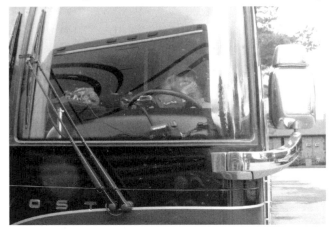 ear to ear grin. So pleased with himself. Yeah, David's still driving.

I've always enjoyed working with David Crosby. He's such a character and deliberately does things to amuse himself. One of the things he always does that no one would ever notice is he always wears mismatched socks. Always. He also has a fascination with flashlights, and, ever since Mag Lights were invented, he always gives one to everyone in the band and crew when we start off the tour…every tour. I look forward to getting them now…I've saved all of them. I nicknamed him "Santa Cros," and when I call him that, he gives me that big Crosby grin. On the road, every night off is "Croz's Movie Night," as he calls it. David takes whoever wants to go, from the band and crew, out to dinner and to a movie…and he picks up the tab. We usually get a little flier stuck under our hotel room door with the details and everyone who wants to go shows up in the lobby. It's really generous of him and it's become something we look forward to.

Later that same day, we were in the dressing room at a gig in New Hampshire and there was a framed scenic print of a family resort by a beautiful lake hanging on the wall. I looked at Stephen and I could tell what he was thinking. I said, "That picture needs some work." The guys agreed, "Yeah, it needs a great white." Stephen kept looking at the picture…finally he broke. Being a gifted "road artist" by now, he grabbed a magic marker, and said, with tremendous authority, "I'll do it." I was stunned. What leadership skills! I held my breath while he drew a great white shark jumping clear out of the water with it's mouth open, about to eat the boat which was pictured in the print. I've seen a lot of Stephen's art, and I felt it was one of his finest works. "Cut out man," props on the stage, Graham and I with cops at our hotel room door, David driving, Stephen drawing…the 2008 CSN tour was right on track.

2008, "Speaking In Drums," "Dancing with Shadows," "Backstage Pass"

What a year! Here I am, writing this book "Backstage Pass" with Susie, producing my son Joe Jr.'s first album "Dancing with Shadows," and releasing my first album in over 26 years "Speaking In Drums," all at the same time. Instead of slowing down, life has sped up to a frantic pace. I love it!

I'd been writing new songs since I'd put out Plantation Harbor in 1982, and had decided I'd try to put out another solo album…and started sending demos out to record companies around ten years ago. I was also working with Joe Jr. as his producer, so we sent out demos of his album, too. We both were getting a lot of rejection. We kept hearing that the music business had changed…that it was no longer about the songs, but it was now about marketing. We even tried combining our songs on one album with a band name, thinking that it might be a better marketing idea. We each sent out around two hundred packets over the years. Both albums were turned down by every major record label in America, but we never gave up. I heard, "These are hit songs, but how would we market you?", the ever popular, "I'm sorry, but we're only signing urban rap and hip hop," and my personal favorite, "The instruments and vocals in these songs are in tune. Can't you fix that? It doesn't sound like a garage band, and there are guitar solos. No one does that anymore."

Since we weren't about to degrade the music and replace tracks with out-of-tune music, we decided to put out both records and the book ourselves, sell them over the Internet, and try to get them into record and book stores. We formed two labels: Susie and I own Hit Records and Marinara Music and Publishing, and Joe Jr. owns Vari Loud Records and Vari Loud Musik.

Susie had the book outlined and had been doing research for several years. She started writing it and finally convinced me to start working on it with her. Even though friends and interviewers kept telling me I should write a book, I just didn't think people would want to read it. It took a lot to convince me, so Susie invited some of our friends over for dinner and taped me telling them some of the stories. They enjoyed the stories and it encouraged me to consider the book idea. Then we started taping me telling her the stories, sometimes over the phone while I was on the road. The book started to take shape. We asked some friends and family to read the first seven chapters and tell us what they thought…were the stories interesting? Would people want to read it?

We didn't look for a publisher because we wanted to have control over writing the stories and the number of photographs we used… everyone told us we'd never get to use many. We literally went through several thousand photographs to pick out my favorites and decided to put nearly 100 pages of colored photos in the book, not including the black and white ones scattered throughout the stories. I asked Graham if the three CSN guys would write a foreward for my book. He immediately agreed and after reading the first fourteen chapters, each of them sent me one. I can't tell you how much that's meant to me.

Joe Jr., Susie, and I did all three projects at the same time. When the albums were finished, I mixed the songs. I didn't have access to an automated board, so that took a LONG time. Susie and Joe Jr. did the photography and album design, and Joe Jr. did the digital audio editing graphics and layout. It's been an enormous and seemingly endless amount of work, but the songs on the albums, the stories in the book, and the artwork and photographs are very personal and exactly what we wanted. My good friend Thom Lowry had worked with Ted Jensen and called

Ted Jensen & Me at Sterling Sound.

him about mastering our albums. Ted had mastered my second solo album, Plantation Harbor" and remembered me. Thom called me and said he'd talked to Ted and that I should give him a call. I didn't think someone of Ted's stature would want to master two albums released by an independent label, so I didn't call him. To my surprise, Ted called me. He did an unbelievable job on both of the albums. I can never thank him enough.

Some of the songs on my album were written as long as twenty-five years ago, and some are new this year. For me, the music business is still about the songs and there's some fantastic guitar work on the albums. Besides my son, Joe Jr., I have my good friends, Tom Bukovac, Doug Breidenbach, Dan Fleishour, and Jason Rivera on guitar...and yeah, there are guitar solos and the music is in tune!

Joe Jr. started writing songs when he was eleven years old, and continued to learn everything he could to further his career. He's taken years of drum, guitar and vocal lessons, taught himself digital recording, editing, video, photography, web design, and graphics. He's sacrificed years and years of his life to write and record his album with little financial reward. While his friends have gotten married and pursued their careers, Joe Jr. has steadfastly pursued his dream. He just kept pressing on, working more hours day after day than you can imagine. His song lyrics reflect frustration and facing adversity and rejection, relying on God and coming out with victory, stronger, but definitely changed. He could have never written the lyrics to those songs if success had come easily to him. I'm so proud of the quality of his song writing and lyrics, and his musical ability on guitar, drums, percussion, vocals, keyboards, bass, editing and production. But mostly, I'm proud of the person he is. He has a quality of character that goes beyond excellence. Hey, I'm his Dad. I get to say these things about him!

It's been hard to produce my son, Joe, because we have differences in our musical tastes and sometimes there's no right or wrong artistic answer. We disagreed, we butted heads, and we were frustrated. We've had to step back from that father and son relationship thing and approach the songs as musicians. In the end, they're his songs and they have to be the way he'll be happy with them…and the album is something we're both very proud of.

One of our many musical discussions...

Joe Jr. has also forced me to join the current century, and has introduced me to email, lap tops, websites, MySpace and digital recording. It's amazing to me how a song can be edited today in ways that would have been impossible before digital. There are still a lot of things I can't do, and I get really frustrated that things have changed so much and I don't know how to do everything…but I'm learning. On the other hand, it's unbelievably great that I can email and keep in contact with my friends, send songs over the Internet, have a website and actually read email from fans. I enjoy seeing songs I put on my MySpace page getting so many hits and it gives me such tremendous feedback and encouragement. I appreciate that a lot.

My website is: www.joevitaleondrums.com
My MySpace page is: www.myspace.com/joevitaleondrums

Joe Jr.'s website is: www.joevitalejr.com
Joe Jr.'s MySpace page is: www.myspace.com/joevitalejr

The Internet has also opened up communication and opportunities in ways I never could have imagined. We've got both albums and the book up for sale on the Internet, but when I tell people to look up "Joe Vitale," to make sure they've gotten the right one. Apparently, there are MANY "Joe Vitales." There's a state senator from New Jersey, some guy who makes mugs, a hockey player, and a motivational speaker and writer. This makes perfect sense…the two favorite Italian names are "Joseph" and "Mary." I just happen to have a popular Italian name! I really get a kick out of it when people come across my website and send me emails thinking they're contacting the motivational speaker, asking for psychological and financial advice…I mean, don't they look at the website? Do they think he plays drums, too? Anyway, since they're asking for MY opinion regarding financial advice, I usually email back and tell them to sell everything and buy a boat!

So, you've read some of my stories and have seen some of my photos. It's been wonderful for me to be able to remember and share my good times. Here I am, nearing sixty, and still playing drums, writing and touring, decades longer than I would have ever dreamed possible. I'm so grateful that I've been able to write this book and thank some of the wonderful people I've met and worked with over the years. I feel blessed that my career has continued year after year, and although the music business has changed, I still love playing my drums and writing music…and I'm looking forward to, hopefully, many more years of stories and memories from this crazy rock & roll life.

As I'm concluding writing this book, I'm packing my drums to start a three week European tour, playing drums with The Stephen Stills Blues Band…with Stephen, Kenny Passarelli on bass and Todd Caldwell on organ and keyboards. The tour starts in Rome and we have shows in several other Italian cities as well, before moving on to other European countries. It's always been a dream of mine to visit the Coliseum in Rome, and I'm finally going to be able to make that dream come true. I can already picture myself standing there. They say, "When in Rome, do as the Romans do." Since I'm Italian, I figured I'd arrive in appropriate attire. Yeah…many more years and stories ahead.

Joe Vitale Discography

1965 The Chylds: You Make Me Feel Good (Single)
1967 The Chylds: I Want More (Lovin) (Single)
1967 The Chylds: Psychedelic Soul (Single)
1968 The Chylds: No More Tears (Single)
1972 Joe Walsh: Barnstorm
1973 Rick Roberts: She Is a Song
1973 Michael Stanley: Rosewood Bitters
1973 Joe Walsh: The Smoker You Drink, the Player You Get
1973 Michael Stanley: Friends & Legends
1974 Rick Derringer: All American Boy
1975 Joe Walsh: So What
1976 Joe Vitale: Rollercoaster Weekend
1976 Jay Ferguson: All Alone In The End Zone
1976 Stephen Stills: Illegal Stills
1976 Stills/Young: Long May You Run
1976 Joe Walsh: You Can't Argue with a Sick Mind
1976 Bill Wyman: Stone Alone
1977 Crosby, Stills & Nash: CSN
1977 Dan Fogelberg: Netherlands
1977 The Outlaws: Hurry Sundown
1978 Stephen Stills: Thoroughfare Gap
1978 Joe Walsh: But Seriously Folks
1978 Joe Walsh: Best of Joe Walsh
1979 Rick Roberts: The Best of
1979 Jay Ferguson: Real Life Ain't This Way
1979 CBS Various Artists: Havana Jam
1979 Peter Frampton: Where I Should Be
1980 Crosby, Stills & Nash: Replay
1980 Graham Nash: Earth & Sky
1980 The Henry Paul Band: Feel the Heat
1980 Boz Scaggs: Middle Man
1980 Eagles: Eagles Live
1981 Mickey Thomas: Alive Alone
1981 Dan Fogelberg: Innocent Age
1981 Joe Walsh: There Goes the Neighborhood
1981 John Entwistle: Too Late the Hero
1982 Joe Vitale: Plantation Harbor
1982 Al Kooper: Championship Wrestling
1982 Crosby, Stills & Nash: Daylight Again
1982 Dan Fogelberg: Greatest Hits

1982 Eric Carmen: Solo Album
1983 Crosby, Stills & Nash: Allies
1983 Michael Brewer: Beauty Lies
1983 Don Felder: Airborne
1983 Joe Walsh: You Bought It: You Name It
1984 Dan Fogelberg: Windows & Walls
1985 Melvin James: Passenger
1987 Joe Walsh: Got Any Gum?
1987 Tom Kimmel: 5 to 1
1987 Michael Stanley: Michael Stanley Band
1988 Crosby, Stills, Nash & Young: American Dream
1989 David Crosby: Oh Yes I Can
1990 Crosby, Stills & Nash: Live It Up
1991 Joe Walsh: Ordinary Average Guy
1991 Crosby, Stills & Nash: Crosby, Stills & Nash Box Set
1991 Father Guido Sarducci: Santa's Lament
1992 Michael Stanley: Right Back at Ya (1971-1983)
1992 Joe Walsh: Songs for a Dying Planet
1992 Rock of the 70's: Rock of the 70's, Vol. 3
1994 Ringo Starr: Old Wave
1995 Joe Walsh: Robocop: The Series Soundtrack
1995 Joe Walsh: Look What I Did.. Anthology
1996 Zakk Wylde: Book of Shadows
1996 Republica: Republica
1996 Rick Derringer: The Best of Rick Derringer
1996 Outlaws: Best of the Outlaws: Green Grass & High Tides
1996 John Entwistle: Thunderfingers: The Best of John Entwistle
1996 Michael Stanley: Coming up for Air
1996 John Entwistle: Anthology
1997 Joe Walsh: Rocky Mountain Way
1997 Prefontaine Movie Soundtrack: Prefontaine
1997 Dan Fogelberg: Portrait: The Music of Dan Fogelberg
1997 Saison: So in Love
1997 Joe Walsh: Greatest Hits: Little Did He Know
1998 Crosby, Stills & Nash: Carry On
1998 TV Soundtrack: Drew Carey Show
1999 Crosby, Stills, Nash & Young: Looking Forward
2000 Saison: I Believe
2000 Dan Fogelberg: Something Old, Something New, Something
       Borrowed, And Some Blues
2002 Bobby Gatewood: Finally Home
2002 Graham Nash: Songs for Survivors

2005 <u>Stephen Stills</u>: Man Alive
2005 <u>Crosby, Stills & Nash</u>: Greatest Hits
2005 <u>John Entwistle</u>: So Who's The Bass Player? (Anthology)
2006 <u>Various Artists</u>: Nicolette Larson Tribute/ Live
2007 <u>Stephen Stills</u>: Just Roll Tape
2008 <u>Jack Black & Wyatt Issac</u>: Autism: The Musical
2008 <u>Brian Vander Ark</u>: Brian Vander Ark
2008 <u>Joe Vitale Jr.</u>: Dancing With Shadows
2008 <u>Joe Vitale</u>: Speaking In Drums

Joe Vitale Resume

PRIMARY INSTRUMENT: DRUMS
Additionally: Vocals / Percussion / Keyboards / Flute

Joe Vitale is a veteran musician whose career has spanned over thirty years of touring, recording, and song writing and production with legendary and Rock 'N Roll Hall of Fame artists. His drumming encompasses all styles of music. A dedicated professional, his quality of performance is evident in his resume.

TOURS / LIVE PERFORMANCES

Eagles	Crosby, Stills & Nash
Joe Walsh	Crosby, Stills, Nash & Young
Dan Fogelberg	Peter Frampton
Neil Young	Jackson Browne
Glenn Frey	Ted Nugent
Linda Ronstadt	Bonnie Raitt
Stephen Stills	Beach Boys
John Fogerty	Don Felder

RECORDING

Eagles	Crosby, Stills, & Nash
Joe Walsh	Crosby, Stills, Nash & Young
Stephen Stills	Graham Nash
Dan Fogelberg	David Crosby
Peter Frampton	Neil Young
Jackson Browne	Glenn Frey
Ted Nugent	Ringo Starr
Rick Derringer	John Entwistle
John Lennon	Al Jardine
Michael Brewer	Mickey Thomas
Eric Carmen	Don Felder
Boz Skaggs	Al Kooper
Bill Wyman	Carl Wison
Jay Ferguson	Albert Collins

Bobby Whitlock	Firefall
Zakk Wylde	Stephen Stills
Keith Richards	(3) Joe Vitale solo LP's
Ronnie Wood	Van Morrison
Jack Black	Joe Vitale Jr.
Tom Bukovac	Bobby Gatewood

Official Joe Vitale Website: www.joevitaleondrums.com
Joe Vitale MySpace: www.myspace.com/joevitaleondrums

ENDORSEMENTS

DW Drums	Sabian Cymbals
Evans Drum Heads	Vic Firth Drumsticks
Yamaha Electronics	Audix Microphones
Sony Creative Software	Fishman Pickups

SONGS WRITTEN / CO-WRITTEN

Songs	*Artist*
"Pretty Maids All In A Row"	Eagles
"Rocky Mountain Way"	Joe Walsh
"Mother Says"	
"Giant Bohemoth"	
"Book Ends"	
"Days Gone By"	
"At The Station"	
"Theme from Boat Weirdos"	
"Alphabetical Order"	
"Up All Night"	
"School Days"	
"Malibu"	
"Fun"	
"Bones"	
"I.L.B.T.'S"	

"Space Age Whiz Kids"	
"Theme from Island Weirdos"	
"Vote For Me"	
"Coyote Love"	
"Live It Up"	CSN, Stephen Stills, Graham Nash
"Beaucoup Yumbo"	Crosby, Stills, Nash & Young
"TV Guide"	
"That Girl"	
"Chuck's Lament"	
"Soldiers of Peace"	
"Shadowland"	
"Don't Say Goodbye"	
"Faith In Me"	
"Around Us"	
"Night Owl"	Don Felder
"How Ya Doin'?"	Joe Walsh
All songs on (3) solo Joe Vitale albums	

ALBUM PRODUCTION / CO-PRODUCTION

Live It Up,   Crosby, Stills & Nash
Ordinary Average Guy,   Joe Walsh
Songs For A Dying Planet,   Joe Walsh
"Sanibel" (song),   Crosby, Stills, Nash & Young
"Faith In Me" (song),   Crosby, Stills, Nash & Young
"No Tears Left" (song),   Crosby, Stills, Nash & Young
Man Alive, Stephen Stills
Dancing With Shadows, Joe Vitale Jr.
Speaking In Drums, Joe Vitale

Awards

Special Citation of Achievement

presented by

BMI

to

Joey Vitale

in recognition of the great national popularity
as measured by over **1** million broadcast performances
attained by

Rocky Mountain Way

James W. Preston
President and C.E.O.

Special Citation of Achievement

presented by

BMI

to

Joey Vitale

in recognition of the great national popularity
as measured by over **2** million broadcast performances
attained by

Rocky Mountain Way

Del Bryant
President and C.E.O.

Joe Walsh
"The Smoker You Drink,
The Player You Get"
Gold

Joe Walsh
"So What"
Gold

The Stills-Young band
"Long May You Run"
Gold

Crosby, Stills & Nash
"CSN"
Gold

Crosby, Stills & Nash
"CSN"
Platinum

Joe Walsh
"But Seriously Folks"
Platinum

Joe Walsh
"But Seriously Folks"
Platinum (UK)

Eagles
"Eagles Live"
Platinum

Dan Fogelberg
"Innocent Age"
Platinum

Crosby, Stills & Nash
"Daylight Again"
Platinum

Dan Fogelberg
"Greatest Hits"
Platinum

Dan Fogelberg
"Windows and Walls"
Gold

Crosby, Stills, Nash & Young
"American Dream"
Gold

Crosby, Stills, Nash & Young
"American Dream"
Platinum

Crosby, Stills & Nash
"CSN Box Set"
Gold

Some of my 45 singles

My "animals playing instruments" collection.

I am telling you the truth! His head was this big!!

*Judy & Mark Berens, Me, Eric & Diana Van Horn, & Joe Jr.
listen to my stories after dinner.*

More cutout man!